Ana Pia Q C

SketchUp 8
for Interior Designers

Daniel John Stine

ISBN: 978-1-58503-816-9

SDC Publications

www.SDCpublications.com

Schroff Development Corporation

Schroff Development Corporation
P.O. Box 1334
Mission KS 66222
(913) 262-2664
www.SDCpublications.com

Publisher: Stephen Schroff

Examination Copies:

Books received as examination copies are for review purposes only and may not be made available for student use. Resale of examination copies is prohibited.

Electronic Files:

Any electronic files associated with this book are licensed to the original user only. These files may not be transferred to any other party.

Foreword:

This book has been written with the assumption that the reader has no prior experience using Trimble **SketchUp** (formerly *Google SketchUp*). With this book, the reader will be able to describe and apply many of the fundamental principles needed to develop compelling SketchUp models.

The tutorials introduce the reader to SketchUp, an easy to use 3D modeling program geared specifically towards interior design. Several pieces of furniture are modeled. The process is broken down in the fundamental concepts of 2D line work, 3D extraction, applying materials, and printing.

Although the book is primarily written with a classroom setting in mind, most individuals will be able to work through it on their own and benefit from the tips and tricks presented. ENJOY!

For a little inspiration, this book has several real-world SketchUp project images throughout.

About the Author:

Dan Stine is a registered Architect with twenty-one years of experience in the architectural field. He currently works at LHB (a 200 person multidiscipline firm; www.LHBcorp.com) in Duluth, Minnesota as the CAD Administrator, providing training, customization and support for two regional offices. Mr. Stine has presented at Autodesk University (au.autodesk.com) and at the Revit Technology Conference (revitconference.com).

Dan has worked in a total of four firms. While at these firms, he has participated in collaborative projects with several other firms on various projects (including Cesar Pelli, Weber Music Hall – University of Minnesota - Duluth). Dan is a member of the *Construction Specification Institute* (CSI) and the *Autodesk Developer Network* (ADN) and also teaches *AutoCAD* and *Autodesk Revit* classes at Lake Superior College, for the Architectural Technology program; additionally, he is a Certified Construction Document Technician (CDT). Mr. Stine has also written the following textbooks (published by SDC Publications):

- *Interior Design using Hand Sketching, SketchUp and Photoshop (with co-author Steven H. McNeill)*
- *Interior Design using Revit Architecture 2013*
- *Residential Design using Revit Architecture 2013*
- *Commercial Design using Revit Architecture 2013*

- *Design Integration using Revit 2013 (Architecture, Structure and MEP)*
- *Residential Design using AutoCAD 2013*
- *Commercial Design using AutoCAD 2013*
- *Chapters in Architectural Drawing (with co-author Steven H. McNeill, AIA, LEED AP)*

Mr. Stine likes to spend time with his family, camping, watching movies, fishing and much more! Dan also enjoys riding his bicycle along the shoreline of Lake Superior, and to work when there is no snow on the ground. The total ride distance is only 4 miles but the elevation gain is over 500 feet. Luckily the uphill part is after work!

You can contact the publisher with comments or suggestions at **schroff@schroff.com**.

Please do not email with SketchUp questions unless they relate to a problem with this book.

Thanks:

I could not have done this without the support from my family; Cheri, Kayla & Carter.

Many thanks go out to Stephen Schroff and Schroff Development Corporation for making this book possible!

Table of Contents

NOTES:

Section 1
Introduction to SketchUp

What is SketchUp® used for?

It might be easier to answer what SketchUp is not used for. SketchUp is an all-purpose 3D modeling tool. The program is primarily developed around architectural design but it can be used to model just about anything. The program's relative ease of use and low cost (the basic package being free) makes it a very popular tool within the AEC design community.

SketchUp models are also used to populate Google Earth with real buildings which have been modeled to scale. Check out this website for more info: http://sketchup.google.com/yourworldin3d/index.html.

It should be pointed out that SketchUp was recently sold by Google to Trimble. The software is still being developed by the same folks in Colorado; they just get their paychecks from someone else. Trimble is a leading manufacturer of survey equipment and GIS software.

Why use SketchUp?

As just mentioned, it is easy to use and free! It is a simple way to quickly communicate your design ideas to clients or prospective employers. Not only can you create great still images, SketchUp also is able to produce walk-thru videos!

When creating interior designs using SketchUp you have access to a massive amount of content with via **Trimble's 3D Warehouse**. You can take a peek now if you want: **http://sketchup.google.com/3dwarehouse/**. Keep in mind that this link may change at some point, due to the recent acquisition by Trimble.

SketchUp versus other Applications?

There are several other 3D modeling applications (aka programs) on the market which compete with SketchUp to varying degrees. Every program has its strengths and weaknesses when compared to another. SketchUp is mainly geared towards concept designs rather than construction documentation. Its ability to quickly develop and present the designer's ideas makes it very popular. However, it is not very good at adding notes and dimensions, but it is getting better at that with each new version. So at some point the SketchUp design typically needs to be exported to a CAD format, such as Autodesk's DWG format and finished in AutoCAD or a similar program.

Another popular modeling approach is Building Information Modeling (BIM). SketchUp is not a BIM application. However, SketchUp can still have a place in the BIM workflow. An application such as Autodesk's Revit® Architecture does have several SketchUp-like features, but many designers prefer the simplicity and limited scope (i.e., SketchUp is designed to do one thing, and it does that one thing very well – similar to Five Guys burgers!). Plus, Revit can import SketchUp models.

SketchUp is primarily a face-based modeling program, as opposed to a solid modeling program. This has its pluses and minuses. It is great for concept modeling as it keeps the size and complexity of the model down to a minimum. This allows the designer to quickly spin around the model and zoom in and out, whereas a solids-based model could take nearly a minute to spin around where SketchUp could do it in seconds. This is all relative to the project size – a small simple project would not be a problem in either case, but a 200,000 square foot school or hospital likely would be. Speed also depends on the power of your computer of course; processor speed, RAM (quantity and speed), video card, video card memory, video card software driver. Notice the emphasis on video card? This is because SketchUp is a graphics intense program, and benefits from high quality video cards when spinning around the model, while displaying textures (e.g. an image of brick) and generating shadows.

This may be considered debatable by some SketchUp experts, but a solids-based model is generally easier to make changes to when the model is complex. SketchUp Pro now has the ability to create some solids so the playing field is leveling out.

One of the drawbacks to face-based modeling is the designer cannot get information from the model such as cubic foot of material for a concrete wall. Luckily nobody really cares about that in the early stages of design! A similar problem is that elements in section look hollow in SketchUp whereas in a solids-based program they would not. This can be seen in the example below:

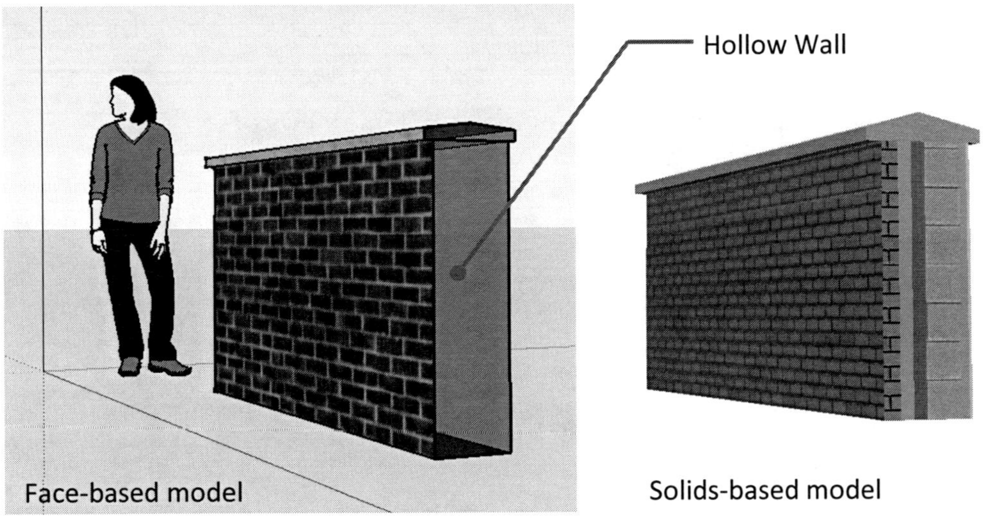

FIGURE 1.1 SketchUp is a face-based program, not solids-based.

The left image shows a masonry wall cut using the section tool. Notice the wall appears hollow. SketchUp does not know this is a masonry wall, or even a wall for that matter. The image on the right is a BIM model – notice the solid core.

As already mentioned, it is possible to export a SketchUp model to a CAD program such as AutoCAD. This format does not work too well in a BIM program such as Revit – but it can be used to varying degrees. It is also possible to export a BIM model to a format that can be imported into SketchUp – thus allowing some of SketchUp's tools to be used; hand sketch effect, easy navigation and simple animation setup and creation.

SketchUp Pro versus the Free version?

The free version of SketchUp is very powerful and can model just about anything. The Pro version, which costs $495 at the time of this printing, has several advanced features such as:

- Technical support
- Solid modeling
- Import and Export AutoCAD DWG files
- Layout 3
    - A separate program used to compose multiple views of the same model on a page
    - More printing options
- Style Builder
    - A separate program used to transform your model into a unique hand drawing.

You can see a more detailed comparison of the free versus pro version at the following web address:

- http://www.sketchup.com/intl/en/product/whygopro.html

For most design firms the pro version is a must, if just for the ability to use and export AutoCAD DWG files. For example, you might import a 2D DWG file provided by the client and use that line work to quickly start modeling the existing conditions. SketchUp also has network license options which a company can purchase. This allows a firm to have the software installed on everyone's computers, but the number of people who can access the program, at any given time, is limited to the number of network licenses the company owns. So, if your firm has six licenses available on the server, the seventh person gets a denial message. That person can keep trying until a license becomes available or, better, make a few calls or send out an email to see if someone can get out!

Given the introductory nature of this textbook, only the tools and techniques found in the free version of SketchUp will be covered. Once you understand the concepts covered in this book you most likely will be able to figure out the other tools on your own.

Mac versus PC?

SketchUp has been designed to work on either the Apple Macintosh or Microsoft Windows based computer system. Most Architectural and Interior Design offices tend to favor the PC due to cost and general availability of other programs geared towards the industry. However, there is not much that cannot be done on a Mac, especially with its ability to run Windows when using Mac's *Boot Camp* or a virtual environment (e.g. *Parallels*).

All screen shots in this book are from a PC running Windows 7 64bit. If the reader is using a Mac or another version of Windows there might be slight differences in some screen shots. However, the main SketchUp *User Interface* should be the same; the User Interface is covered next.

Warning!

Because you are using this book, you are obviously interested in Interior Design and SketchUp is great for that. But, just so you know (and to provoke a little smile), there are some things SketchUp is not allowed to be used for. The following is an excerpt from the End User License Agreement you are required to agree to before downloading and using the software:

> NONE OF THE SOFTWARE IS INTENDED FOR USE IN THE OPERATION OF NUCLEAR FACILITIES, LIFE SUPPORT SYSTEMS, EMERGENCY COMMUNICATIONS, AIRCRAFT NAVIGATION OR COMMUNICATION SYSTEMS, AIR TRAFFIC CONTROL SYSTEMS, OR ANY OTHER SUCH ACTIVITIES IN WHICH CASE THE FAILURE OF THE SOFTWARE COULD LEAD TO DEATH, PERSONAL INJURY, OR SEVERE PHYSICAL OR ENVIRONMENTAL DAMAGE.

Staying in the loop

Be sure to follow the office SketchUp blog to learn about the latest updates, tips and tricks. You can also read about how others are using the product. **http://sketchupdate.blogspot.com/**

Project Example: Waiting Area. *Image courtesy of LHB; www.LHBcorp.com*

Section 2
Overview of the SketchUp User Interface

The first step in learning any new computer program is figuring out the **User Interface** (UI). SketchUp has a traditional user interface, consisting of menus across the top, toolbars that can float or be docked to a side, a status bar across the bottom and a large area in the middle to do your design work. SketchUp has chosen not to implement the *Ribbon* as a number of other software makers have (e.g., Microsoft and Autodesk). Which UI style is better is a hotly debated subject.

The image on the next page highlights the primary components of the *User Interface*. A few of the items identified are not really considered a part of the UI, but help paint a better overall picture for the new user. Take a little time to familiarize yourself with the terms presented, as they will be used throughout this textbook.

Project Example: Custom Casework. *Image courtesy of LHB; www.LHBcorp.com*

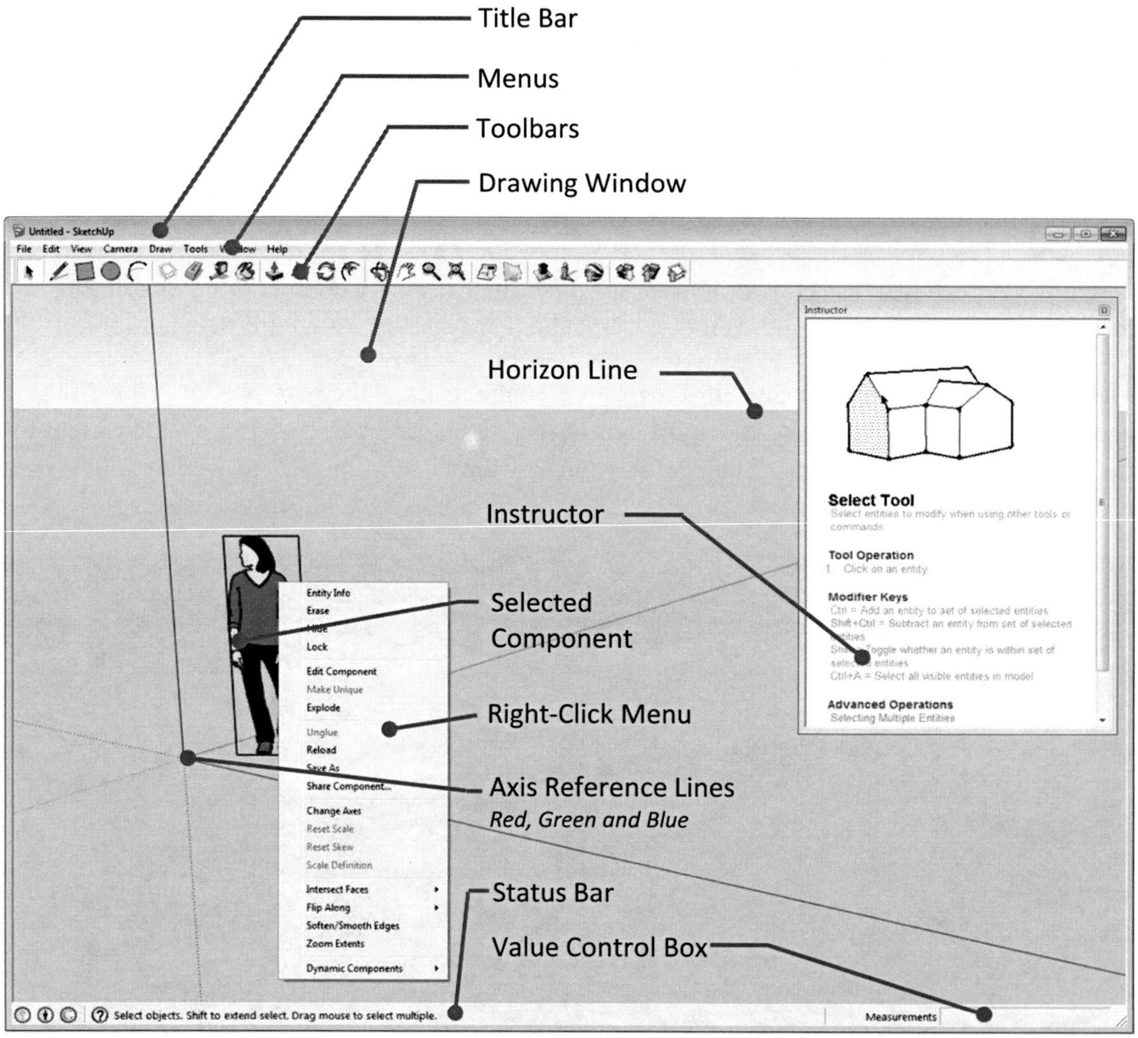

FIGURE 2.1 SketchUp User Interface

Title Bar:

The program title bar displays the name of the file currently being worked on, *TFDM Office Building Remodel.skp* in this case. And just in case you forgot, the name of the program you are using is listed to the right of the file name: *SketchUp*, right? On the far right are the typical controls for the application's window: minimize, maximize/restore down, close.

FIGURE 2.2 Title Bar

Menus:

Below the title bar are several pull-down menus; these are the words across the top (File, Edit, View, etc.). When clicked on, these menus reveal a list of commands. The menus are a way to break the list of commands down into smaller, task specific lists. A *menu* is closed when a command is selected or the **Esc** key is pressed.

Notice in the image provided (Figure 2.3), the **Camera** menu is expanded. Some items have a check mark on the left to show that item is active (projection type in this case). Also, some items in the list are fly-out menus. A fly-out menu can be identified by the black arrow pointing to the right (**Standard Views**, for example). Hovering over a fly-out menu item reveals another sub-set of menu options. Whenever a command or toggle has a keyboard shortcut, it is listed on the right. Finally, any command or toggles which are not relevant to the current tool or drawing will be grayed out to avoid any confusion.

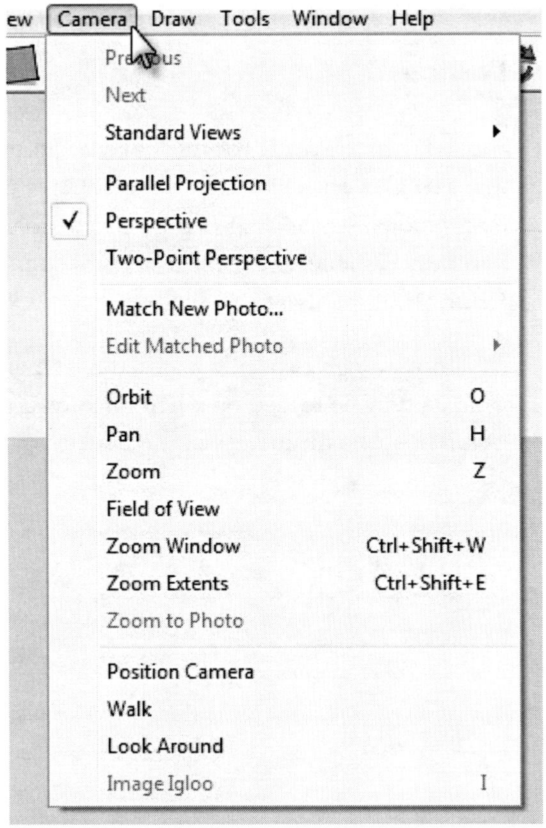

FIGURE 2.3 Menus

When reference is made to a command within the menu system it will be shown as such:

Camera → Parallel Projection

This means: click the **Camera** menu and then click the **Parallel Projection** command in the list as shown in the image to the right (Figure 2.4).

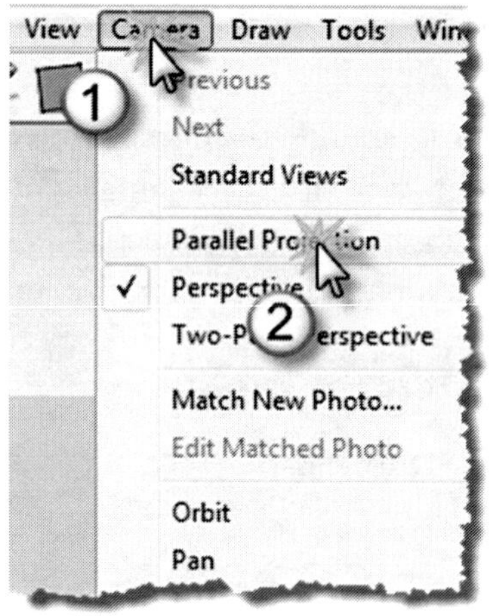

FIGURE 2.4 Menu selection

Toolbars:

Toolbars are a favorite for most SketchUp users as they provide small graphical images and are only a single click away. When SketchUp is first started (after being installed), only the *Getting Started* toolbar is showing (Figure 2.5). Additional toolbars can be toggled on and off via **View → Toolbars**. Whenever a toolbar is visible on the screen, it can be dragged so it is "docked" along the perimeter of the drawing window, or it can "float" anywhere on the screen.

The book will give specific instructions when certain toolbars are required. It is recommended that toolbars only be turned on when instructed to minimize any possible confusion and so the reader's screen matches the images in the book.

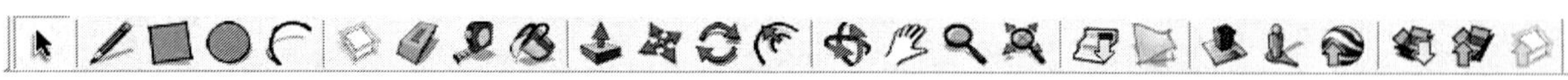

FIGURE 2.5 Toolbars

Drawing Window:

The drawing window is, of course, where all the modeling is done! Using various tools from the menus, toolbars and keyboard shortcuts, you create and interact with your model in the drawing window.

Status Bar (and Value Control Box):

The *Status Bar* is found across the bottom of the application (Figure 2.6). On the far left are three small round icons; hover your cursor over them to see what they are. Next you have a circle with a question mark which toggles the *Instructor* visibility on and off (see the next topic for more on this feature). The next section provides prompts for any command you are currently using. The example shown is letting you know SketchUp expects you to pick a point in the model to define one of the corners while using the **Rectangle** tool. Finally, on the right hand side of the *Status Bar* is the *Value Control Box*. This box shows the length or size of an object being drawn. It is not necessary to spend a lot of time moving the mouse into just the right location so the dimension reads correctly, as you can more quickly (and accurately) type this information in (either before or after picking your last point).

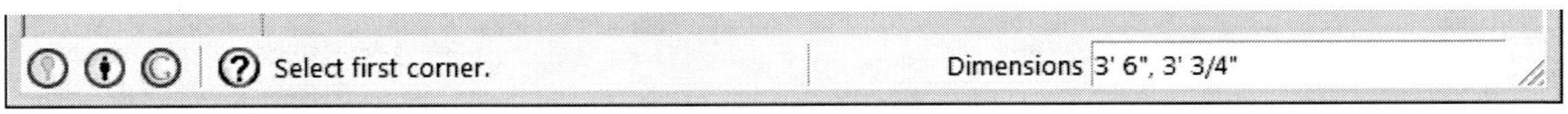

FIGURE 2.6 Status Bar

Instructor:

The *Instructor* is not necessarily part of the *User Interface*, but it automatically appears on the screen when SketchUp is opened. This feature is intended to help new users understand how to use various tools. For example, when you select the **Rectangle** tool the *Instructor* provides an animated graphic and steps on how to sketch a rectangle (Figure 2.7). This feature compliments this book in that it will remind you how various tools are used. This book works through many of SketchUp's commands in a systematic way, and once a command is covered it is not typically covered again in as much detail.

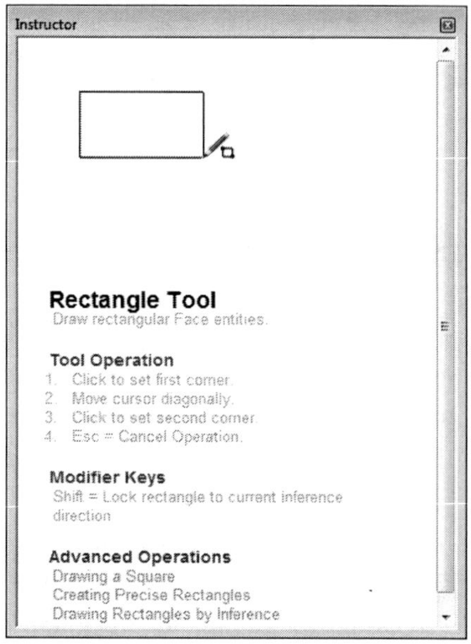

FIGURE 2.7 Instructor window

Once you become familiar with SketchUp, you will want to turn off the *Instructor* in order to free up more screen space. This can be done via **Window → Instructor**; clicking this toggles the *Instructor* on and off. Also, as mentioned in the previous section, the question mark icon on the *Status Bar* will turn the *Instructor* on, if off – and it will also minimize it if already on.

If you have a dual monitor computer system, the *Instructor* can be moved to the second monitor to increase the usable portion of the *Drawing Window*.

Right-Click Menu:

SketchUp allows you to right-click on something to both select it and present a contextual pop-up menu which provides quick access to tools used to manipulate the selected component, line/edge or face. Notice in Figure 2.8a that there are fewer options to choose from when an edge is selected than for a component (Figure 2.8b). Also, some options, in the right-click menu, have a black triangle pointing to the right. Hovering over these reveals a sub-menu with additional tools, similar to the pull-down menus.

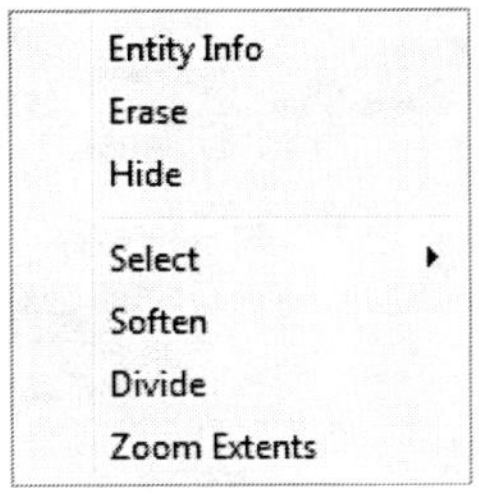

FIGURE 2.8A
Right-click menu: Edge Selected

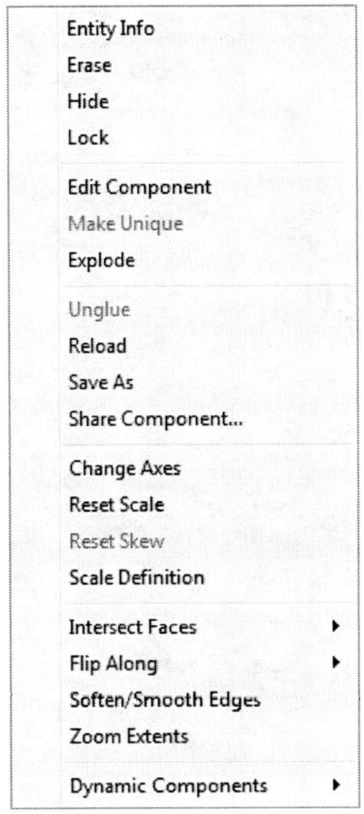

FIGURE 2.8B
Right-click menu: Component Selected

Clicking a tool from the right-click menu or pressing the **Esc** key closes the right-click menu.

Project Example: Retail Counter. *Image courtesy of LHB; www.LHBcorp.com*

Section 3
Open, Save and Close

Opening **SketchUp** is just like opening most any other program. You can either locate the file, i.e. the 3D model, using *Windows Explorer* (aka, *My Computer* or just *Computer*) and then double-click on the file, or you can open SketchUp and then create a new file or open one previously created.

If SketchUp is properly installed on your computer, you can launch the program from the Windows *Start* menu. To do this, make the following clicks within the *Start* menu (Figure 3.1):

Start → All Programs → SketchUp 8 → SketchUp

Or double-click the **SketchUp 8** icon from your desktop.

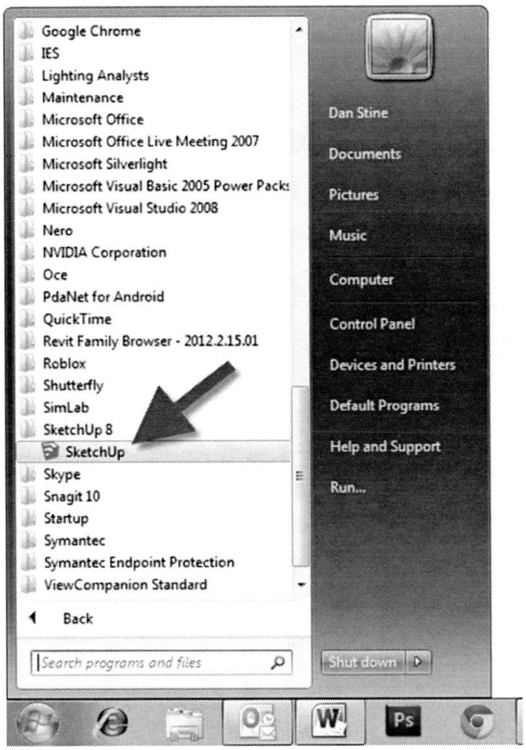

FIGURE 3.1 Welcome to SketchUp Interface

This may vary slightly on your computer depending on the version of Windows you are using (or if you are using a Mac); see your instructor or system administrator if you need help. It is possible to have more than one version of SketchUp installed on a computer. Make sure you are using version 8 to gain access to all the new features and to ensure your screen matches the images in this book!

Open a New SketchUp Model:

By default, SketchUp will open in the *Welcome to SketchUp* dialog as shown (Figure 3.2). Here you have access to more ways to help yourself learn SketchUp and the various templates provided. Make sure you select the correct template before clicking the **Start using SketchUp** button.

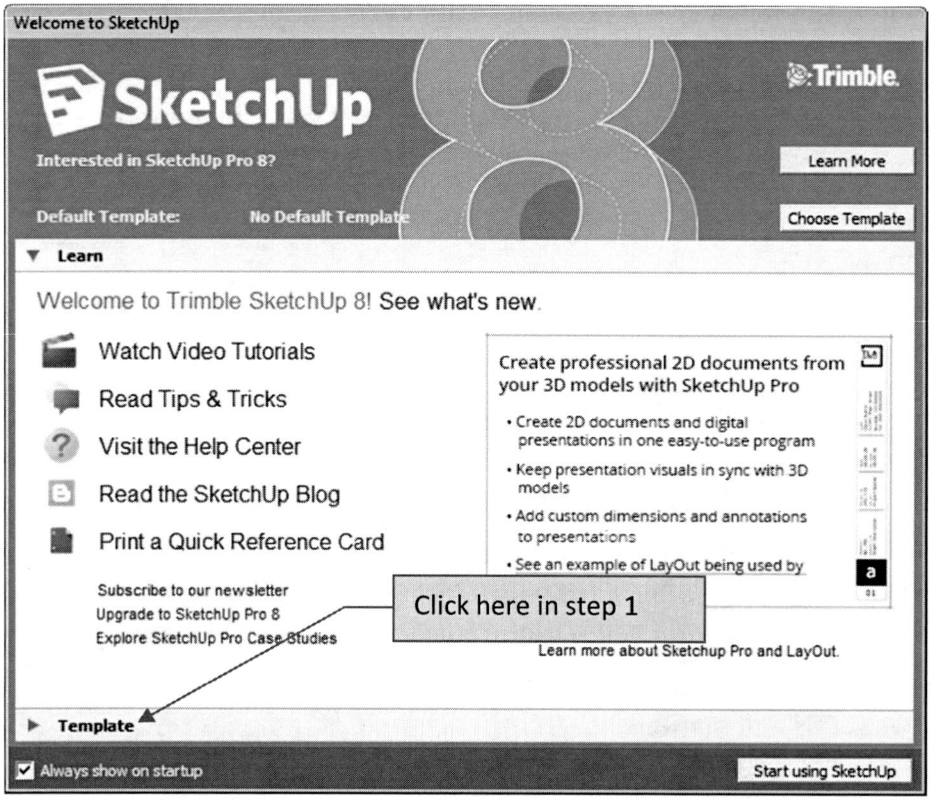

FIGURE 3.2 Welcome to SketchUp Interface

> ***TIP:*** *Experienced SketchUp users will uncheck the "Always show on startup" option in the lower left so they can get right to work. You should NOT uncheck this option until you consider yourself somewhat proficient in the program.*

Here you will learn how to open a new SketchUp model.

1. Click the arrow next to the word *Template* (pointed out in the Figure 3.2).

SketchUp provides several templates. You will be selecting the one set up with the architect and interior designer in mind: Architectural Design – Feet and Inches.

2. Click to select **Architectural Design – Feet and Inches** from the list of available templates (as shown in the image below).

   FYI: *This will be the default template selected the next time SketchUp is opened.*

3. Click the **Start using SketchUp** button in the lower right (Figure 3.3).

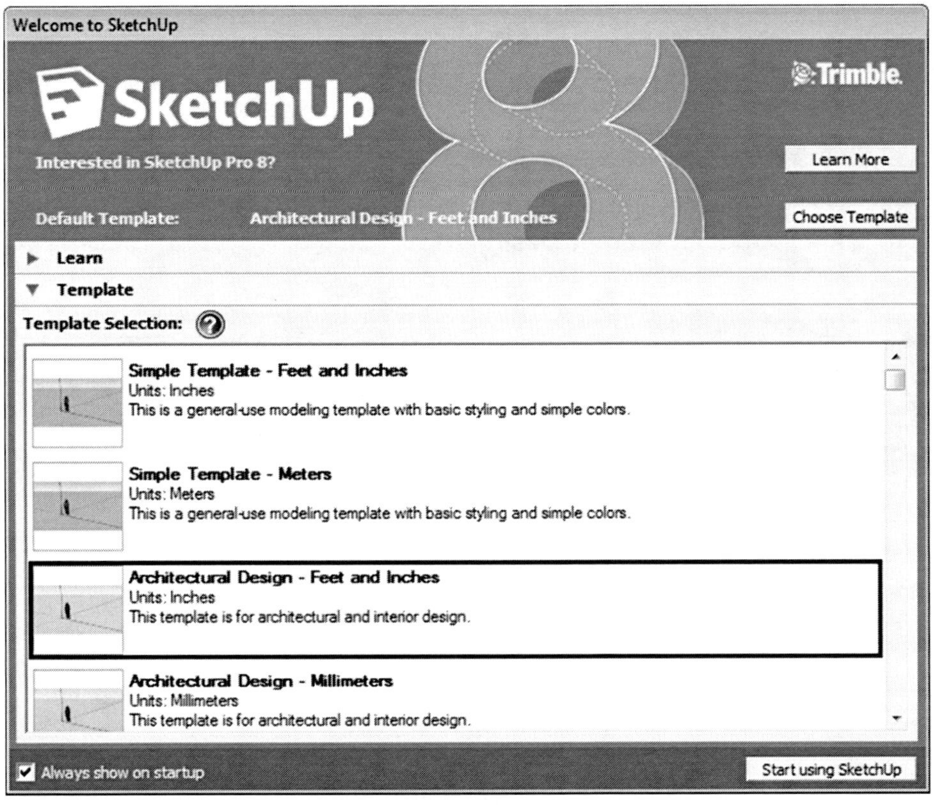

FIGURE 3.3 Welcome to SketchUp - Templates

You are now in a new SketchUp file! Notice the red, green and blue axis lines, the person pre-loaded (which is a great scale reference), and the implied ground which extends to the horizon. At this point you are in an unnamed file. The first time you click **Save**, you will be prompted to select a location and provide a file name; make sure you pay close attention to where you save the file and what you call it!

Open an Existing SketchUp Model:

Now that you know how to open SketchUp and create a new file in which to model, you will open an existing SketchUp file. You will select a sample file provided on the book's webpage.

4. Download the "Required Files" from www.SDCpublications.com (Figure 3.4).

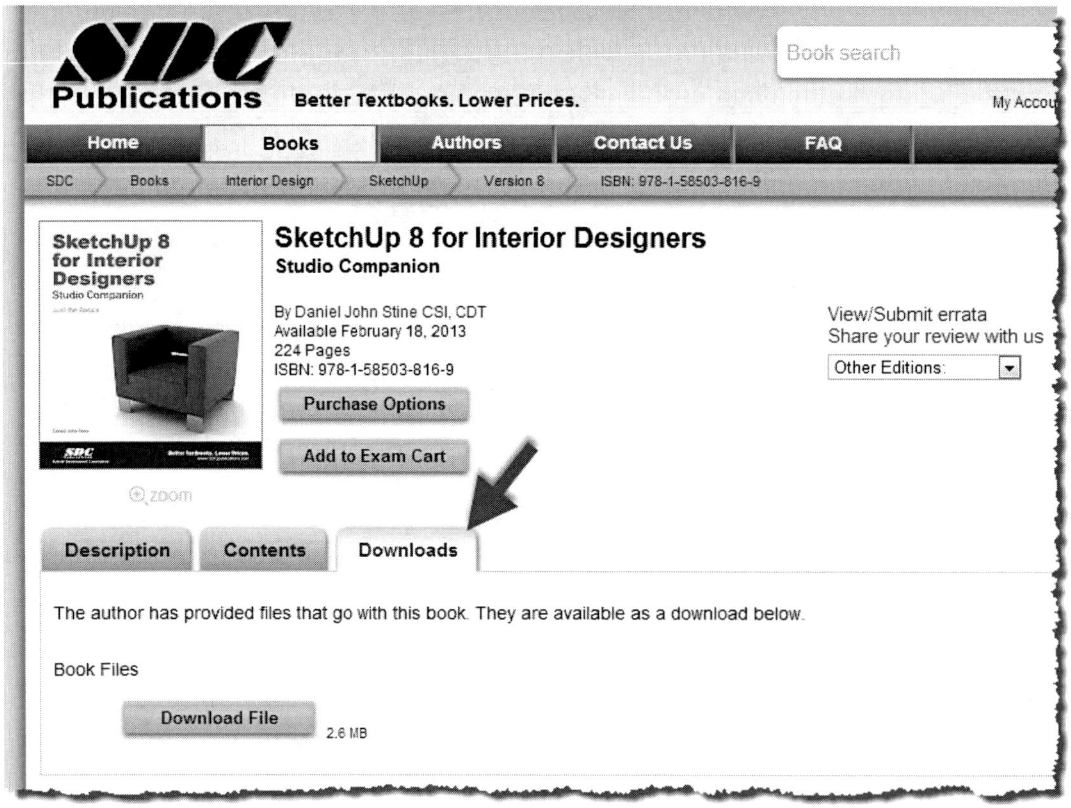

FIGURE 3.4 Download required files for this book

5. In a new SketchUp model, Select **File → Open**.

   ***TIP:** Pressing **Ctrl + O** will also get you to the Open dialog.*

6. In the *Open* dialog, browse to your hard drive where you save the files you downloaded and select **Office Building.skp**.

7. Click **Open**; if you are prompted to save the current model, choose **No**.

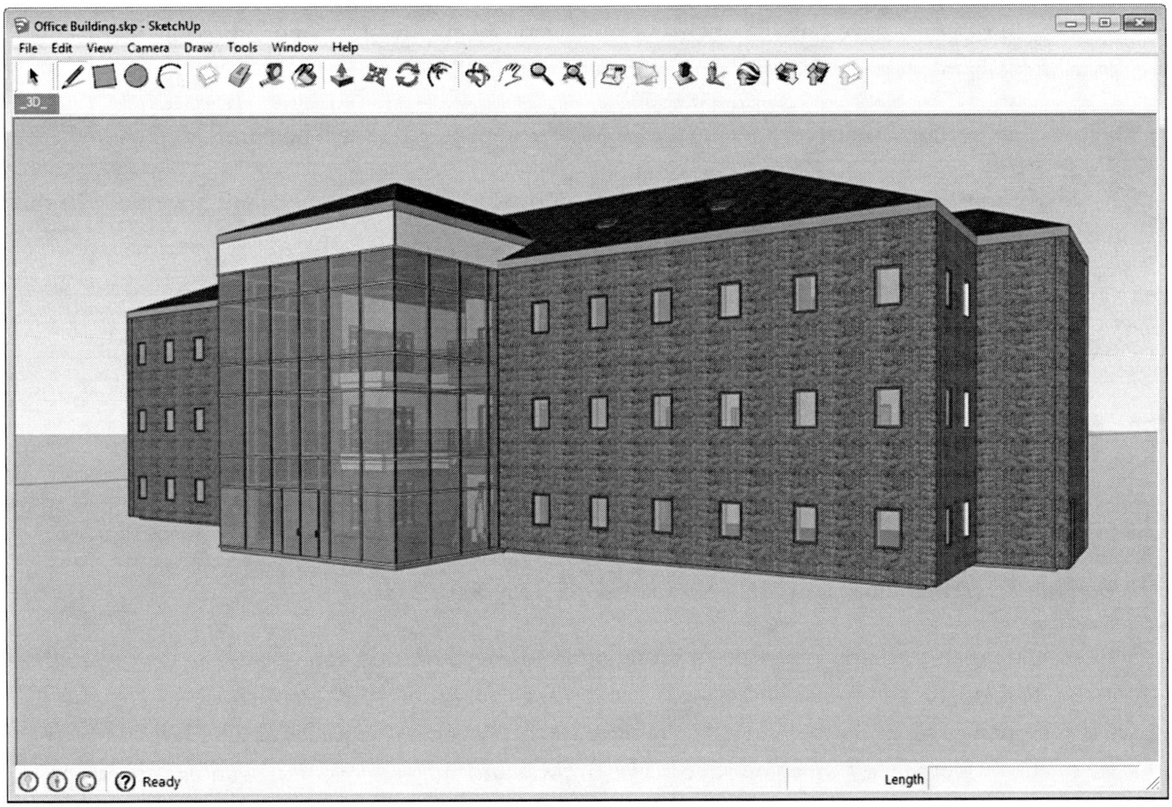

FIGURE 3.5 File opened

You are now in the *Office Building* file (Figure 3.5). Because you did not do any work in the new file you had just created, SketchUp discards that file in favor of the file you are opening. However, if you made any changes, SketchUp would have prompted you to save before closing the file. In

SketchUp you can only have one file open at a time, but it is possible to have multiple sessions of SketchUp open – each with a different file.

> ***TIP:*** *To open multiple copies of SketchUp, simply double-click on the desktop icon or the SketchUp icon via Start menu.*

Closing a SketchUp File:

Because you can only have one file open at a time, and one file must be open, the only way to "close" a file is to open another file or exit SketchUp altogether.

The previous section discussed opening a file, and exiting SketchUp will be coming up soon.

If you have not saved your file yet, you will be prompted to do so before SketchUp closes. **Do not save at this time**.

Saving a SketchUp Project:

> ***NOTE:*** *At this time we will not actually save a project.*

To save a project file, simply select **Save** from the **File** menu. You can also press **Ctrl + S** on the keyboard.

When the *Standard* toolbar is open, you can also click the **Save** icon. 

You should get in the habit of saving often to avoid losing work due to a power outage or program crash. The program automatically creates a backup file every time you save; that is, the current SKP file is renamed to SKB. So the SKP file will have the most current model and the SKB will be the state of the model the last time you saved. The backup and auto-save options can be set via **Window** (menu) → **Preferences** (Figure 3.6).

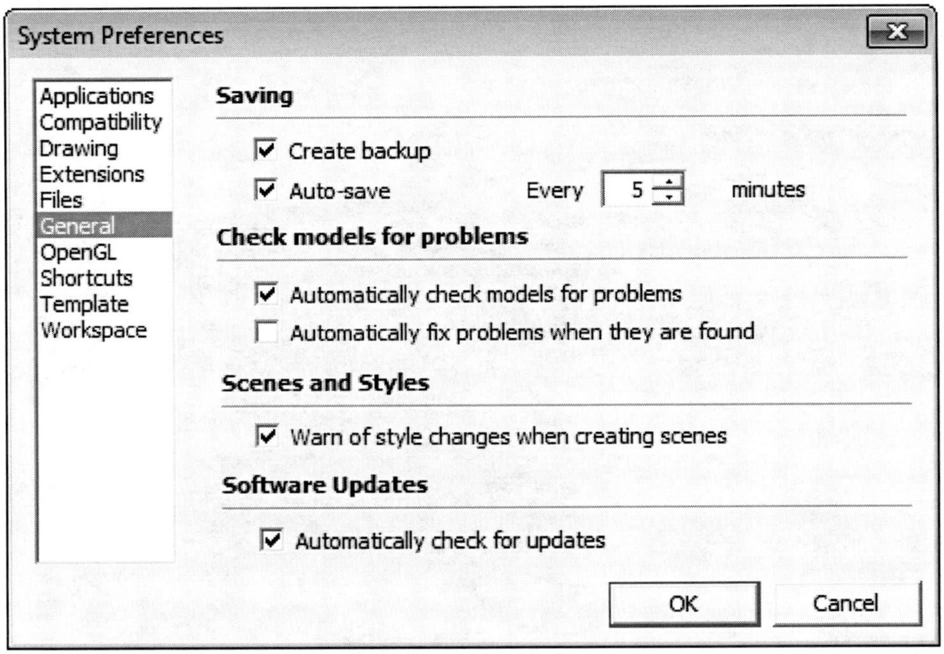

FIGURE 3.6 System Preferences Dialog

Auto-save files are saved in the same folder as the file. If SketchUp crashes, the file can be used to recover what would otherwise be lost work. When SketchUp closes properly, the auto-save file is deleted and thus cannot be accessed.

Closing the SketchUp Program:

Finally, from the **File** menu select **Exit**. This will close the current file and shut down SketchUp. Again, you will be prompted to save, if needed, before SketchUp closes. **Do not save at this time**.

You can also click the red "X" in the upper right corner of the SketchUp application window.

Project Example: Reception Desk. *Image courtesy of LHB; www.LHBcorp.com*

Section 4
Viewing SketchUp Models

Learning to get around in a SketchUp model is essential to accurate and efficient design and visualization. We will review a few tools and techniques now so you are ready to use them with the first design exercise.

You will select a sample file from the files downloaded previously in Section 3.

1. Open SketchUp and then select **File → Open**.

2. Browse to the folder where you saved the files downloaded from the publisher's website: www.SDCpublications.com. If you did not download the files yet, refer back to Figure 3-4 for more information, if necessary.

3. Select the file **Office Building.skp** and click **Open** (Figure 4.1).

You should see a view of the SketchUp model similar to that shown in Figure 4.1.

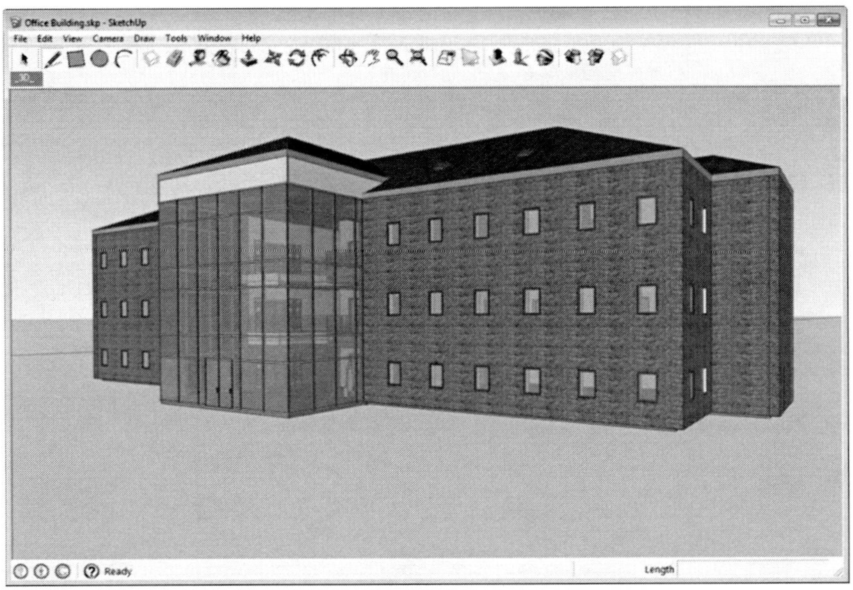

FIGURE 4.1 Office Building.skp model

Using Zoom and Pan Tools:

You can access the navigation tools from the *Getting Started* toolbar – shown in the image below. The tools are, from left to right: *Orbit*, *Pan*, *Zoom* and *Zoom Extents*.

These tools do the following:

- Orbit: Fly the camera view around the model
- Pan: Pan the camera view vertically and/or horizontally
- Zoom: Zooms in or out – centered on current view
- Zoom Extents: Zooms view so everything in the model is visible

You will now have an opportunity to try each of these tools in the sample model.

Orbit

4. Select the **Orbit** icon from the *Getting Started* toolbar. *Keyboard Shortcut*: **O**

5. Drag your cursor across the screen from right to left – holding down the left mouse button. Stop when your view of the building looks similar to Figure 4.2.

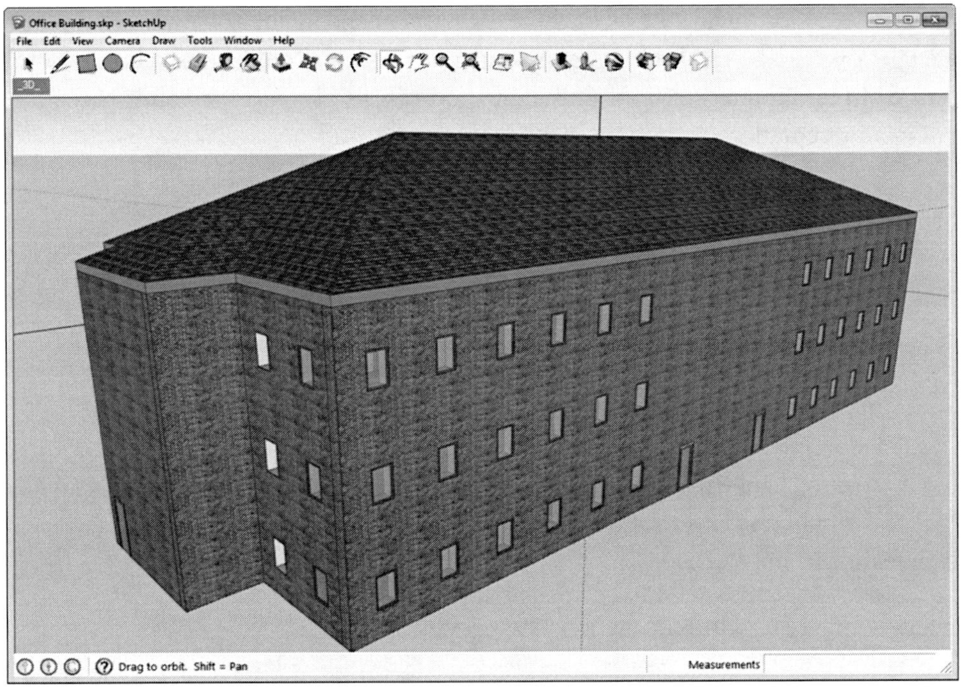

FIGURE 4.2 Using the Orbit tool

Spend a little time using the *Orbit* tool, looking at the model from the top, bottom and each side.

FIGURE 4.3 Scene tab

6. Click the **Select** icon to cancel the current tool and get back into the default mode of being able to select things in the model.

7. Once you are done experimenting with the *Orbit* tool, you can quickly get back to your original view by clicking the "_3D_" **scene tab** (Figure 4.3).

Additional *scene tabs* can be added, saving views of different parts of the building – both interior and exterior. The scene tabs can also be used to define the outline of an animation, where SketchUp smoothly transitions from location to location. This animation can also be exported and shared with others or used in a presentation.

Pan

The ***Pan*** tool allows you to reposition the camera left/right or up/down relative to the current view direction. This is helpful if a portion of the building extends off the screen and you want to see it, but you do not want to change the angle of the view (i.e. see more of the side rather than the front) – as the *Orbit* tool would do. This tool will be particularly useful when composing interior views. Next you will test-drive the *Pan* tool.

8. If your view is not reset, do so now per the previous step.
9. Click the **Pan** icon from the *Getting Started* toolbar. *Keyboard Shortcut*: **H**

Notice how the cursor has changed to a hand symbol to let you know the *Pan* tool is active.

10. Drag the cursor from right to left until the view looks similar to Figure 4.4).

As you can see, the camera moved, which is similar to you walking by a building. As you walk by, you see a little more of what is around the corner than when you were right next to the front. Later you will learn how to toggle between **Perspective** and **Parallel Projection**, the first being more realistic with vanishing lines, the latter is like a flat 2D drawing. When the view is in *Parallel Projection* mode, you do not see more or less of anything – the view stays the same, it is just being moved around on the screen.

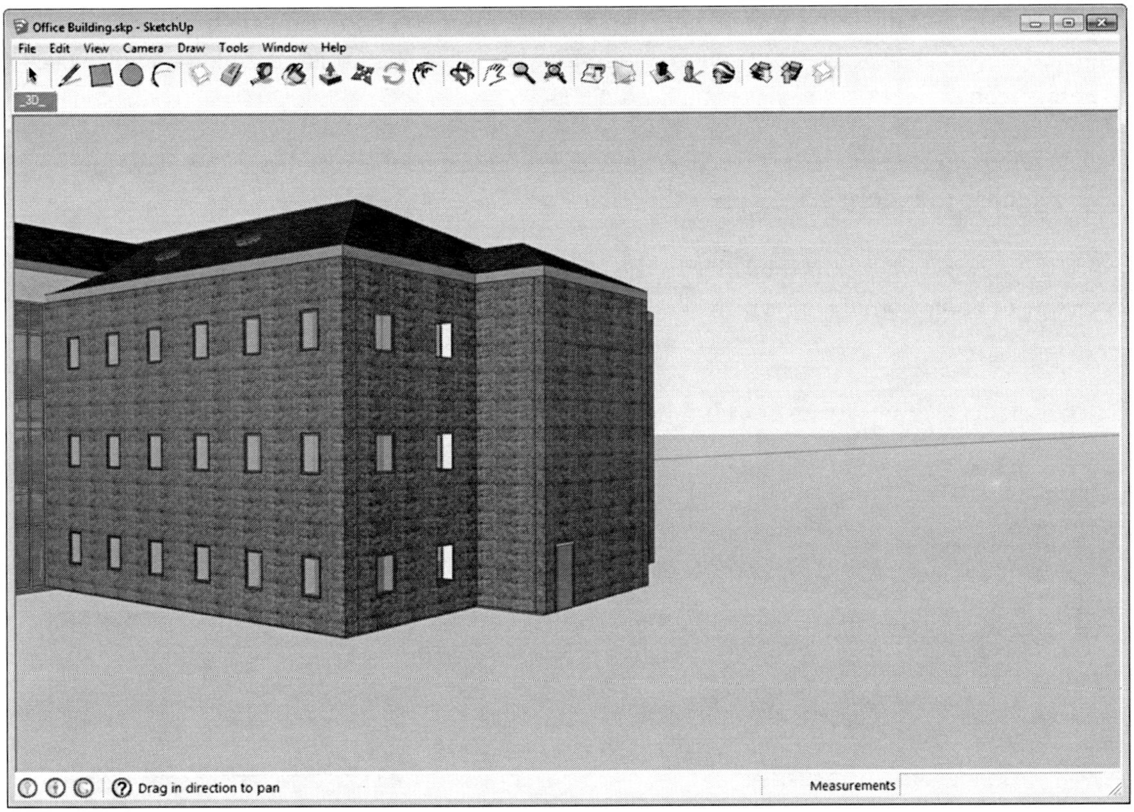

FIGURE 4.4 Using the Pan tool

 Zoom

The ***Zoom*** tool basically does what the name implies… it zooms in and out of your model. Keep in mind it is not changing the size of anything. This feature is not the same as zooming in and out on your camcorder. With the camcorder analogy, in SketchUp you would actually be walking closer to the building when zooming rather than simply magnifying an area. In fact, you can zoom in so far you actually enter the building. Don't forget, you can click the *scene tab* to quickly restore your view if things get messed up.

11. Select the **Zoom** icon from the *Getting Started* toolbar. *Keyboard Shortcut:* **Z**

Notice the cursor changes to a magnifying glass symbol to let you know you are in the *Zoom* command. This will be active until you press the **Esc** key, click to start another command or click the **Select** icon.

12. Drag your cursor from the bottom of the screen to the top, until the view looks similar to Figure 4.5.

Notice the view is only zoomed relative to the center of the drawing window. You will learn a better way to zoom coming up, which allows better control of where you zoom.

Notice how the high quality textures (i.e. building materials) appear more realistic the closer you get.

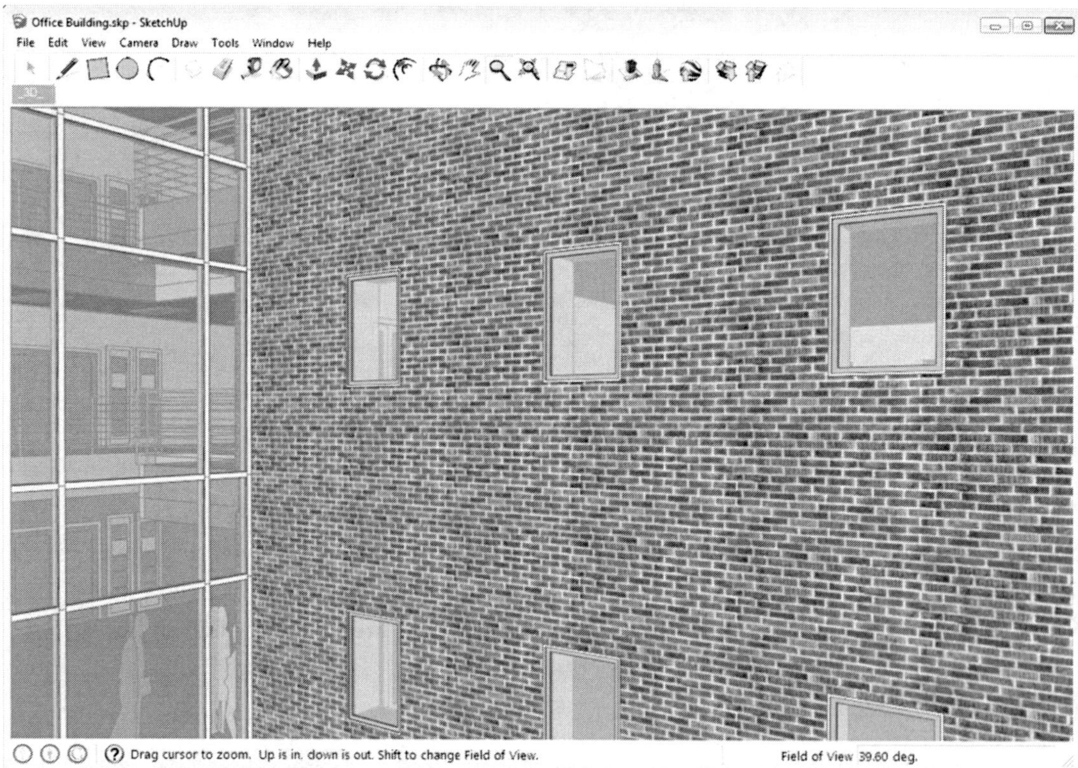

FIGURE 4.5 Using the Zoom tool

Sometimes you need to make several dragging motions with your mouse to zoom in far enough (because there is not enough room on the desk or your arm simply will not reach). To do this, click and drag as far as you can, and then release the mouse button, move your mouse back, and then repeat the process (i.e. click and drag).

Dragging the mouse in the opposite direction zooms out.

13. Try zooming out, using the ***Zoom*** tool, dragging from top to bottom.

14. When finished testing the *Zoom* tool, click the ***scene tab*** to reset the view.

    FYI: *Holding down the* Shift *key while zooming changes the field of view degrees. This is similar to changing the lens on a camera. A larger angle gives you a wide-angle view, allowing you to see more in a smaller space. However the view can be more distorted as the angle is increased*

Zoom Extents

The ***Zoom Extents*** tool is a quick way to make sure you are seeing everything in the model from your current vantage point. You simply click the icon and SketchUp does the rest. This can be tricky if something is floating way out in space because using *Zoom Extents* will show a stray line and the rest of your model on the same screen – which means your model might be a tiny dot on the screen somewhere.

15. Try the ***Zoom Extents*** tool:

    a. Zoom in on the building (similar to Figure 4.5).

    b. Click the **Zoom Extents** icon. *Keyboard Shortcut*: Shift + **Z**

In this example this would not be any faster than clicking the *scene tab*. However, there will not always be a corresponding *scene tab* for every angle from which you will be looking at your model. So the *Zoom Extents* tool is very useful.

Using the Scroll Wheel on the Mouse

The scroll wheel on the mouse is a must for those using SketchUp. In SketchUp you can *Zoom* and *Orbit* without even clicking the *Zoom* or *Orbit* icons. You simply **scroll the wheel to zoom** and **hold the wheel button down to orbit**. This can be done while in another command (e.g., while sketching lines). Another nice feature is that the drawing zooms into the area near your cursor, rather than zooming only at the center of the drawing window. Give this a try before moving on. Once you get the hang of it you will not want to use the icons. The only thing you cannot do is *Zoom Extents* so everything is visible on the screen.

To use the ***Pan*** feature (aka, *hand* tool), simply hold down the **Shift** key while pressing the center wheel button.

Project Example: Waiting Area. *Image courtesy of LHB; www.LHBcorp.com*

Section 5
Help System

Using the *Help* system is often required when you are having problems or trying to do something advanced. This section will present a basic overview of the *Help* system so you can find your way around when needed. It is important that you don't skip this section as it can help reduce your stress level when/if you run into problems.

1. Open SketchUp, if not already open. It does not matter if you are in a blank file or a sample file.

2. Select **Help → Help Center**.

3. Your default internet browser opens and you are in SketchUp's *Help* system (Figure 5.1). The entire *Help* system is internet based, thus allowing Trimble the ability to make revisions and additions as needed.

Project Example: Art Glass Feature Wall. *Image courtesy of LHB; www.LHBcorp.com*

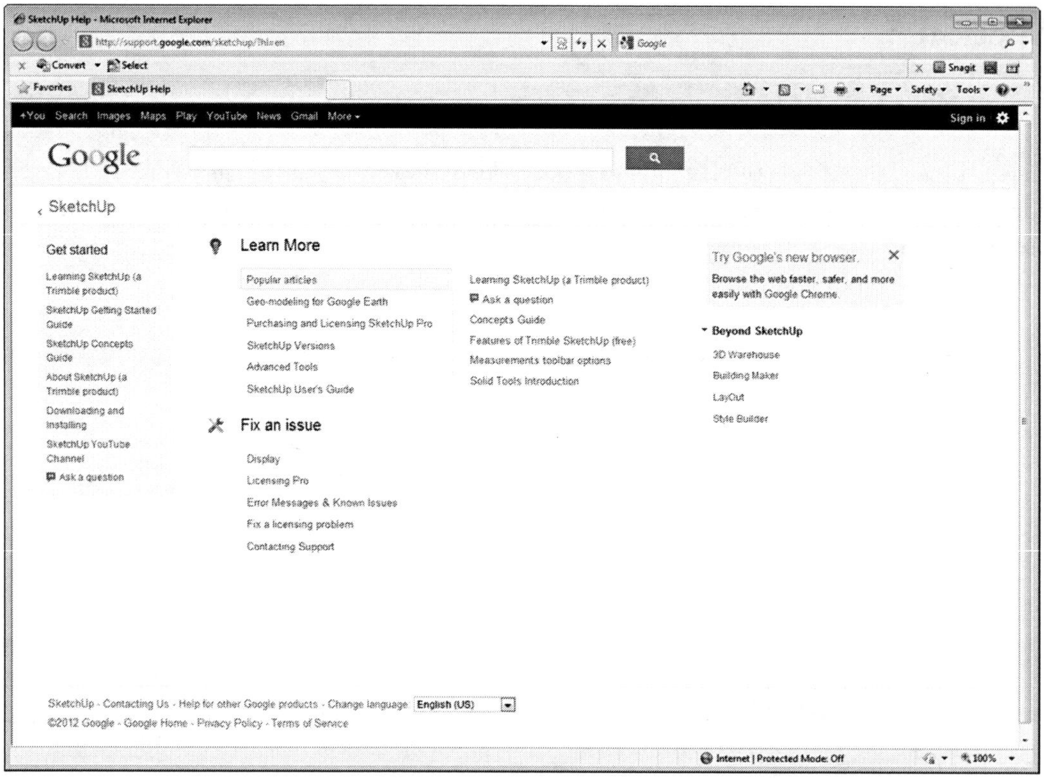

FIGURE 5.1 Help system interface

Searching for answers

The various links found on the *Help* page speak for themselves. However, most of the time you can just type a command name and press **Enter** to get a refined list of options from which to choose. You will try that now.

4. Click within the search box and type **ORBIT**.

5. Press **Enter** or click the **Search Help** button to the right.

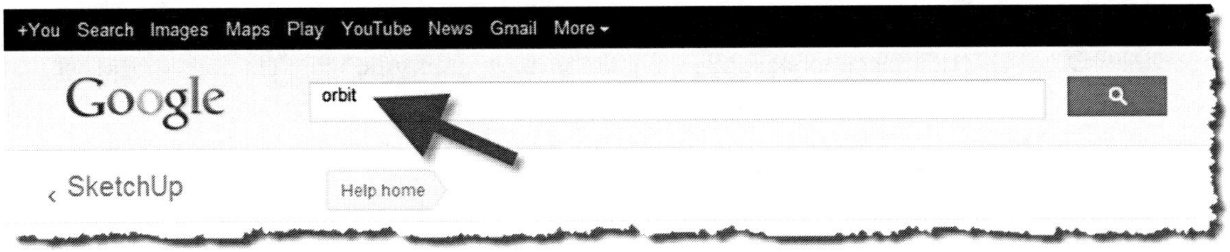

FIGURE 5.2 Entering a word to search for within Help

Trimble SketchUp uses the Google search engine to return help topics related to your search parameters (remember, SketchUp used to be owned by Google). The image below shows the results (Figure 5.3). Since this is a web based search, the results can change over time. Of course, you also need internet access for the search to work.

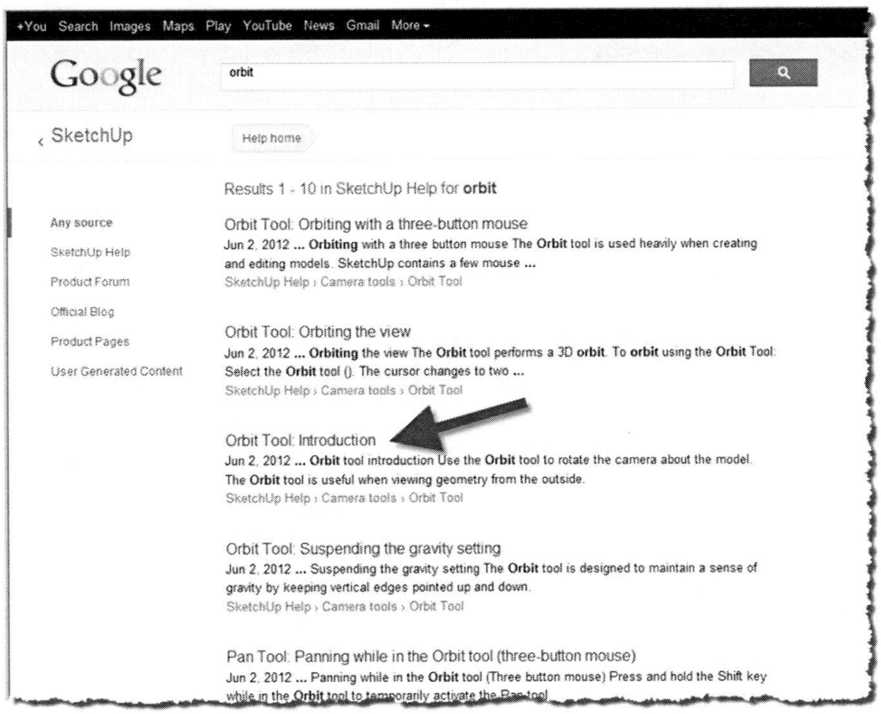

FIGURE 5.3 Search results for "orbit"

The most relevant item may not always be first. The example's first item relates more to the mouse rather than *Orbit*. The first place to start might be the introduction link, which is third in the list (Figure 5.3). Also notice the word(s) you typed is bold in the title and description.

6. Click on the link titled **Orbit Tool: Introduction**.

Your result should look similar to Figure 5.4. Notice the various items: basic description, keyboard shortcut, tabs to display additional information on this topic (on the left) and a quality control-type survey at the bottom.

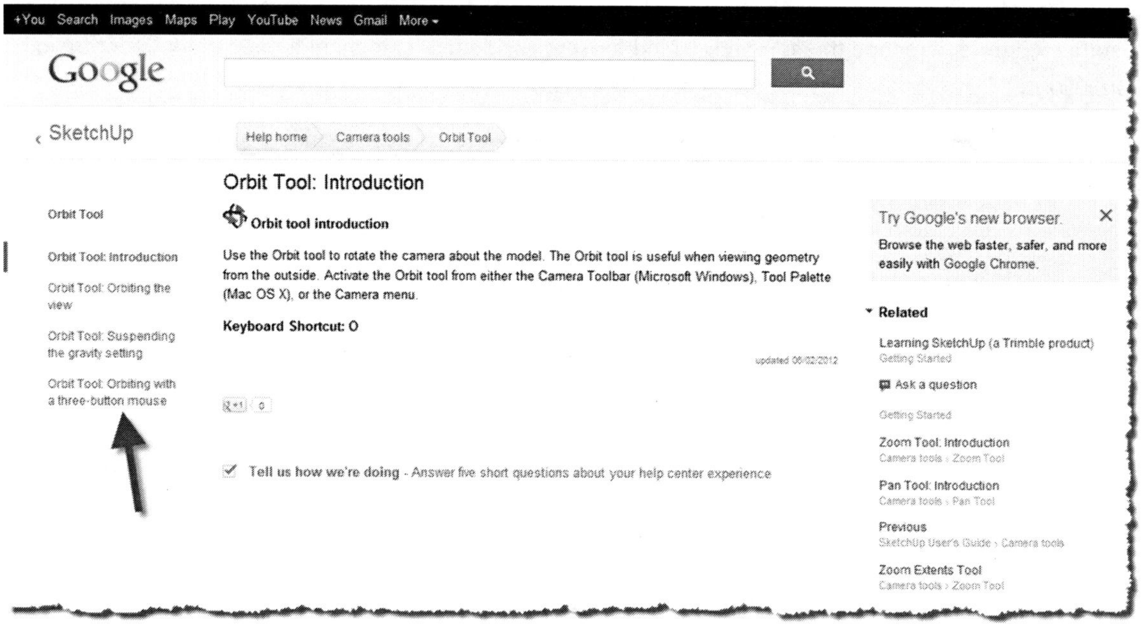

FIGURE 5.4 Sample help item

7. Try clicking on the links on the left (i.e., *Orbiting*, *Suspending* and *Mouse*) to see the information that is shown (see arrow in image above).

Most of the results come from the formal SketchUp *Help* system. However, some of the help results point to the SketchUp user-to-user forum (Figure 5.4). The green text below the description indicates where the information is coming from (hard to show in a black and white textbook). The forums can be a great source of information, but you do need to understand that this is not official SketchUp advice – so users beware.

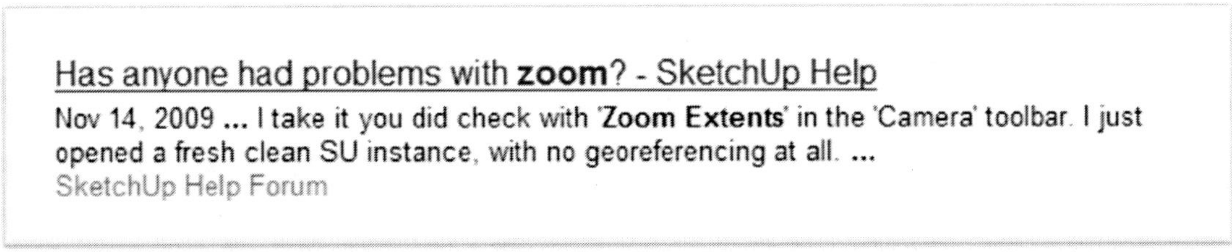

FIGURE 5.5 Search result pointing to user forum

If you are searching for a multi-word tool it is best to add quotation marks around the entire search text to narrow the search. For example, if you want to search for information on the *Zoom Extents* tool, you should enter:

- "zoom extents" rather than: zoom extents

Google will show results with both words, but if quotation marks are not used, it will also show results with just one of the words.

Anytime you want to return to the initial help screen you can click the "Help home" link in the upper left.

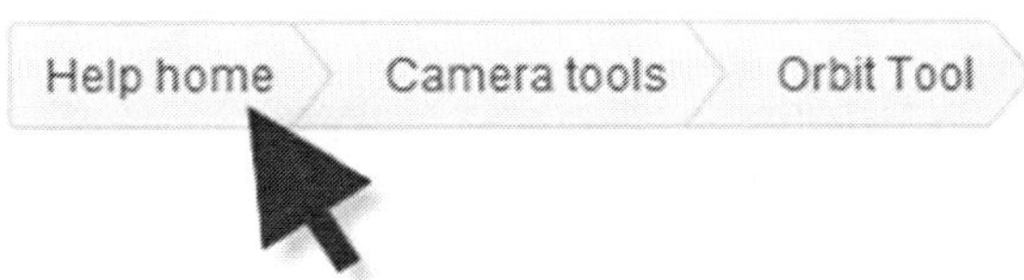

SketchUp User's Guide

Another way to learn and do research on SketchUp is via the user's guide. This is an indexed list which makes it easy to find information on a specific topic (e.g., placing a camera). You might not even know the name of the command you want to use. In the user's guide you can look for it by process of elimination. This is a great way to stumble across information you were not even looking for – similar to randomly opening a book to a page and something catches your eye, so you start reading about it.

The user's guide can be found via a link on the initial help page. The highest level of the index tree is shown to the right (Figure 5.6).

Be sure to refer to the *Help* system anytime you get stuck to see if it can help you find the answer to your problem.

User Interface
Principle Tools
Drawing tools
Modification tools
Construction tools
Camera tools
Walkthrough tools
Sandbox tools
Solid Tools
Google Toolbar
Advanced Camera tools
Model settings and managers
Entities
Input and output
Common tasks
Technical Reference

FIGURE 5.6 User's guide index

Project Example: Hallway Flooring. *Image courtesy of LHB; www.LHBcorp.com*

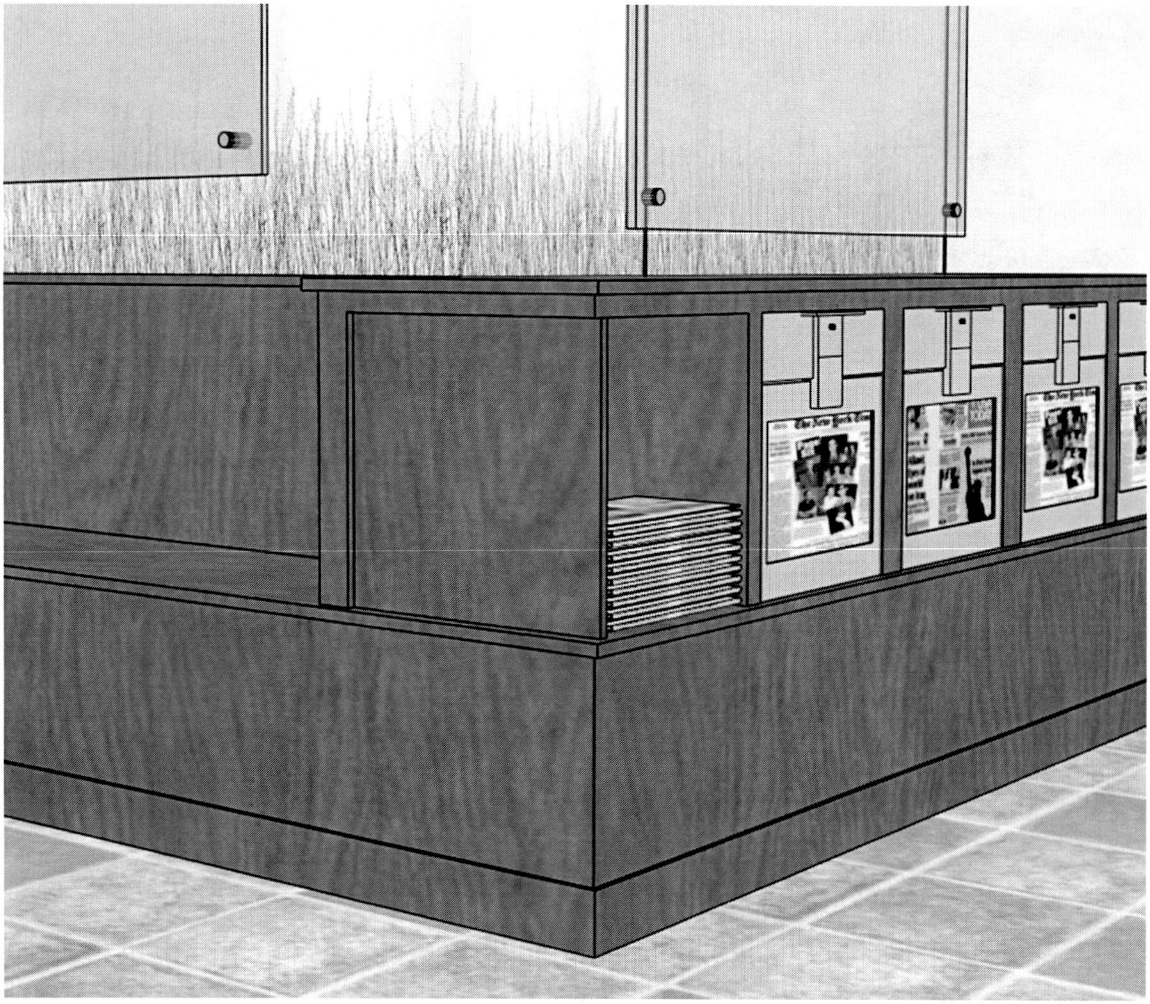

Project Example: Custom Casework. *Image courtesy of LHB; www.LHBcorp.com*

Section 6
The Basic Entities

Given the amazing images one can create using SketchUp, it may be somewhat surprising that there are mainly eight types of entities which can be added to a model.

They are:

- Edges
- Surfaces
- Annotation
  - Dimensions
  - Text
  - 3D Text
- Components
- Groups
- Guide (reference line)

The next few pages will provide a brief overview of each of these entity types.

Edges

SketchUp is a face-based program, and all surfaces (i.e. faces) must be defined by an edge. This is the fundamental building block of a SketchUp model.

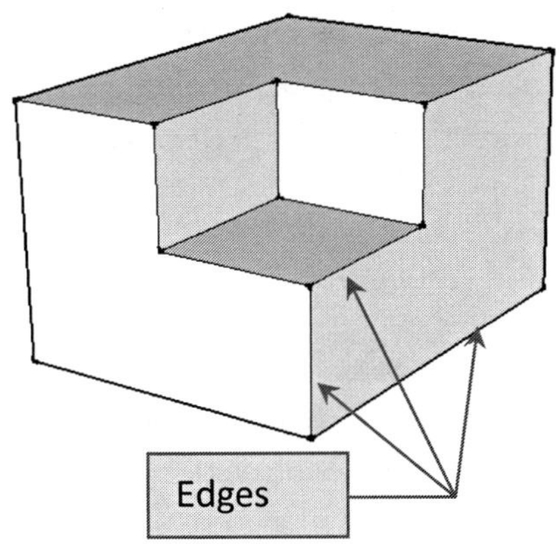

FIGURE 6.1 Edges pointed out

Edges are created with one of the *Draw* tools:

- Line
- Circle
- Arc
- Rectangle
- Polygon
- Freehand

Edges can be created with very specific length (or radius), or arbitrarily by clicking anywhere within the drawing window. It is easy to snap to one of the three planes (axes) while drawing lines. This makes it possible to draw 3D shapes from a single 3D view (more on this later).

A basic cube has twelve edges. Figure 6.1 has 21 edges and Figure 6.2 has two edges.

Even circles are made up of small edges. When one is being created, the *Value Control Box* (on the *Status Bar*) lists the number of sides that will be used to approximate the circle. This number can be increased to make larger circles smooth, or decreased to make smaller circles less complex (which can be a burden on model performance).

Later in this chapter you will get some practice drawing edges and editing them.

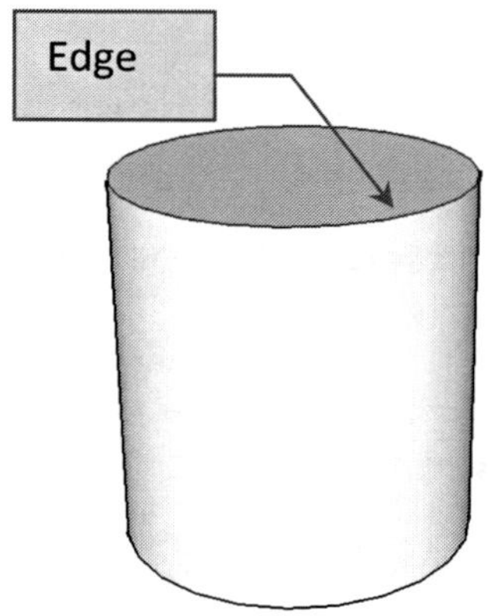

FIGURE 6.2 Edge pointed out

Edges can be modified with a number of tools. For example, an edge can be scaled, rotated, divided, copied, offset and erased. These tools are accessible from the *Tools* menu, toolbars (which may not be visible yet), right-click menus (when the edge is selected) and keyboard shortcuts.

Edges can also be placed on *Layers* in order to control visibility. A *Layer* can be turned off, making everything assigned to that *Layer* invisible.

Surfaces

A surface is the second most significant type of entity in SketchUp. You might be surprised to learn that no tool exists to create a surface! They are created automatically when the conditions are right.

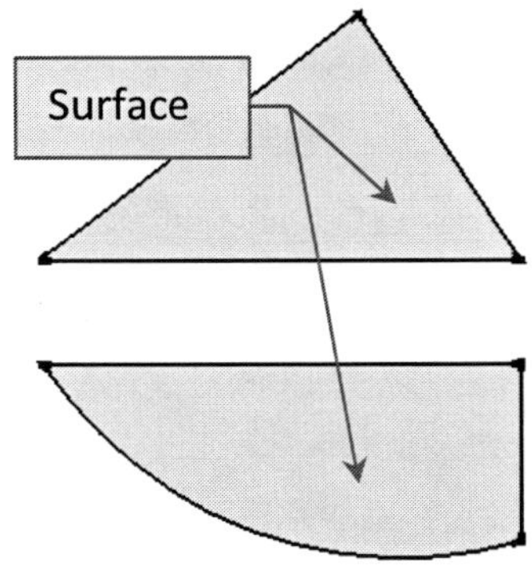

FIGURE 6.3
Surfaces defined by at least three edges

What are the conditions in which a surface is automatically created? The simple answer is that **a series of edges forms an enclosed area**. When the last edge is drawn which defines an enclosed area, a surface is created. This can be as few as three edges – forming a triangle.

The image to the right (Figure 6.3) shows two examples of three connected edges defining a *surface*. Note the edges can be a combination of straight and curved lines.

If an *edge* is erased, the *surface* is also erased, seeing as it no longer has a boundary.

In addition to *edges* forming a closed perimeter, there is another important requirement a new modeler needs to be aware of; that is, **all the lines forming the enclosure must be coplanar**.

Project Example *Image courtesy of LHB; www.LHBcorp.com*

If you don't already know, the easiest way to describe coplanar is to think of all the edges as lines drawn on a flat piece of paper. As long as all the lines are in the same plane (i.e., on that flat piece of paper) a *surface* will be created.

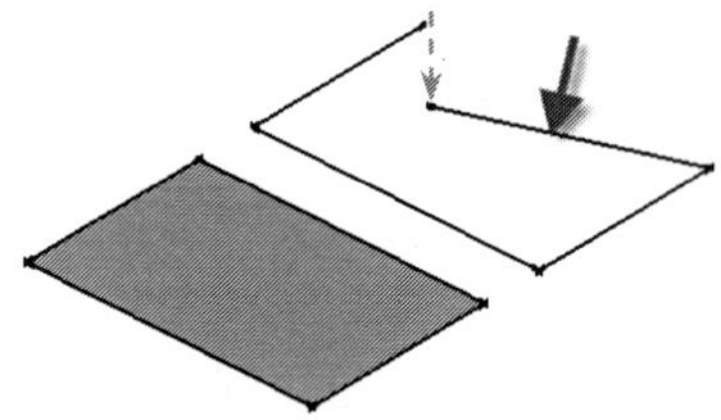

FIGURE 6.4
Coplanar on left, not on right

Surfaces may have materials painted on them. They can also be placed on *Layers* in order to control visibility.

A surface can be deleted; simply select it and press the **Delete** key on the keyboard. The only way to get another surface is to draw a line directly on top of one of the existing *edges*. SketchUp will then create a surface and delete the extra line, as it does not allow two lines to exist directly on top of each other.

FIGURE 6.5 Another angle of Figure 6.4

Dimensions 

Dimensions can be added to your SketchUp model. These are smart entities; they are not sketched lines and manually entered text. A *dimension* entity becomes a permanent part of the model, unlike the *Tape Measure* tool (which is used to list distances without drawing anything).

To place a dimension you simply pick three points; the first two are what you want to dimension and the third is the location of the dimension line and text. SketchUp automatically displays the correct length.

The dimensions are associative, relative to the first two points picked. The dimension will grow or shrink if the geometry is modified. However, if the geometry is deleted the dimension will remain (but is no longer associated to anything).

Dimensions can be tricky in that they may appear correctly and legibly from one angle (Figure 6.6a) but not another (Figure 6.6b). But the visibility of a *dimension* can be controlled by *Layers* or by *Scene* (more on what scenes are later).

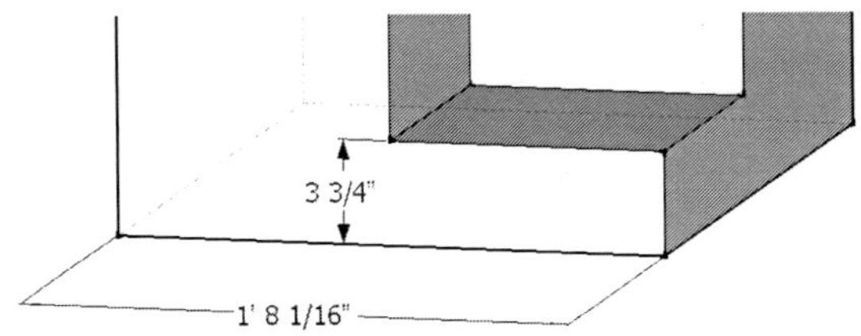

FIGURE 6.6A Dimensions added while viewing the model from this angle

To adjust various settings related to how dimensions are created, go to **Window → Model info** and then click **Dimensions** in the list on the left.

Text

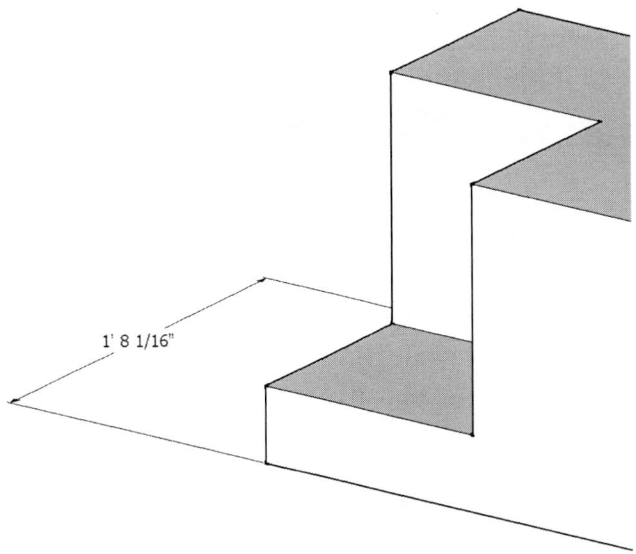

FIGURE 6.6B One dimension still visible when view angle is changed using orbit

SketchUp has a tool which allows you to add notes with leaders (i.e., pointing at something). To place a *Text* entity, you make two clicks and then type (or accept the default value). Default value? If you point to a *surface*, SketchUp will automatically list the area of that surface. If an *edge* is pointed to, SketchUp will list its length. An example of each can be seen in the image on the next page (Figure 6.7).

If you don't want a leader, simply click in empty space and you can just type text. The text "Option A" is an example of text without a leader (Figure 6.7).

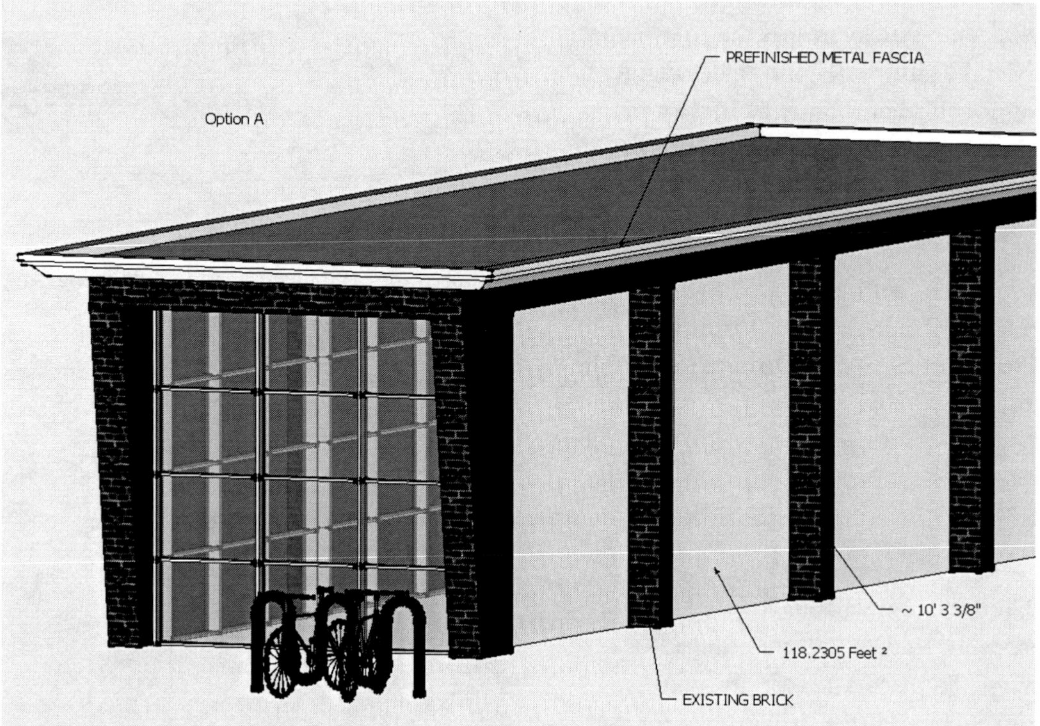

FIGURE 6.7 Notes added using the Text tool

Similar to dimensions, text entities remain visible when the vantage point is changed, using *Orbit* for example. As you can see in the Figure 6.8, this can get a bit messy. *Text* visibility can also be controlled with *Layers* and *Scenes* like *dimensions.*

For the most part, notes and dimensions are left until the end of the modeling or added outside of SketchUp – in LayOut or a CAD program such as AutoCAD or Revit.

When text is right-clicked on, a menu pops up which allows you to change the arrow type and leader (Figure 6.9). These options, plus the ability to change the font, are available via the ***Entity Info*** dialog. This can be turned on from the *Window* pull-down menu.

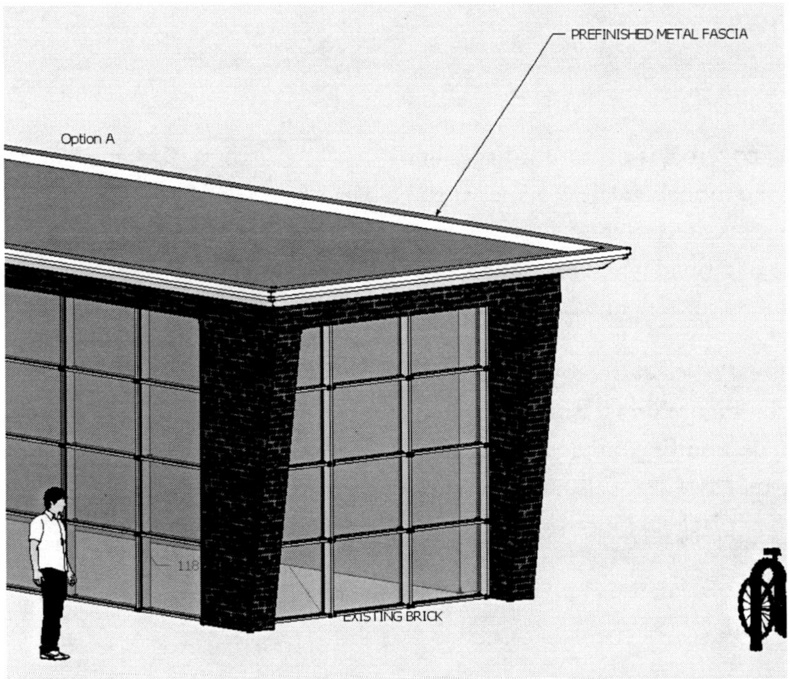

FIGURE 6.8 Notes still visible when model rotated using orbit

The default settings for text can be changed via **Window → Model Info**, and then selecting **Text** from the list on the left.

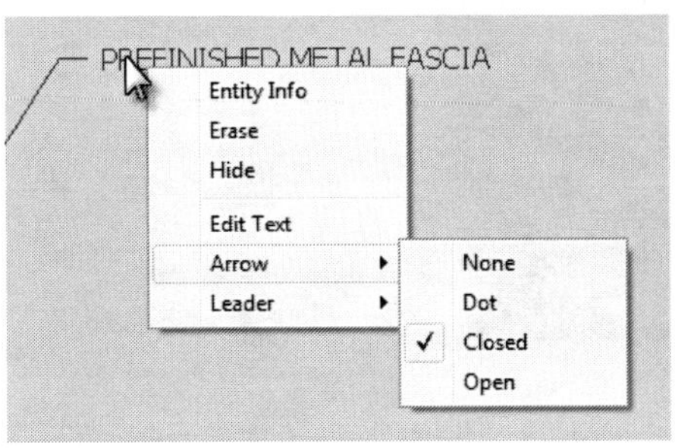

FIGURE 6.9 Right-click options for text

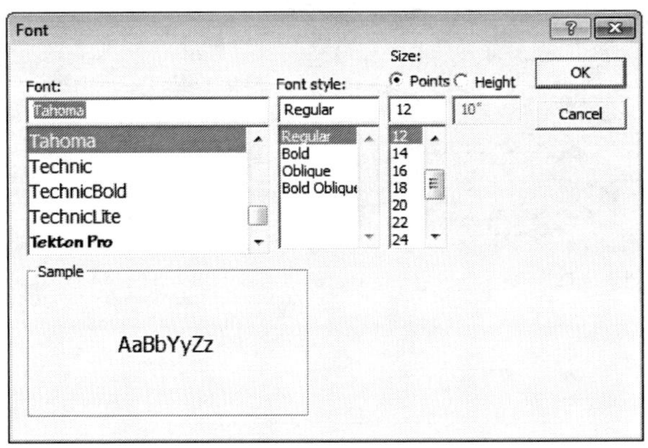

FIGURE 6.10 Changing font for text entity

3D Text

The *Text* tool, just covered, is meant for notes and comments about the model. *3D Text* is meant to be part of the model. This tool is used to model text on signs or letters on the face of a building. Unlike notes created with the *Text* tool, *3D Text* stays right where you put it.

FIGURE 6.11 Adding 3D Text

Placing *3D Text* is easy. Select the tool, and the *Place 3D Text* dialog appears (Figure 6.11). Enter your text and select the options desired for font style, height and thickness (i.e., extruded). Click **OK** and then pick a location on a face to place it.

Once the 3D Text is placed, the *Paint Bucket* tool can be used to apply a material.

FIGURE 6.12 3D Text placed

Once the text is created, it becomes a *Component* that cannot be easily edited (in terms of typing new words).

It is possible to see the properties for *3D Text*, or anything else selected, using the ***Entity Info*** dialog (Figure 6.13). This can be turned on from the *Window* pull-down menu. The information presented varies depending on what is selected. This dialog can remain open while modeling.

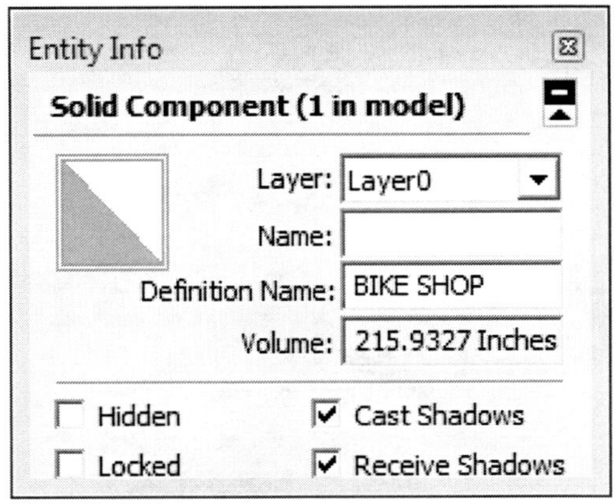

FIGURE 6.13 Entity Info dialog

Components

In SketchUp one can think of *Components* being something like clipart in a word processing program – but clipart on steroids! They are pre-built models which can be reused in your SketchUp model. Some *Components* are flat 2D models while others are complex 3D models. The simple, flat *Components* reduce the resources required of your computer, making it easier to smoothly orbit and inspect your model. For example, many of the trees which designers use in SketchUp are 2D due to the number typically needed. If 3D trees were used, the file would be large and unmanageable. The 2D *Components* can be setup so that they always face you – plus they cast shadows (see Figures 6.14 and 6.15).

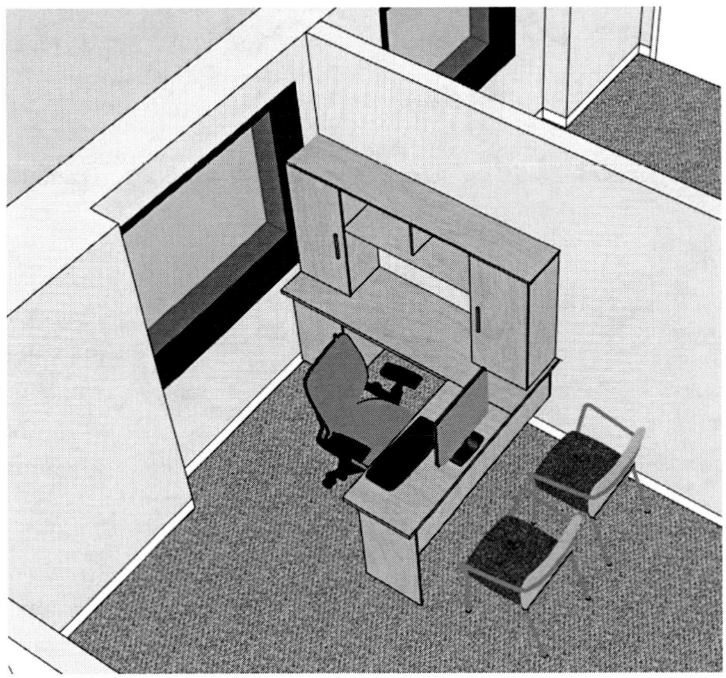

Image courtesy of LHB; www.LHBcorp.com

FIGURE 6.14 2D vs. 3D components; two items are 2D and two are 3D.

Right-clicking on a *Component* allows you to edit it, explode it (reduce it down to individual entities) and add parameters and parametrics using the advanced ***Dynamic Components*** functionality.

Editing a *Component* causes all instances of that *Component*, in your model, to instantly update. You will see an example of this in the next section.

FIGURE 6.15 Rotated view of previous image

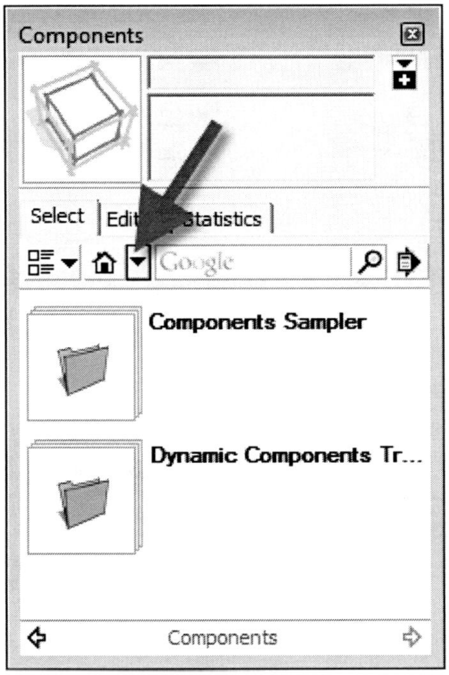

FIGURE 6.16 Components dialog

One of the truly great things about using SketchUp is the amount of content the designer has access to. Google hosts a site called ***Trimble 3D Warehouse*** which has thousands of *Components* ready for the taking.

Some of the content found on *Trimble 3D Warehouse* is provided directly by Google, while other content comes from manufacturers of products (who hope you will ultimately buy or specify their products) or from end users like you.

Of course, *users beware* on anything one downloads and uses in their design. As a design professional (or would-be, someday, design professional) you are responsible for code and performance compliance. So you cannot just assume the toilet or the door you downloaded is the correct size. You need to double-check it with the manufacturer's data sheets. Now, if the content was created by the manufacturers, it is highly probable that it is the correct size.

The *Components* dialog (Figure 6.16) is the easiest way to add *Components* to your model. This can be accessed from the *Window* menu. The down arrow highlighted reveals a menu which provides shortcuts to groups of content, such as *Architecture*, *People*, *Playground*, etc.

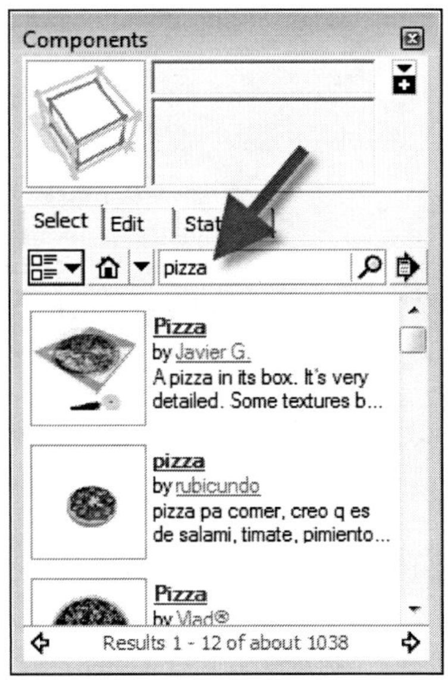

FIGURE 6.17 Components search

It is also possible to search for *Components.* You may be surprised at what you can find. Figure 6.17 shows some of the results when searching for "**pizza**"! Notice the author of the component is listed directly under the name.

Try a few searches to see what you can find – maybe try goat, newspaper, or snowboard.

See the next section for more on *Components.*

Groups

A *Group* is similar to a *Component* in that you can select one part of it and the entire representation is selected (selecting potentially hundreds of entities with a single pick). However, that is about all that is the same between them.

Groups are meant for one-off type items; that is, a unique reception desk, a built-in entertainment center, etc. A *Component* is used when your model will contain many instances of an object.

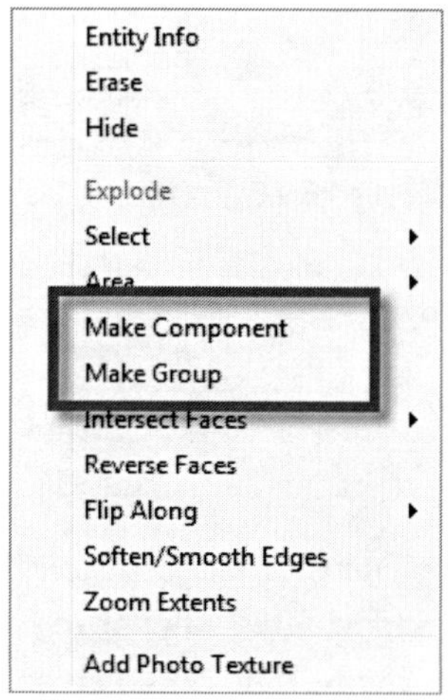

FIGURE 6.18 Right-click menu

Both *Groups* and *Components* are easy to create. You simply model something, select it and then right-click (on it). At this point you can select either **Make Group** or **Make Component** (Figure 6.18).

Both *Groups* and *Components* can be copied around the model (using the *Move* tool and holding down Ctrl). They both can also be edited, by right-clicking and selecting "edit" from the pop-up menu.

It is important to note that editing a *Group* only changes the specific *Group* you are editing. But editing a *Component* instantly causes all instances of that *Component* to update (see Figures 6.20 and 6.21). This means SketchUp duplicates all information required to define each copy of a *Group.* A single definition is all that is needed for multiple instances of a *Component.* Of course, this means a file with many copies of a *Group* will be larger than one with many copies of a *Component.*

The main thing to keep in mind is that *Groups* are quick and require minimal decisions. *Components* can be much more sophisticated and take a lot of time setting up (creating parameters and parametric relationships, and adding formulas).

When you right-click and select **Make Group**, SketchUp just makes it without asking any questions. It can be selected and named via the *Entity Info* dialog if you wish.

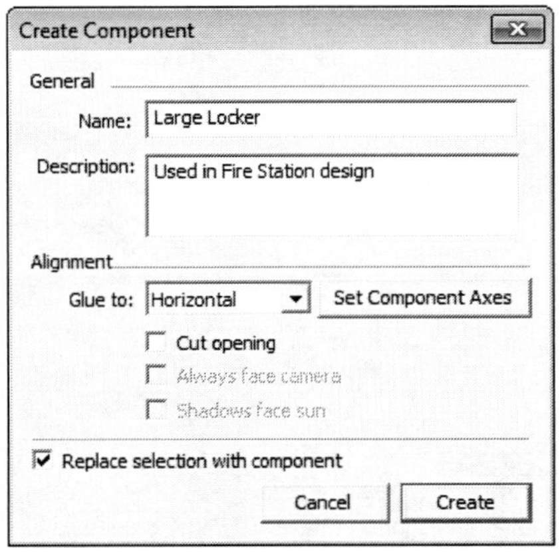

FIGURE 6.19 Right-click menu

When creating a *Component*, the *Create Component* dialog appears (Figure 6.19). Notice the various options:

- Glue to – does the tree stick to the ground or float in the air?
- Always face the camera – this is ideal for flat two-dimensional items.
- Replace selection – turn the current selection into one of the *Components* you are creating.

The images below compare what happens when a *Component* is edited versus a *Group*. Notice all instances of the *Component* are updated, whereas only the selected *Group* being edited is updated (even though the other *Groups* are copies of the one being edited).

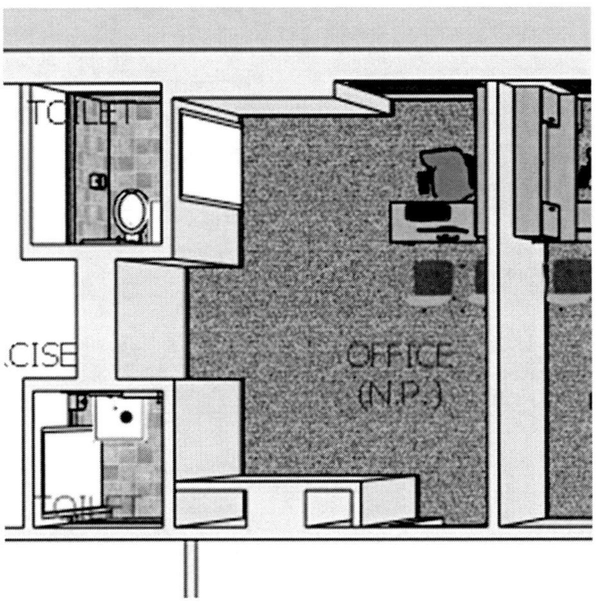

Image courtesy of LHB; www.LHBcorp.com

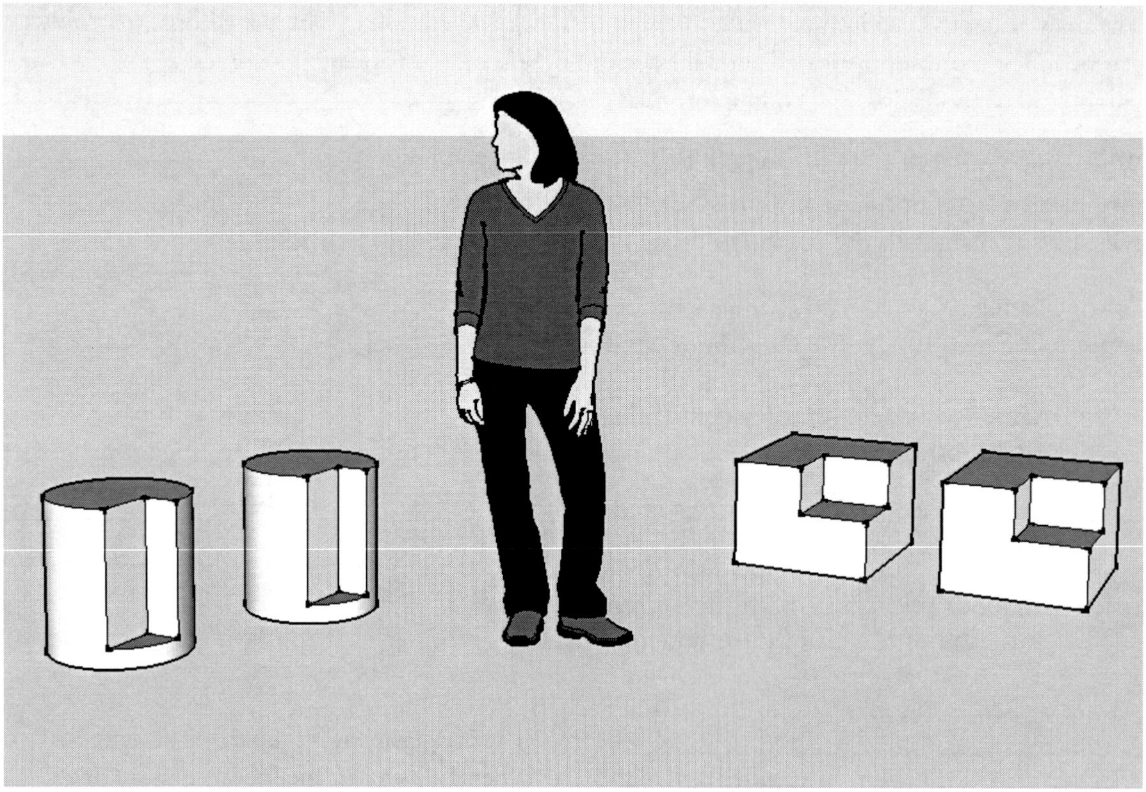

FIGURE 6.20 Components vs. Groups – Components on the left; Groups on the right

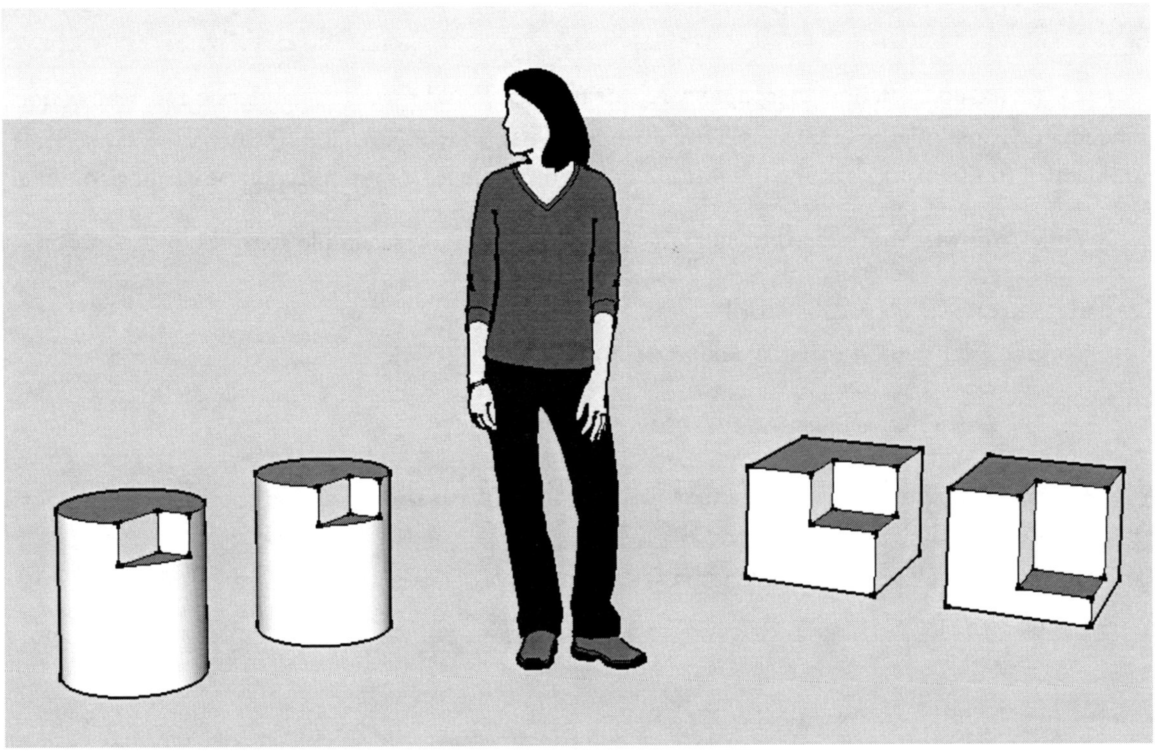

FIGURE 6.21 Components vs. Groups – all Components update; only selected Group updates

Guides

Guide lines (or construction lines) are useful for new users and for a general design reference grid. The image below (Figure 6.22) shows the main *Axes* and a few *Guides* at 5′-0″ intervals. These lines are parallel to the main *Axes* and are infinite in length. Note how they converge at the horizon line.

The ***Tape Measure*** tool is used to create *Guide* lines. Follow these simple steps to create one:

- Start the *Tape Measure* tool.
- Click on the *Edge* of any shape or *Axes*.

> ***FYI:*** *Clicking on an endpoint creates a Guide Point.*

- Drag the cursor perpendicular to where you want the *Guide*.
- Release the mouse to locate the *Guide*.
- Type in a length to (retroactively) adjust the *Guide* location.

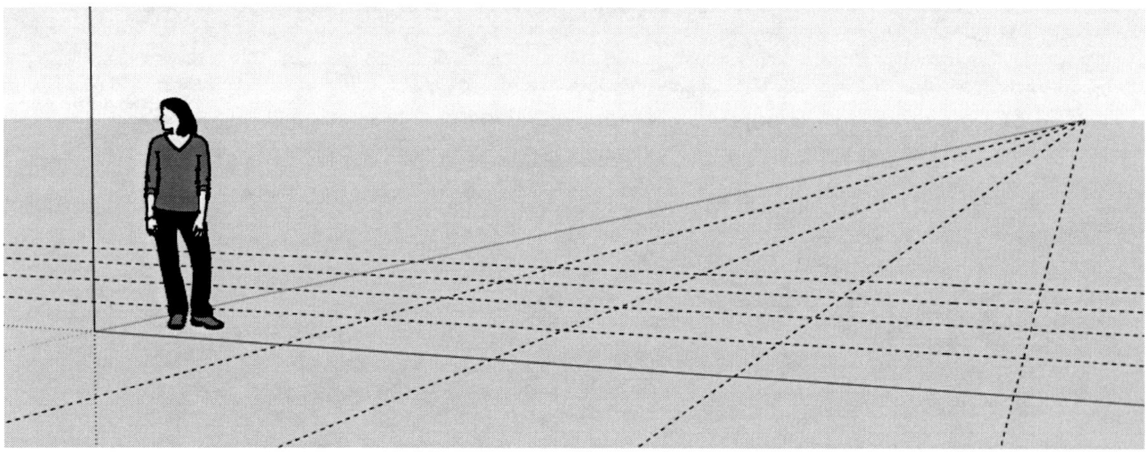

FIGURE 6.22 Guides added at 5′-0″ intervals

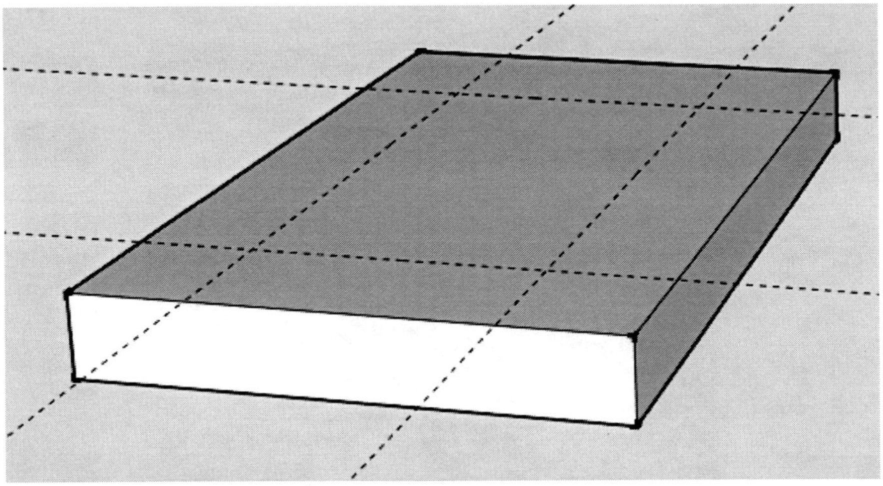

FIGURE 6.23 Guides added on top of a surface

Guides can be selected and deleted. They can also be relocated with the *Move* tool. They can be rotated with the *Rotate* tool as well.

You can quickly hide the *Guides* via the *View* menu (Figure 6.24). Notice the *Axes* can also be toggled off/on here as well.

Guides can also be placed on a *Layer* and hidden. This would allow you to hide some *Guides* while leaving others visible. Simply create a *Layer* using the *Layer* dialog (*Window* → *Layers*). Then select the *Guide(s)* and switch them to another *Layer* via the *Entity Info* dialog (see page 45).

If you can see *Guides* on the screen, they will print. You need to hide them before printing if you do not want them to print.

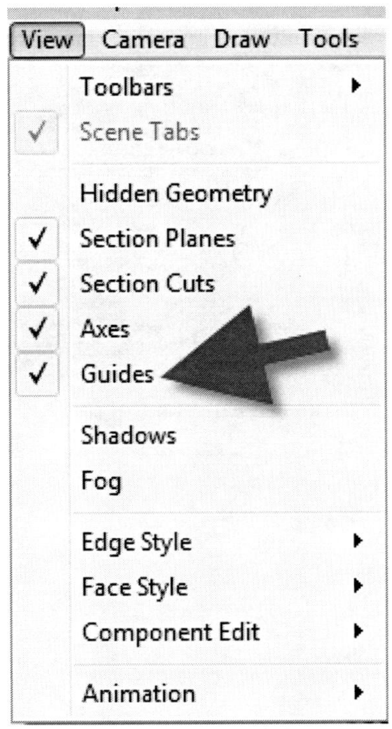

FIGURE 6.24 Guides visibility

Project Example: Reception Desk. *Image courtesy of LHB; www.LHBcorp.com*

Section 7
Beginning with the Basics

In this section you will practice sketching basic 2D lines and shapes to get the hang of using a few of the draw and modify tools, as well as specifying specific dimensions. In the next section you will circle back and see how easy it is to turn these 2D sketches into 3D drawings. Normally you would do the 2D line work and then immediately turn it into a 3D model. But we are breaking the process down and focusing on each part separately.

Setting up the model

The first thing you need to do is start a new model and make a few adjustments. You will complete these steps for each drawing in this section, unless noted otherwise (UNO).

1. Start a new SketchUp model using the **Architectural Design – Feet and Inches** template.

2. Select the person *Component*, and press the **Delete** key, on the keyboard.

To break things down into the simplest terms, you will change to a non-perspective plan (or top) view.

3. From the *Camera* menu, select **Parallel Projection** (Figure 7.1).

4. Also from the *Camera* menu, select: **Standard Views → Top**.

You can also go to **View → Toolbar → Views** to turn on a toolbar which provides quick access to the standard views (top, front, iso, etc.).

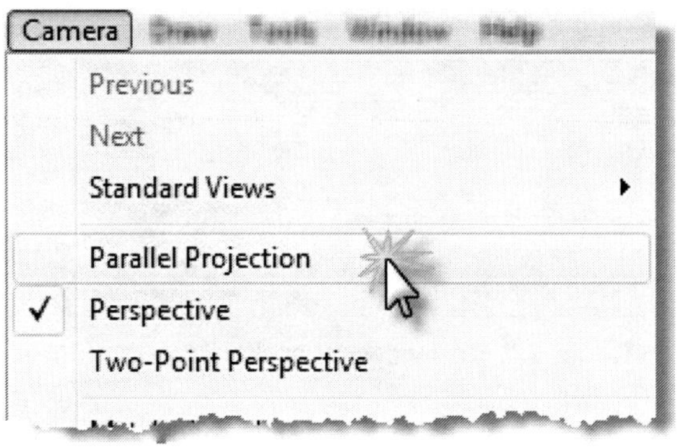

FIGURE 7.1 Parallel Projection mode

You are now looking at a plan view (Figure 7.2). This view is similar to what you would see on a printed out floor plan (aka blueprints or construction documents). Use caution not to press and drag your center wheel button as this action will activate the *Orbit* tool and throw you out of *Top* view; you would still be in "parallel" mode however. If you accidentally do this, simply select "top" again from the *Camera* menu. Selecting *Undo* does not help.

Notice how the *Axes* are centered on the screen.

You can adjust which part of the model you are looking at using the ***Pan*** tool. When finished panning, click the *Select* icon. Do not pan at this time.

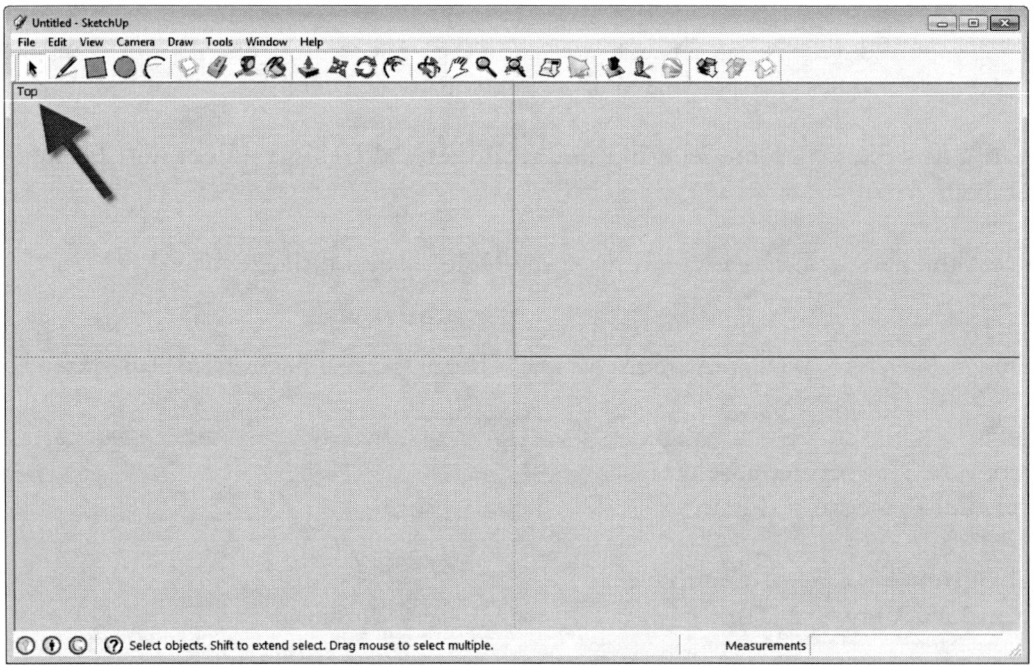

FIGURE 7.2 Top view in Parallel Projection mode

file name: **Bookcase**

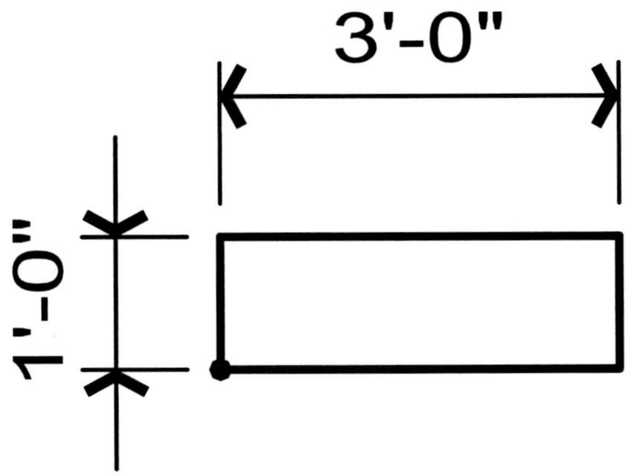

This is a simple rectangle that represents the size of a bookcase. The black dot represents the starting point, which should align with the intersection of the axes. **Do not draw the black dot.**

5. Select the ***Rectangle*** tool.

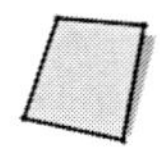

6. **For your first point**, click the intersection of the *Axes* (Figure 7.3).

Be sure your cursor snaps to the *Origin*; you will see a yellow circle and a tooltip appear.

7. **Select your second point** approximately as shown in Figure 7.3.
   a. You can keep an eye on the dimension box in the lower right, but do not worry about getting the number exact as that will be done in the next step.

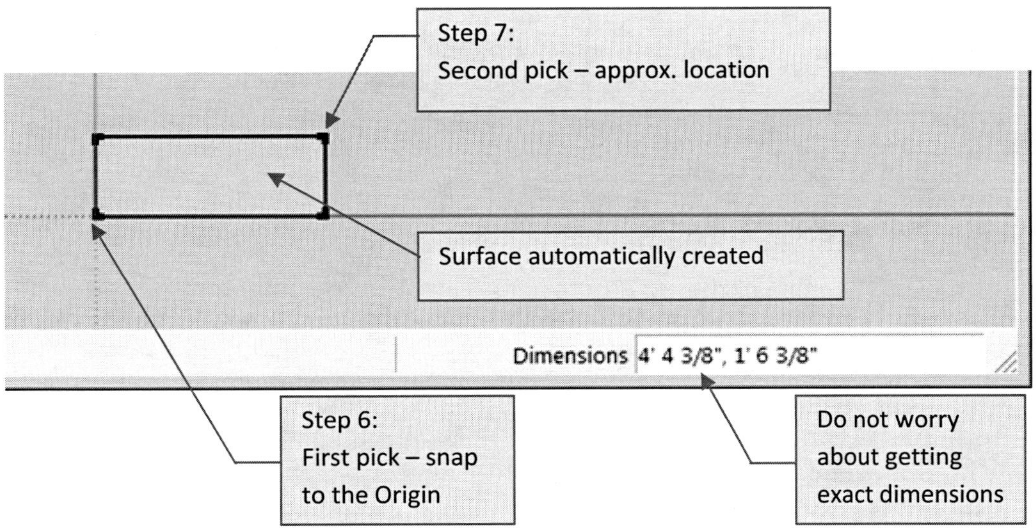

FIGURE 7.3 Sketching a rectangle

8. After clicking the second point (Step 7) and before doing anything else, simply type **3′,1′** and then press **Enter**.
    a. You do not need to click in the *Dimensions* box; just start typing.
9. **Save** your file as **Bookcase.skp**.

Notice the surface which was automatically created once an enclosed area was created. You are done with this file for now. You will come back to it later and turn it into a 3D bookcase.

file name: Coffee Table

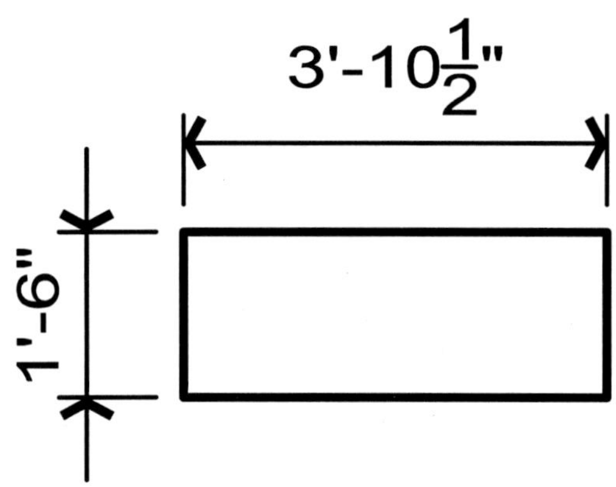

Next you will start a new file, using the steps previously covered (Setting up the Model; Steps 1-4). The previously created file can be closed and set aside for use in the next section.

The *Coffee Table* drawing will introduce you to entering fractional values.

10. Start a new model, following Steps 1-4.

It would be fairly easy to use the *Rectangle* tool again to draw this item, however you will use the basic *Line* tool so you can see how it works and get practice entering specific lengths.

11. Select the **Line** tool from the toolbar. 

12. Snap to the *Origin* (the intersection of the red and green axes).

13. Begin moving your cursor to the right (Figure 7.4):

    a. Ensure your cursor is "snapped" to the horizontal.

    b. When horizontal, you should see the "**On Red Axis**" tooltip.

    c. Once you are pointing in the correct direction and snapped to the horizontal, you may type in a length (see the next step for this).

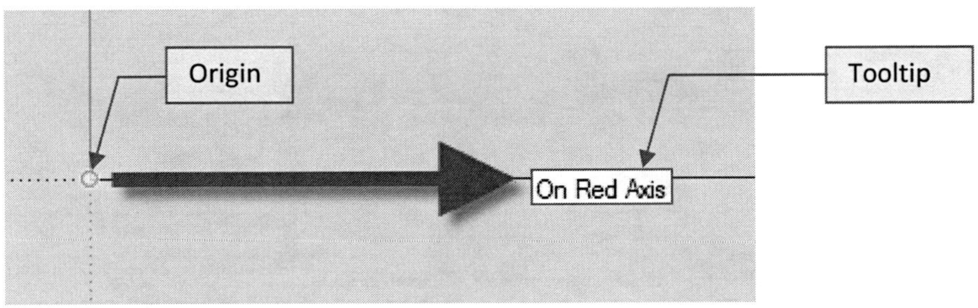

FIGURE 7.4 Sketching a line

14. Without moving the mouse, type **3'10.5** and then press **Enter**.

You always have to enter a foot symbol if feet are needed, however the inch symbol never needs to be typed as it is assumed when nothing is specified.

The *Line* tool will remain active until you pick the *Select* icon or another tool. Next you will draw one of the vertical lines.

15. While the ***Line*** tool is still active (Figure 7.5):

    a. Start moving your cursor straight up.

    b. Ensure the "**On Green Axis**" tooltip is showing, meaning vertical.

    c. Type **1′6** and then press **Enter**.

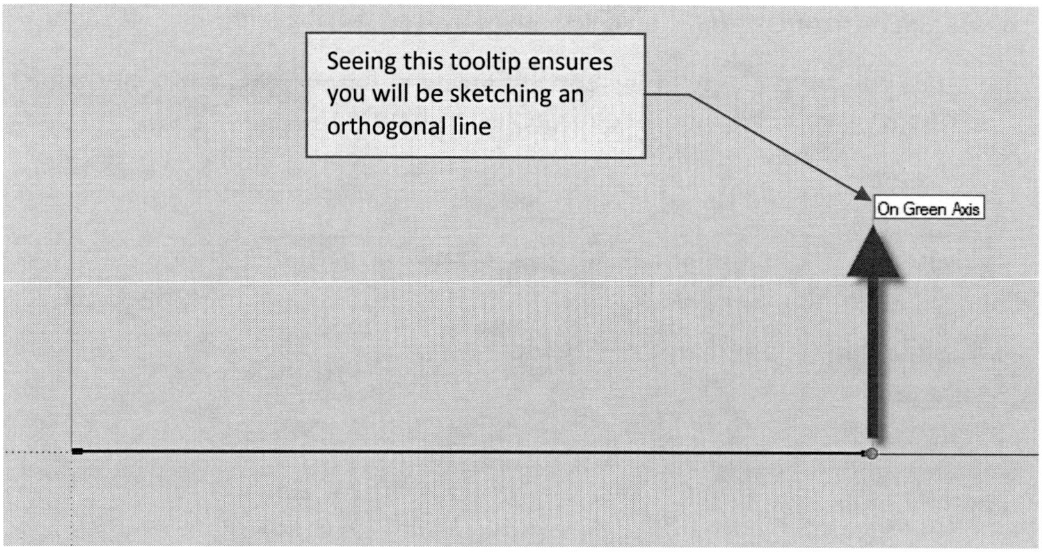

FIGURE 7.5 Sketching another line

16. Using one of the alternative methods of entering 3′ 10½″ (see below), sketch the top horizontal line, from right to left.

Entering fractions: the 3′-10½″ can be entered several ways.

o	3′ 10.5	*Notice there is a space between the feet and inches.*
o	3′10.5	*Notice space can also be left out.*
o	3′ 10 1/2	*Note the two spaces separating feet, inches and fractions.*
o	3′10 1/2	*The second space is always required.*
o	0′ 46.5	*This is all in inches; that is, 3′-10½″ = 46.5″.*
o	46.5	*SketchUp assumes inches if nothing is specified.*

TIP: *Even when you are in a model using imperial units, you can type a metric value and SketchUp will automatically convert it. For example; typing* ***150mm*** *draws a* ***5 7/8″*** *line.*

To draw the last line you could type in the value but you can more quickly snap to the endpoint of the first line drawn. This will complete the rectangular shape.

17. Snap to the **Endpoint** of the first line drawn (Figure 7.6).

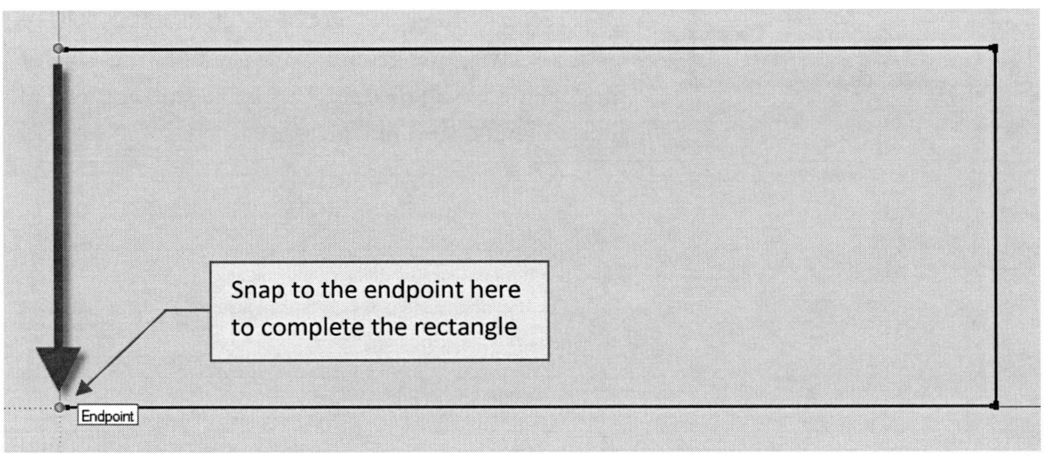

FIGURE 7.6 Completing the rectangle

Once a closed perimeter is defined as your rectangle, a surface is automatically created. You should use the ***Tape Measure*** tool too occasionally to double-check your lengths. Simply select the *Tape Measure* tool from the toolbar and then pick two points in the model. The *Value Control Box* in the lower right of the application lists the measurement. Give it a try!

18. **Save** your file as **Coffee Table.skp**.

file name: Small Desk

Next, you will start another new file and create this rectangular shape.

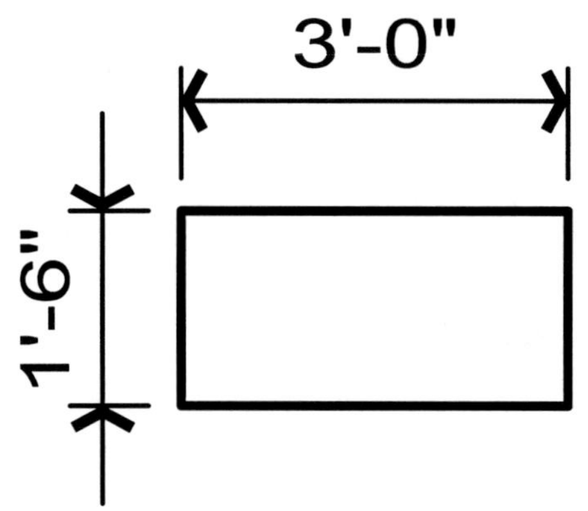

19. Create a new model (per Steps 1-4) and create this small desk using either of the methods just covered.

20. **Save** your file as **Small Desk.skp**.

Don't worry; things will get more challenging. These steps are laying the groundwork for all of the 3D modeling you will be doing! So make sure you take the time to understand this material.

file name: **Night Table**

Obviously, you could draw this quickly per the previous examples. However, you will take a look at copying a *file* and then modifying an existing model.

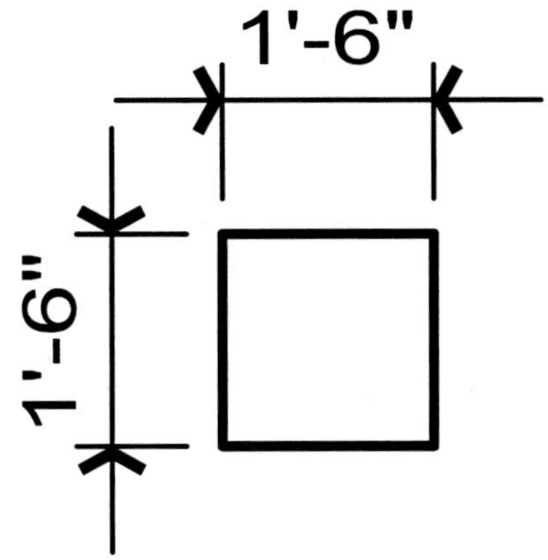

You will use the *Move* tool to stretch the 3′-0″ wide desk down to a 1′-6″ wide night table.

21. With the *Small Desk* SketchUp model still open, select **File → Save As**.

22. Type **Night Table** for the *File name* and click **Save** (Figure 7.7).

You are now in a new file named *Night Table.skp*, and are ready to manipulate the file. The original "small desk" file is now closed and will not be affected.

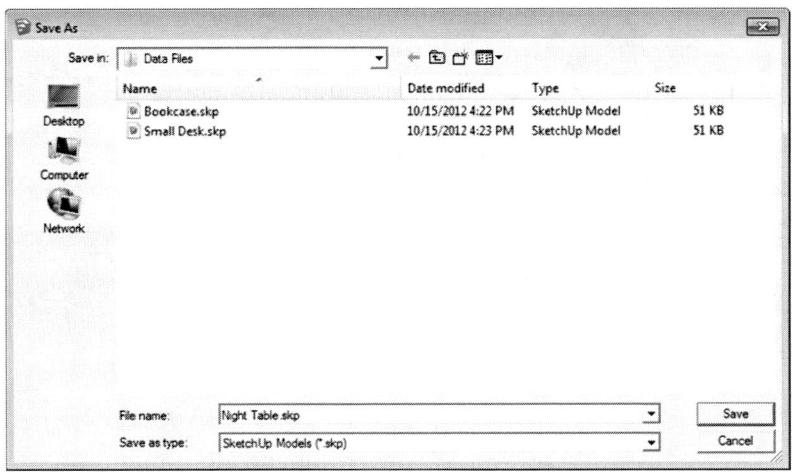

FIGURE 7.7 SaveAs dialog

You will use the *Move* tool to change the location of one of the vertical lines, which will cause the two horizontal lines to stretch with it. SketchUp's *Lines* automatically have a parametric relationship to adjacent lines when their endpoints touch each other.

23. Click the vertical line on the right and then select the **Move** icon on the toolbar (Figure 7.8).

24. Pick the mid-point of the selected line. Move the mouse towards the left – while locked to the vertical (Figure 7.8). **Do not click yet.**

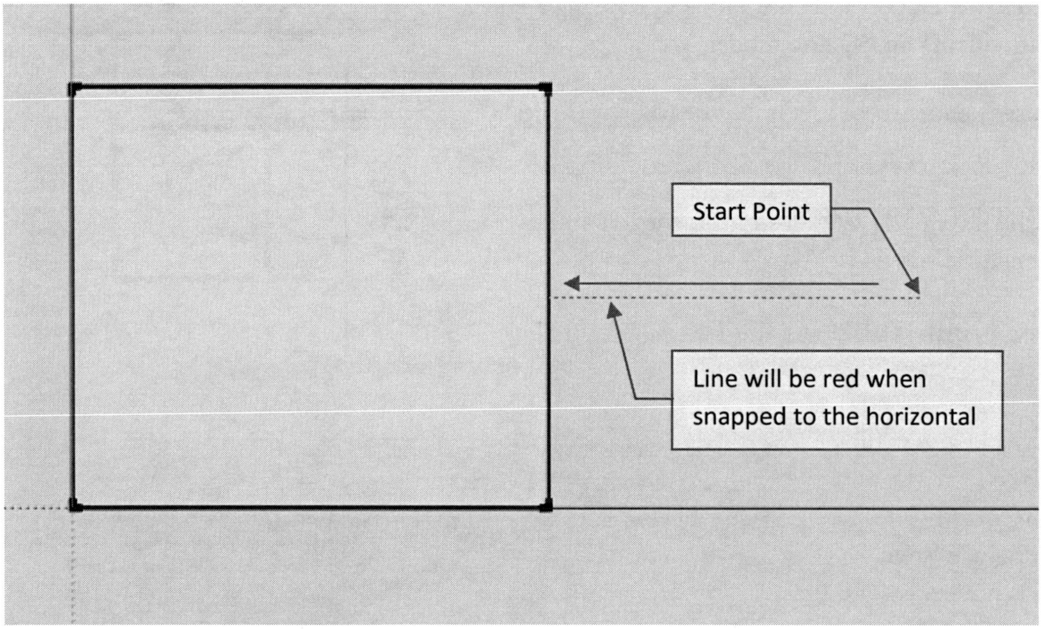

FIGURE 7.8 Moving an edge

25. While in the *Move* command and snapped to the horizontal (i.e., red axis), type **1'6** and then press **Enter**.

That is it! You essentially just stretched the rectangle. The two horizontal lines automatically shrunk in length and the surface resized itself as well.

26. **Save** your *Night Table.skp* file.

file name: **Small Dresser**

file name: **File Cabinet**

27. Draw the *Small Dresser* and the *File Cabinet* per the previous instructions.

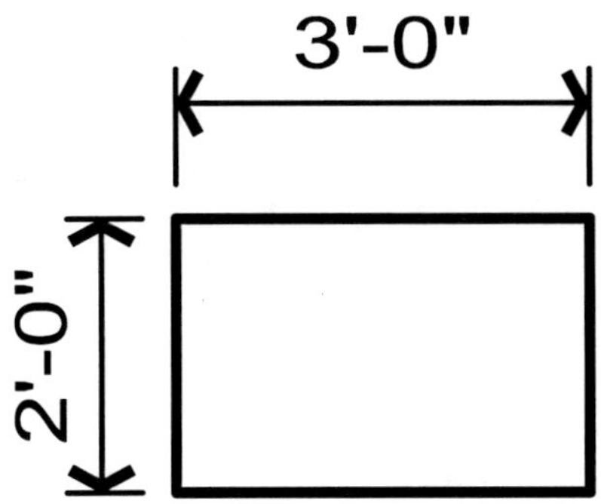

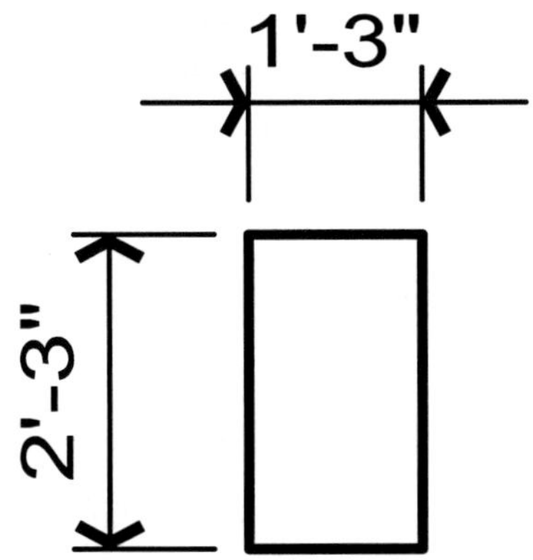

file name: **Square Chair**

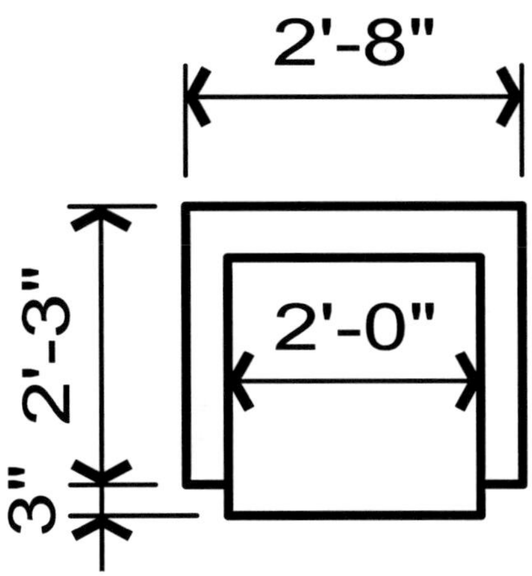

Next you will draw this squarish-styled chair. You could draw this by setting up a few *Guides*, but another method will be shown. It is good to know several ways to accomplish the same thing as one solution may be more efficient than another in certain situations.

28. Start with a 2′x2′ square aligned with the origin.

29. Draw the backrest and armrests as separate rectangles, near the square (Figure 7.9)

30. Use the ***Move*** tool to move the rectangles into position (Figure 7.10).

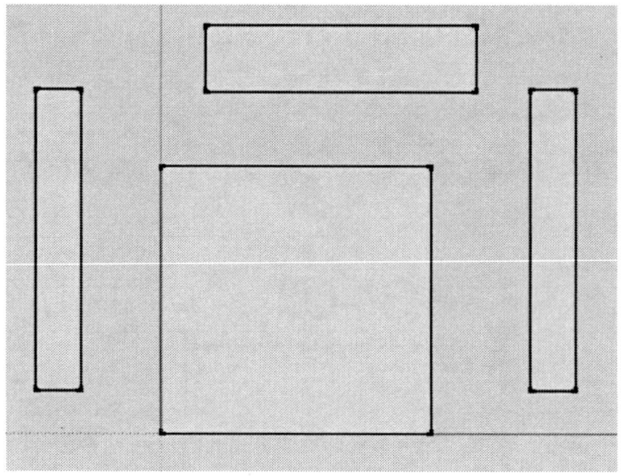

FIGURE 7.9 Creating the chair

SketchUp does not allow overlapping lines. Therefore, when you moved the rectangles into place the lines were merged, with any endpoints remaining. This will allow you to delete the extra lines identified in Figure 7.10.

31. **Delete** the extra lines identified in Figure 7.10; select it and press the **Delete** key on the keyboard.

When the two lines were removed, the surfaces automatically joined together within the newly enclosed area (Figure 7.11). At this point you only have two surfaces defined, each of which can be extruded into separate shapes, which you will do later in the next chapter.

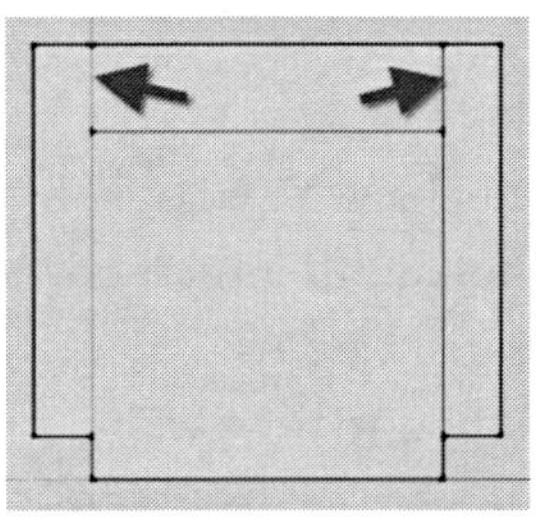

FIGURE 7.10

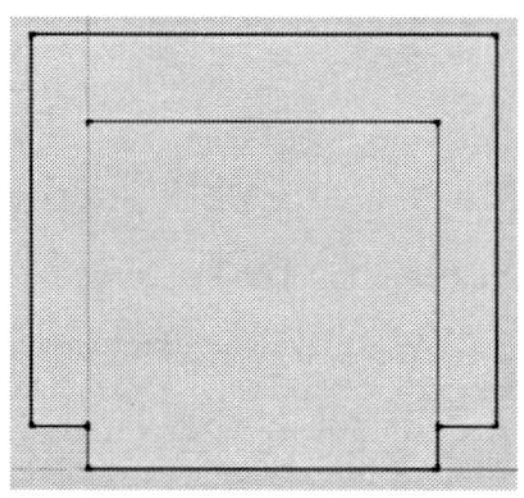

FIGURE 7.11

You have completed the square chair – for now anyway. You can save your file and move on to the next one.

Selecting Objects:

At this time we will digress and take a quick look at the various techniques for selecting entities in SketchUp. Most tools work the same when it comes to selecting elements.

When selecting entities, you have two primary ways to select them:

- Individually select entities one at a time
- Select several entities at a time with a window

You can use one or a combination of both methods to select elements when using the ***Select*** tool.

Individual Selections:

When using the *Select* tool, for example, you simply move the cursor over the element and click; holding the **Ctrl** key you can select multiple objects. Then you typically click the tool you wish to use on the selected items. Press **Shift** and click on an item to subtract it from the current selection set.

Window Selections:

Similarly, you can pick a *window* around several elements to select them all at once. To select a *window*, rather than selecting an individual element as previously described, you select one corner of the *window* you wish to define. That is, you pick a point in "space" and hold the mouse button down. Now, as you move the mouse you will see a rectangle on the screen that represents the windowed area you are selecting; when the *window* encompasses the elements you wish to select, release the mouse.

You actually have two types of windows you can use to select. One is called a **window** and the other is called a **crossing window**.

Window:

This option allows you to select only the objects that are completely within the *window*. Any lines that extend out of the *window* are not selected.

Crossing Window:

This option allows you to select all the entities that are completely within the *window* and any that extend outside the *window*.

Using Window versus Crossing Window:

To select a *window* you simply pick and drag from *left to right* to form a rectangle.

Conversely, to select a *crossing window*, you pick and drag from *right to left* to define the two diagonal points of the window.

file name: Square Sofa

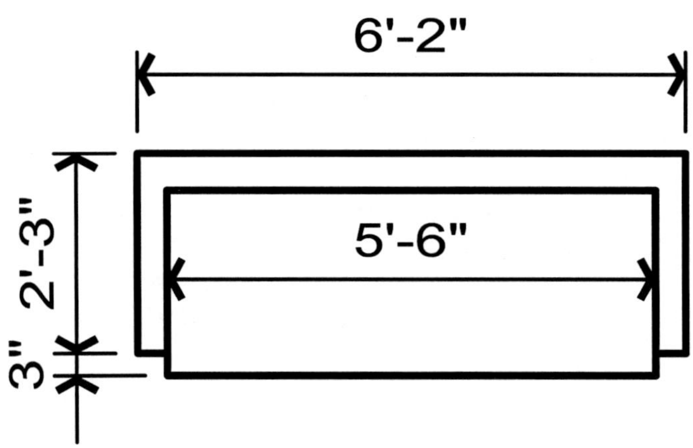

Similar to how you turned the *Small Desk* into a *Night Table*, you will turn the *Square Chair* into this *Square Sofa*.

This is a little trickier as you have to select multiple lines as part of the *Move* command.

32. Once you are sure you saved the *Square Chair* file, do a **Save As** to create the **Square Sofa** file.

33. Select the three lines shown in Figure 7.12.

FIGURE 7.12

Moving these lines will cause the horizontal lines to follow – or stretch, thus growing the chair into a sofa!

34. Select **Move** from the toolbar.

35. Pick anywhere in the drawing area and begin moving the cursor to the right, snapped to the horizontal (i.e., on red axis).

36. Without clicking a second point, type the desired length you wish to move the lines (i.e., stretch the sofa); this is the difference between the chair and the sofa.

Notice how the horizontal lines extended because they have a parametric relationship to them. The surface has also updated.

37. Use the ***Tape Measure*** tool to double-check your dimensions. Make any corrections needed before moving on.

Keep in mind that all these basic steps will be directly applicable to the more advanced 3D modeling coming up.

file name: **Range**

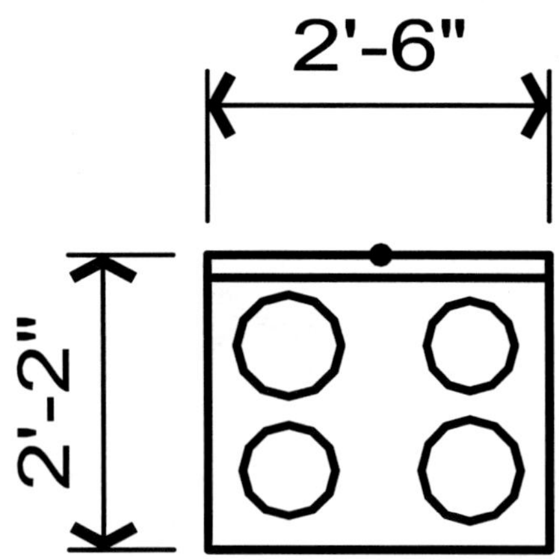

Now you will draw a kitchen range with four circles that represent the burners.

In this exercise you will have to draw temporary lines, called *Guides*, to create reference points needed to accurately locate the circles. Once the circles have been drawn the *Guides* can be erased.

38. In a new file, **Draw** the range with a 2″ deep control panel at the back; refer to the steps previously covered if necessary.

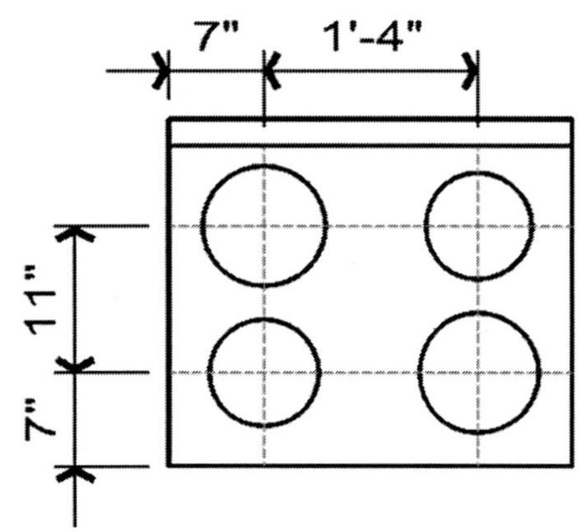

FIGURE **7.13** Adding guides

39. Use the ***Tape Measure*** tool to create the four guides dimensioned in Figure 7.13.
    a. With the *Tape Measure* tool active, click and drag on an edge to create a *Guide* parallel to that edge.
    b. Once you let go of the mouse the *Guide* is created.
    c. Once placed, type the distance and then press **Enter** to position it.

40. Using the ***Circle*** tool, draw two 9½″ Dia. circles and two 7½″ Dia. circles using the intersections of the *Guides* to locate the centers of the circles (Figure 7.13).

41. Using the ***Select*** tool, select each of the *Guides* and press the **Delete** key on the keyboard to remove them from the model.

Circles are made up of several straight line segments. The default number is 24. If your circle is large, the number of edges needs to be increased to maintain the look of a circle. This can be done just before clicking to locate the circle's center, by just typing a number and **Enter**. This number, the radius and *Layer* can all be changed at any time using the *Entity Info* dialog.

file name: Rounded Chair

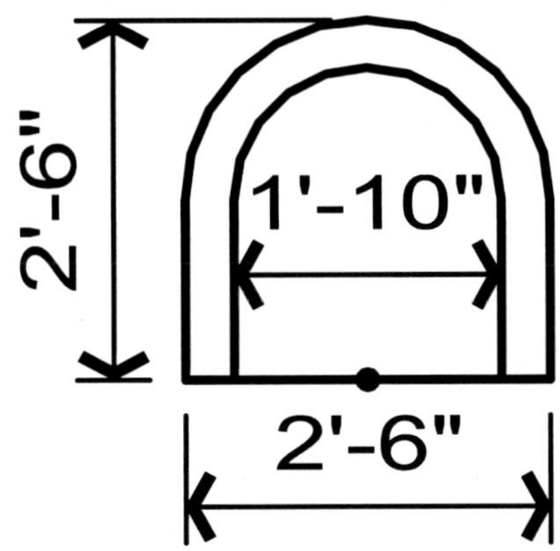

These last two drawings will involve using the *Arc* tool. The *Offset* command will also be utilized.

You will start this chair drawing by sketching the perimeter and then offsetting it inward.

42. Draw the three orthogonal lines shown in Figure 7.14.
    a. The horizontal line is centered on the green axis and aligned with the red axis.
    b. The two vertical lines are 1′-3″ long.

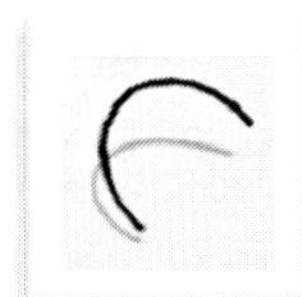

43. Use the ***Arc*** tool to add the rounded backrest.
    a. Pick the three points shown in Figure 7.14.
    b. When picking the third point you should see a "half circle" tooltip before clicking the mouse button.

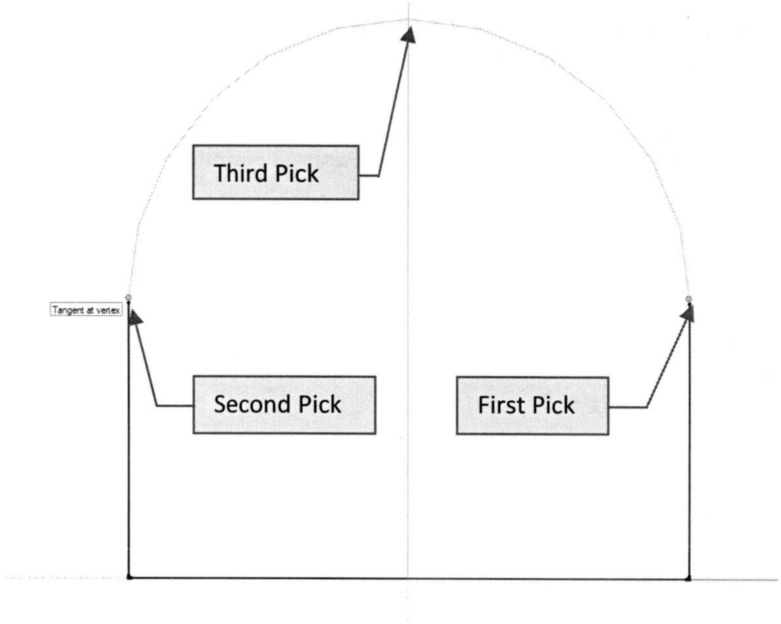

FIGURE 7.14 Sketching an arc

You now have the perimeter of the chair defined. Next you will use the ***Offset*** command to create the backrest.

44. Select the **Offset** tool from the toolbar.

45. Select the arc – just the line, not the surface.

46. Start moving your cursor towards the middle of the chair and then type **4** and press **Enter**.

47. Draw the two remaining vertical lines.

    a. For the first end of the line, snap to the end of the arc.

    b. For the second end of the line, snap to a perpendicular point on the horizontal line.

The 2D version of the chair is now complete. The drawing now has two surfaces, because two enclosed areas exist; the backrest and the seat area. This will make the 3D extrusion process go smoothly.

file name: **Love Seat**

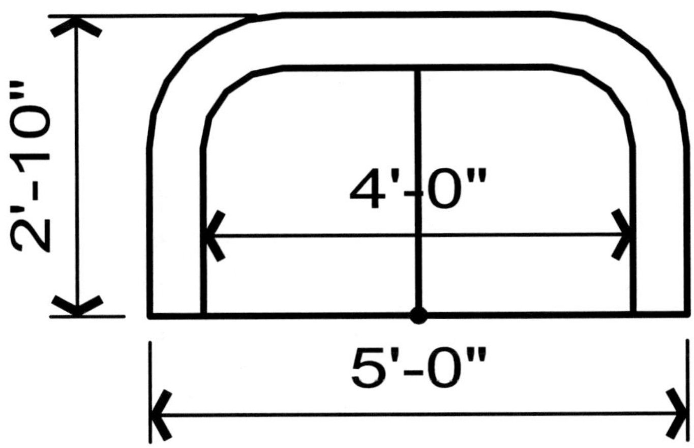

This last 2D exercise will round things off by making quarter round arcs.

One thing that is a little tricky here is setting up points to pick before sketching the arc. When adding an arc, it is easiest if the two endpoints are defined by other line work. Thus, you just have to snap to endpoints for your first two picks and the third defines the radius. In this example you will need to add two temporary lines to define the start and end points of the arc.

The radius of the two arcs is 1′-3″.

48. Add the orthogonal lines shown in Figure 7.15.

    a. All dimensions can be deduced from the information given.

The two 1′-3″ lines are temporary and have only been added to aid in sketching the arcs (which is done in an upcoming step).

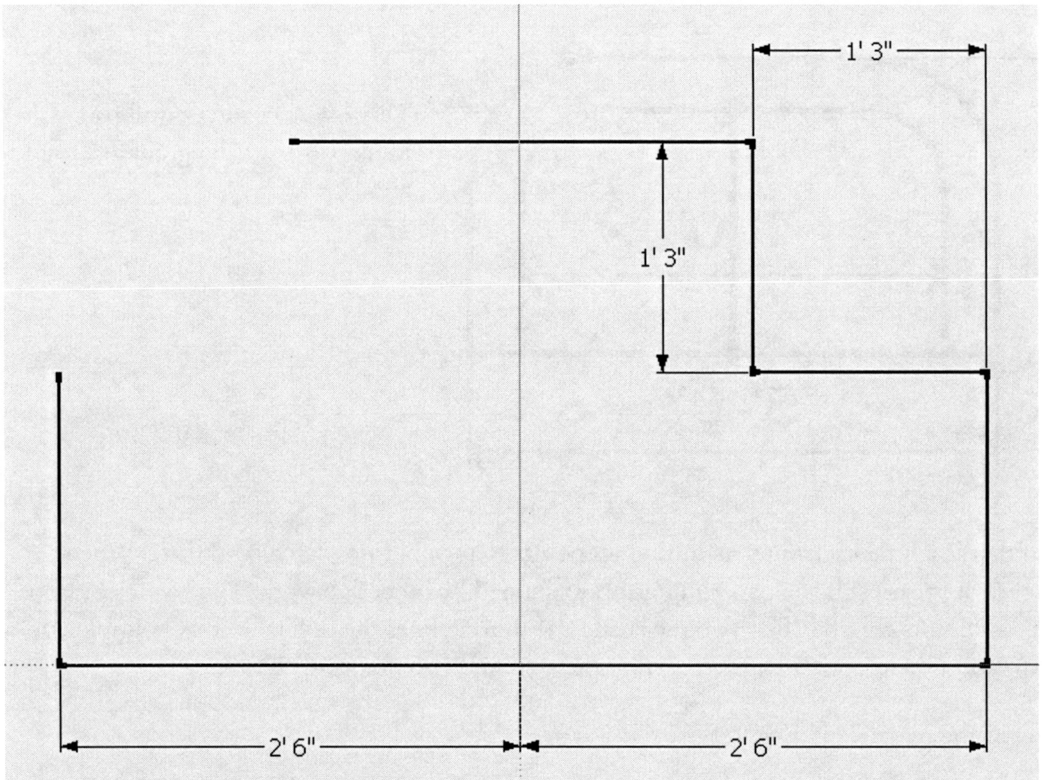

FIGURE 7.15 Setting things up for the arc tool

49. **Delete** the two 1′-3″ lines.

50. Add one of the perimeter arcs.

    a. Pick the two endpoints provided by the orthogonal lines.

    b. Move the cursor until the arc is purple and the tooltip reads "Tangent at vertex" – this will produce a quarter round arc.

51. Add the other arc per the previous step.

Notice that you did not have to specify the radius of the arc because of the preparation done.

52. Offset the two arcs inward **4″** – similar to the rounded chair (Figure 7.16).

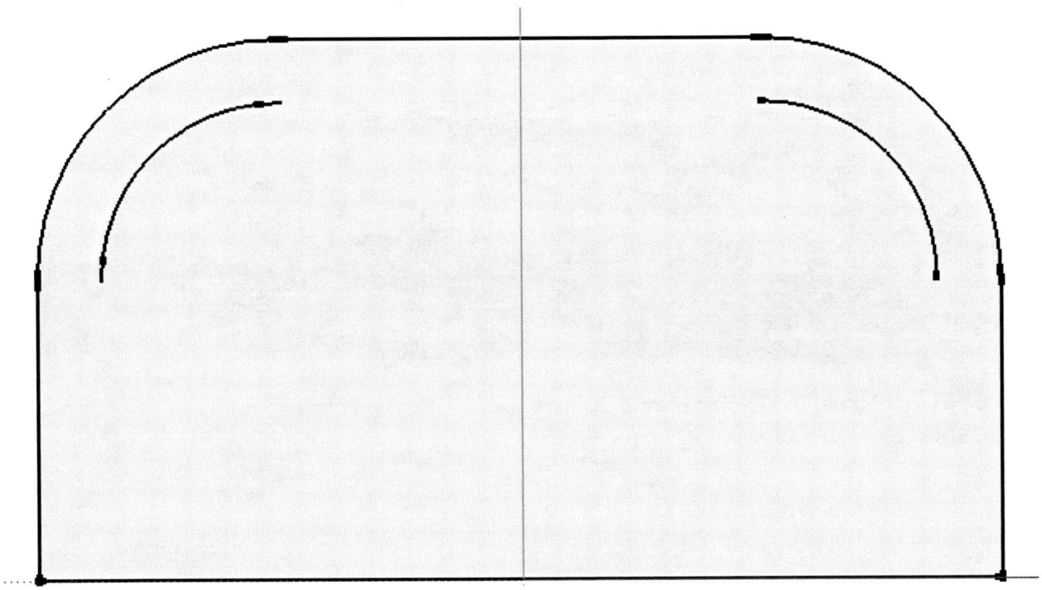

FIGURE 7.16 Offset perimeter arcs inward 4 inches

53. Complete the backrest and armrests by "connecting the dots" via the *Line* tool.

54. Draw the vertical line down the middle, representing the cushions.

55. Save.

Sometimes it is better to extrude a shape into the third dimension before adding extra line work such as the cushion line. This issue will be explored more in a later lesson.

Your drawing should be complete (Figure 7.17). Note that the drawing has three surfaces based on the line work you sketched. Don't forget to save your file.

FIGURE 7.17 Completed 2D love seat

Section 8
3D Modeling

In this chapter you will transform the objects created in the previous chapter into three dimensional models. Once the 3D objects have been developed, you will learn how to apply materials to make them look more realistic.

file name: Bookcase – 3D

You will open the files from the previous chapter and *Save As* to a new file name so the original files remain intact (just in case you need to start over).

1. Open the **Bookcase.skp** file created in the previous chapter.

2. Select **File → Save As**.

3. Save the file as **Bookcase – 3D**. (You may save it into another folder if you wish.)

Next you will turn on the *Views* toolbar to make it easier to switch between 3D and elevation/plan views.

4. Select **View → Toolbars → Views**.

5. Click on the **3D** icon on the *Views* toolbar.

You should now be viewing a 3D view of your bookcase drawing (Figure 5-5.1). Of course it is still just a 2D drawing being viewed from a 3D vantage point. Also recall that the view mode of the model is currently set to *Parallel Projection* rather than the default *Perspective* mode. You will leave it this way for now.

Using the Push/Pull Tool

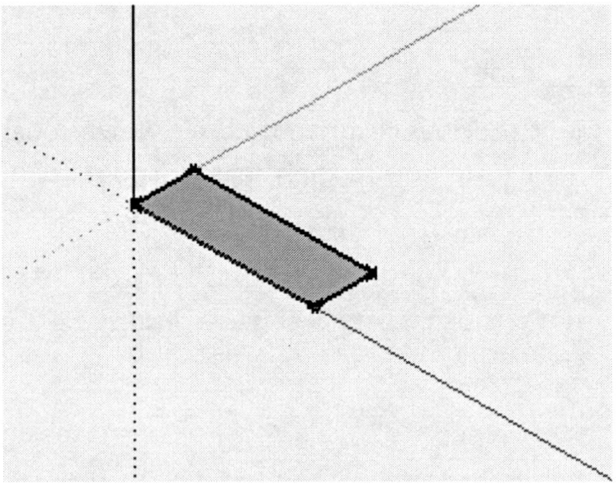

FIGURE 8.1 Parallel Projection 3D view

Now you will use the ***Push/Pull*** tool to quickly turn the 2D outline into a 3D (face based) object. This tool requires you to select a surface, which means an enclosed perimeter is required. The tool takes the previously defined 2D shape and extrudes it into a 3D shape. So the end result is several additional edges and surfaces which give the appearance of a 3D object.

6. From the *Getting Started* toolbar, select the ***Push/Pull*** tool.

Next you will simply click and drag on the surface portion of your bookcase (i.e., rectangle) and start moving the mouse straight upwards. You will not worry about an exact height as the precise value will be typed in immediately after using the *Push/Pull* tool.

7. Move your cursor over the surface until it pre-highlights and then **click and drag the mouse up**.

You can only drag in a direction perpendicular to the surface – in this case, straight up or down.

8. **Release the mouse** button at any time, once the 3D geometry appears in the correct direction (i.e., up versus down below the ground).

9. Immediately after releasing the mouse button, type **4′** and then press **Enter**.

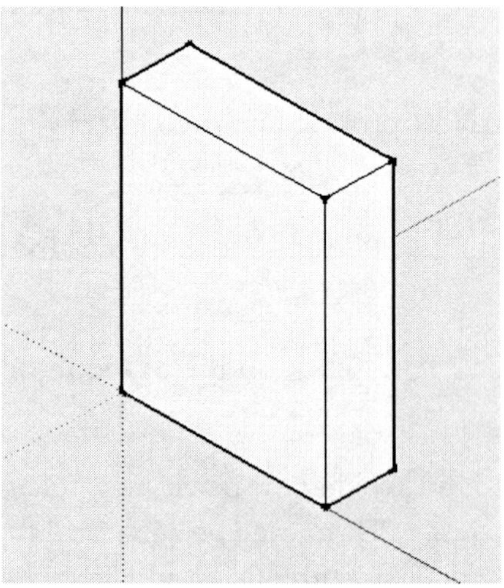

FIGURE 8.2 4′ high extrusion

You now have a 4′-0″ high extrusion which will be further refined to look like a bookcase (Figure 8.2).

In addition to the *Push/Pull* tool making solid (or additive) geometry, it can also be used to make voids (or subtractive) geometry. That is, if you sketch rectangles on the face of the bookcase and then use *Push/Pull* you can create a void by "pushing" into the larger 3D object. Conversely, if you "pull" the rectangular shape you would create a bump-out on the face of the bookshelf.

The following steps can be done in the current 3D view, and are easier once you get used to working in a 3D view. You can try following the next few steps in the current 3D view or you can switch to the front view (per the very next step) to follow along exactly with the book.

10. Click the **Front** icon on the *Views* toolbar.

You are now looking at the equivalent of a 2D elevation. This is only true if you are still in *Parallel Projection* mode; if not, you see more of a 3D view of the front.

11. Select the **Offset** tool from the toolbar.

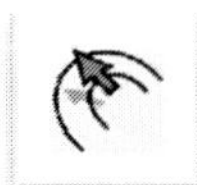

Before you click and drag on the edge you want to offset, you need to see the surface highlight first. This lets you know the edge will offset on the correct plane/direction.

12. Move your cursor over the surface. Once you see it highlight, click on the top edge, drag your cursor downward, and let go of the mouse button (Figure 8.3).

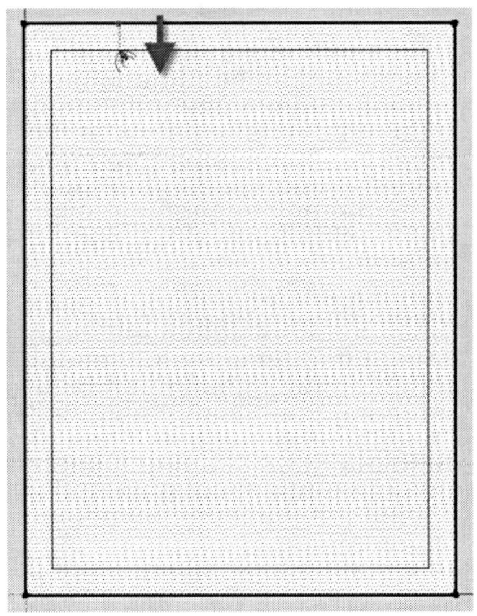

FIGURE 8.3 Offset on front face

13. Type **1″** and then press **Enter** to make the newly created line work one inch away from the perimeter.

14. Click the **Select** tool, and then select the bottom edge of the newly created rectangle.

15. Use the ***Move*** tool and reposition the line **3″** up (Figure 8.4).

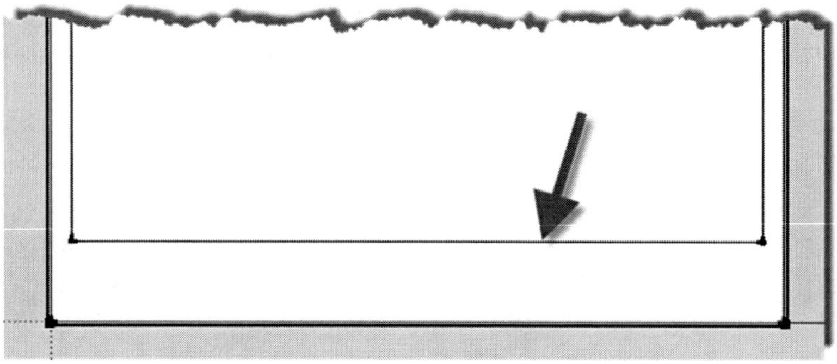

FIGURE 8.4 Line moved, 4″ from bottom edge

Now you will sketch the line work for the shelves.

16. Sketch the two shelves (Figure 8.5):

    a. Each shelf is **1"** thick.

    b. The shelves are **equally spaced**.

    c. Make the shelves equally spaced. Use the *Tape Measure* tool to list the overall distance within the inner rectangle.

    d. Copy the top or bottom line using **Move** (while holding down the **Ctrl** key to get into *Copy* mode).

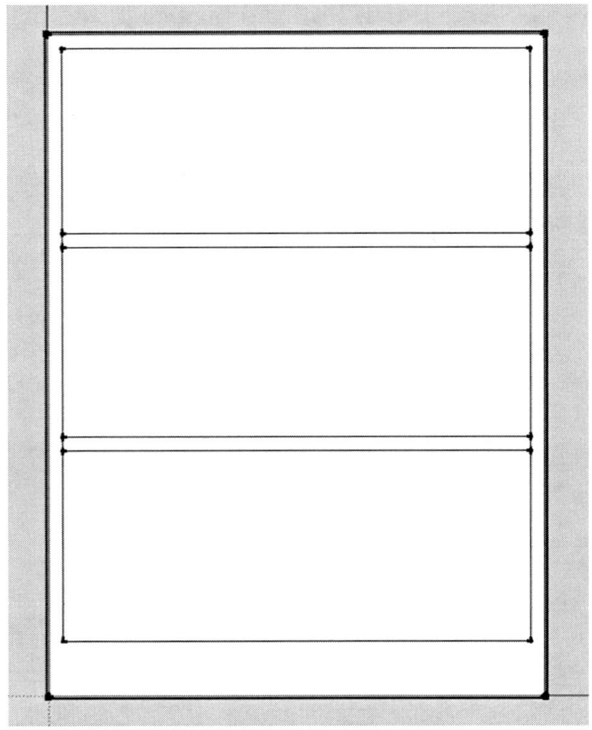

FIGURE 8.5 Lines added for shelves

As you copied the horizontal line up, a new perimeter was defined on the front surface. So SketchUp created a new surface, and modified the previous surface smaller.

Now it is time to switch back to the 3D view and use the *Push/Pull* tool to carve out the shelf areas. The large rectangular surfaces you are about to push will become the inside face of the back panel for the bookshelf. If that did not make sense, it will in a moment.

17. Switch back to the 3D view.

18. Select **Push/Pull** and then click and drag on the larger top rectangle (Figure 8.6).

19. Drag the mouse about halfway into the bookcase and let go of the mouse.

20. Type **11″** and then press **Enter**.

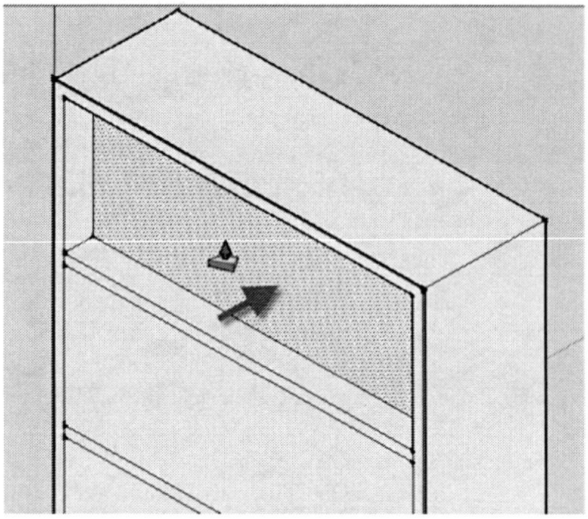

FIGURE 8.6 Push/Pull void

The book case is 12″ deep, so pulling the surface back 11″ gave us a 1″ thick back panel.

21. Repeat this process for the other two larger rectangles (Figure 8.7).

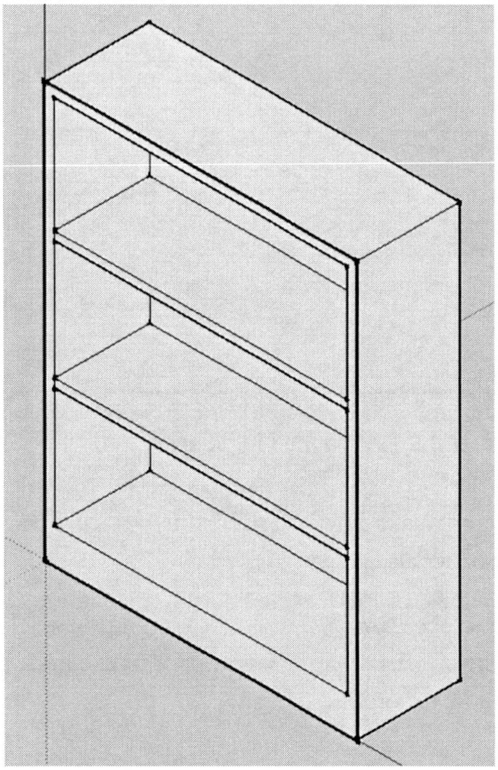

FIGURE 8.7 Final bookcase

The final bookcase should look like Figure 8.7. You can press and hold down your center wheel button and orbit around the bookcase to see it from various angles. When finished, just click the **3D** icon again.

22. **Save.**

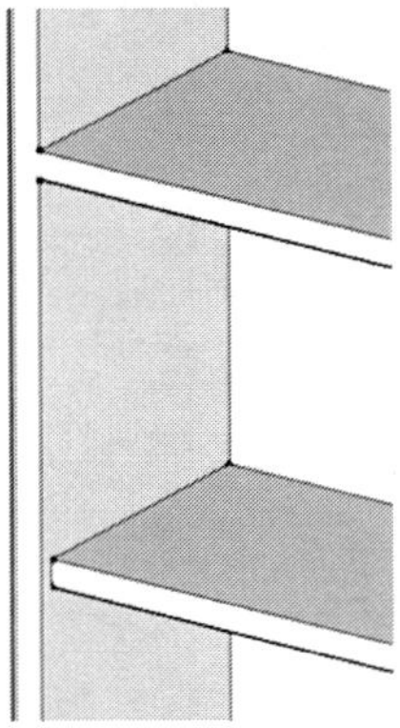

One last comment on the bookcase (Figure 8.8): If you want the face of the shelf to appear flush with the edge panel you can zoom in and erase the small vertical line (top example). Or, if you want the shelf to appear separate or recessed slightly, you can leave the line in place and use the *Push/Pull* tool (bottom example).

FIGURE 8.8 Shelf options

file name: **Coffee Table – 3D**

Using similar techniques to developing the bookcase, you will now create a coffee table.

23. Open the 2D coffee table model and do a **Save As** to **Coffee Table – 3D**.

24. Use the ***Push/Pull*** tool to make the 2D rectangle **2′-0″** high.
    a. See the previous steps for more information on how to do this.

25. Switch to the **Front** view.

This will be a heavy mass looking coffee table. The next steps start to define the thickness of the top and legs as viewed from the front.

26. Using the ***Line*** tool, sketch the 5 lines shown in Figure 8.9.
    a. Create 3″ wide legs and a 3″ thick top.

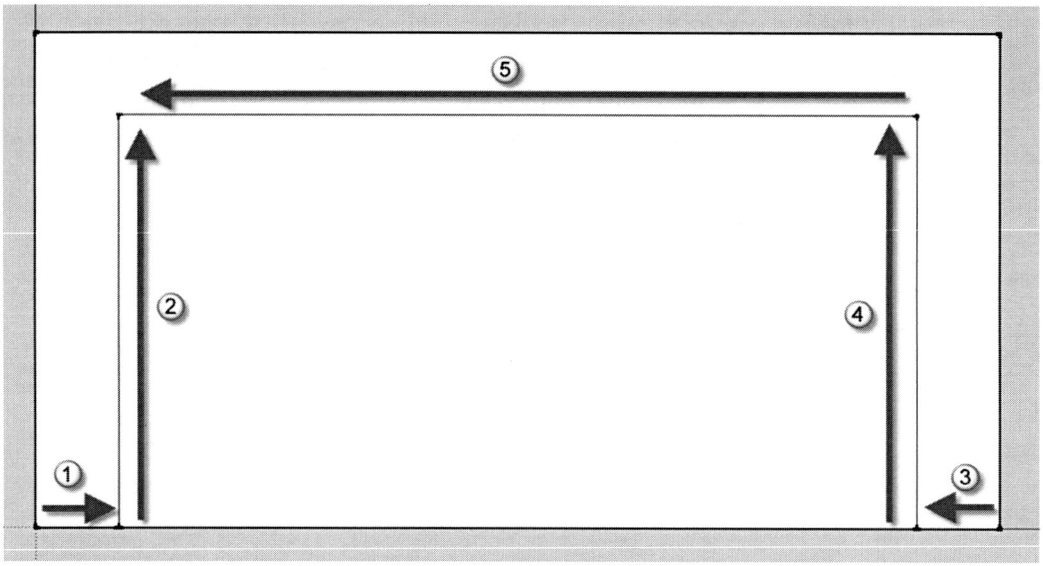

FIGURE 8.9 Coffee table front view with lines sketched

SketchUp does not allow two lines to overlap. So when you sketched lines 1 and 3 the original line across the bottom split into smaller line segments based on where your new line stopped. This is good as it keeps the file less cluttered and it ultimately creates a large surface in the middle; we will use the *Push/Pull* tool to carve out that area.

Keep in mind this could have been done from a 3D view. Once you are more experienced, it will be more efficient to do this in a 3D view. The main trick is making sure you stay on the correct *Axes*.

Next you will define the two side views in the same way the front view was developed. You have to do this for both sides, but not the back view. You will see why in a moment.

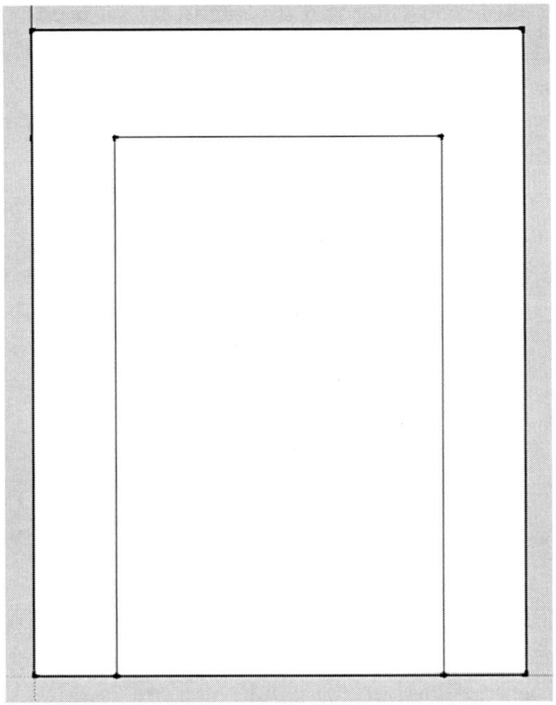

FIGURE 8.10 Right view with lines added

27. Switch to the **Right** view and add the 3″ wide legs and a 3″ thick top, per the previous steps (Figure 8.10).

28. Repeat the previous step for the **Left** side.

You are now ready to switch back to a 3D view and use the *Push/Pull* tool to remove the large mass below the table.

29. Switch to the **3D view**.

30. Use the ***Push/Pull*** tool to select the large rectangular area on the front of the coffee table.

31. Push the surface back into the model until it "snaps" into alignment with the back face of the model. Release the mouse button.

The model should look like Figure 8.11. If not, you can either *Undo* and try again, or grab the surface again using the *Push/Pull* tool. You may need to *Orbit* a little to get a better view (but this should not be necessary). Notice, when the two faces (front and back) come together, SketchUp deleted both and the end result is a void.

If you would have done one of the sides first, you would get the same result. However, now the sides will be a little different due to the top edge now being defined on the back side of the legs. In this case, you will end up needing to manually delete one surface and a line.

32. Use ***Push/Pull*** on one of the side of the table, pushing the surface in to align with the back side of the legs (Figure 8.11).

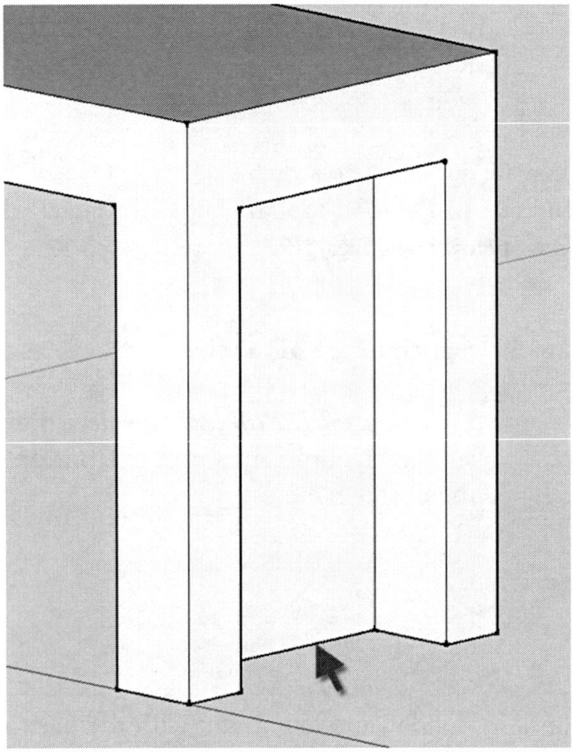

FIGURE 8.11 Right side adjusted

Notice the surface and bottom edge did not automatically get deleted when modifying the side view (Figure 8.11). Again, this is due to the surface ending directly on the edge of the underside of the 3″ thick top (the top edge was created when the front was extruded back).

This is an easy fix.

33. Use the **Select** tool to pick the bottom edge (i.e. line) and press the **Delete** key.

Once the perimeter is gone the surface must go as well. You could have deleted the surface and then the line but that would be more work!

That concludes the coffee table exercise. Be sure to save as a new file name per the first step for this model. Use *Orbit* and *Tape Measure* to inspect your work!

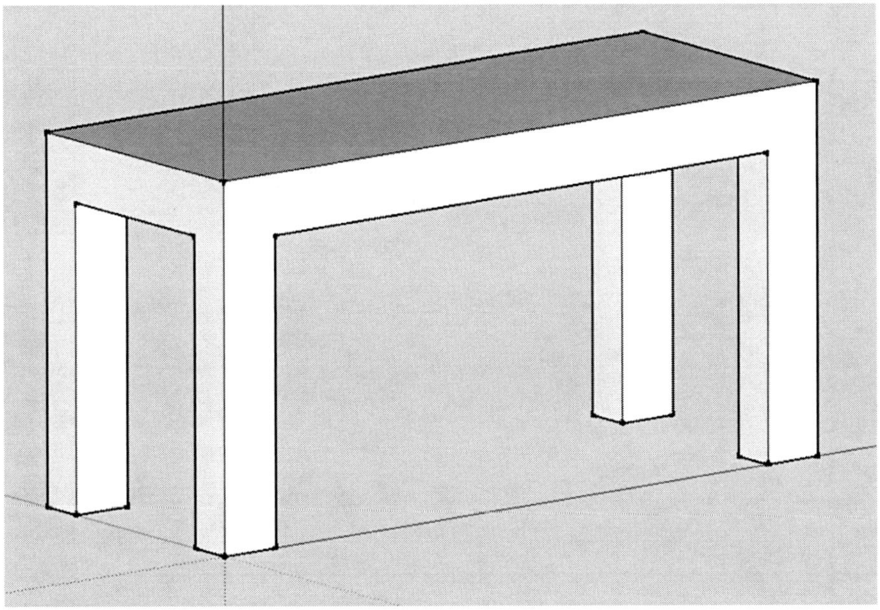

FIGURE 8.12 Completed coffee table

file name: Small Desk – 3D

Here you will continue to build on the concepts covered thus far.

34. **Open** the *Small Desk* file and **Save As** to **Small Desk – 3D**.

35. Extrude the rectangle to be **30" high** using ***Push/Pull***.

36. Switch to the front elevation view and add the line work shown in Figure 8.13. Use the ***Line*** tool and **Move + Alt** to *Copy* lines rather than *Offset*.

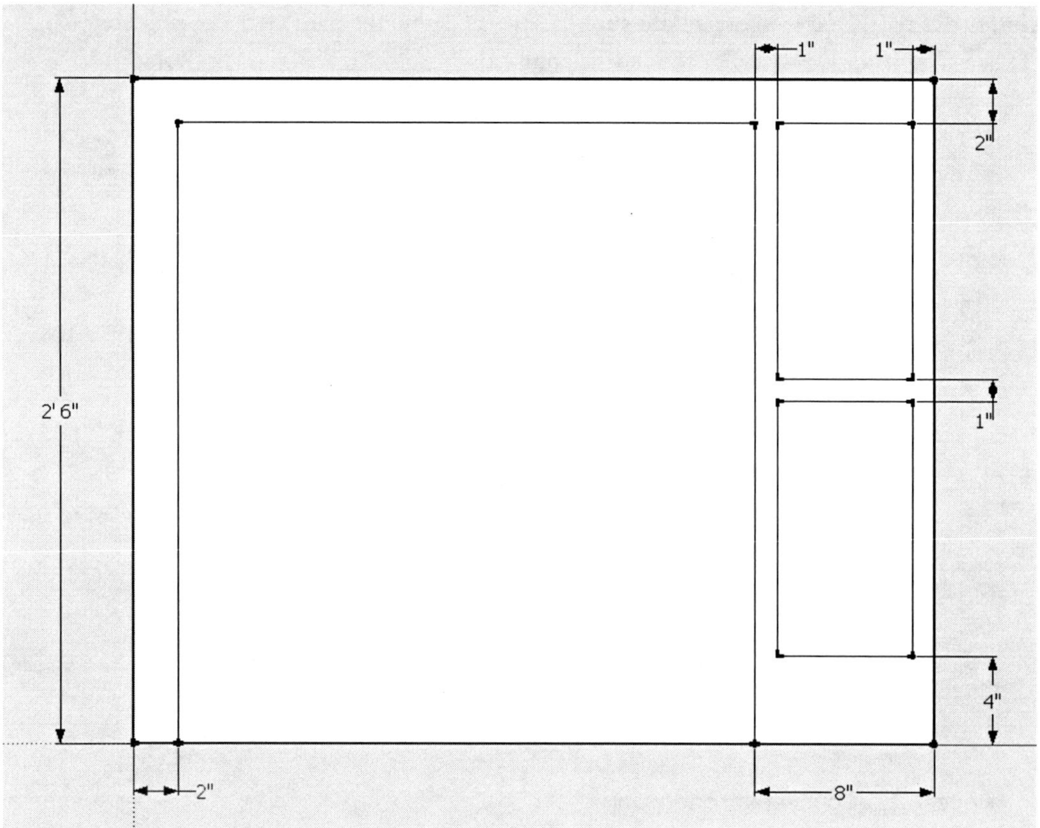

FIGURE 8.13 Front elevation of small desk

Next you will carve out the leg space and bump out the drawer panels. Notice you will not sketch in the pulls (i.e., handles) for the drawers yet. If the handles were sketched now you would have another face that would not *Push* or *Pull* with the rest of the drawer panel. Instead, you will get the drawer panel extruded and then sketch the pull outline on the face of the new panel surface.

37. Use ***Push/Pull*** to modify the desk (Figure 8.14):

    a. Knee space should be 1′-4″ deep.

    b. Drawer panels should be ½″ thick.

Your model should look like this (Figure 8.14).

Next, you will create the pull for the top drawer. This will be a simple pull which will be turned into a *Component* and copied down to the lower drawer.

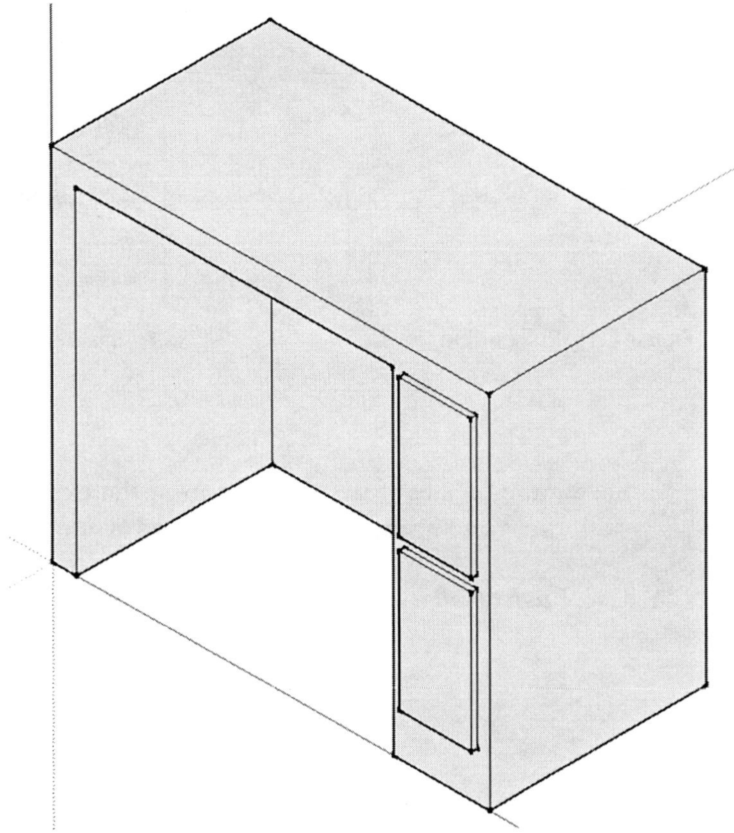

FIGURE 8.14 Modified desk

38. Create the rectangle for the pull on the face of the drawer panel. Exact size and location are not critical; just try and get it close (Figure 8.15).

39. Use ***Push/Pull*** to extrude the pull out from the drawer panel (Figure 8.16).

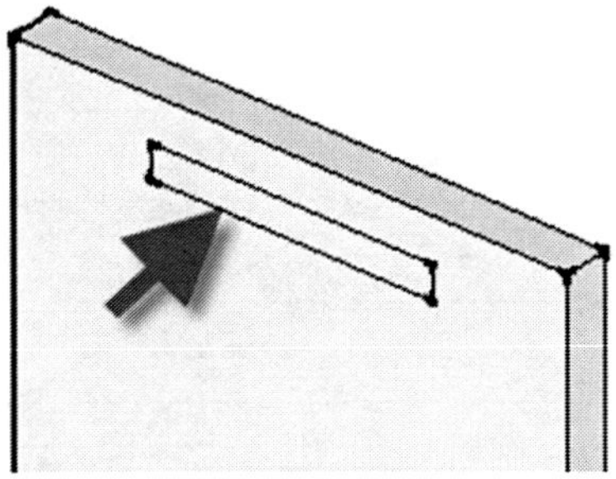

FIGURE 8.15 Pull outline

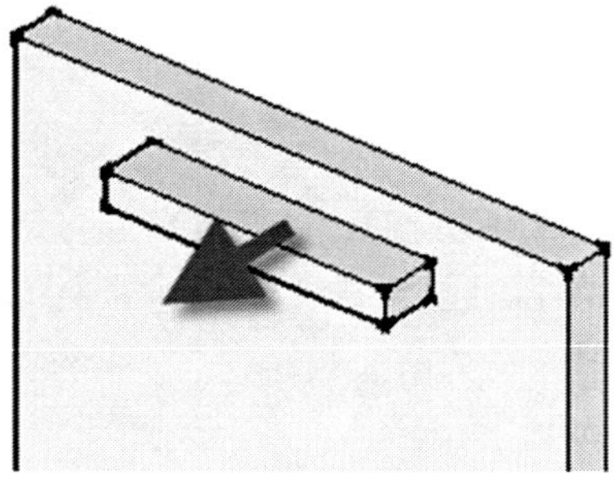

FIGURE 8.16 Pull Extruded

40. Sketch the profile of the pull on top of the extruded shape. This is in the 3D view; wait until you see the tooltip which says "on face" for drawing (Figure 8.17).

41. Use ***Push/Pull*** to carve out the back side of the pull (Figure 8.17).

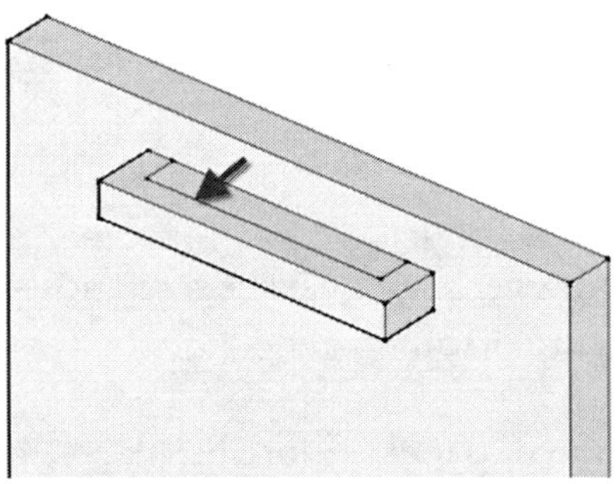

FIGURE 8.17 Pull profile

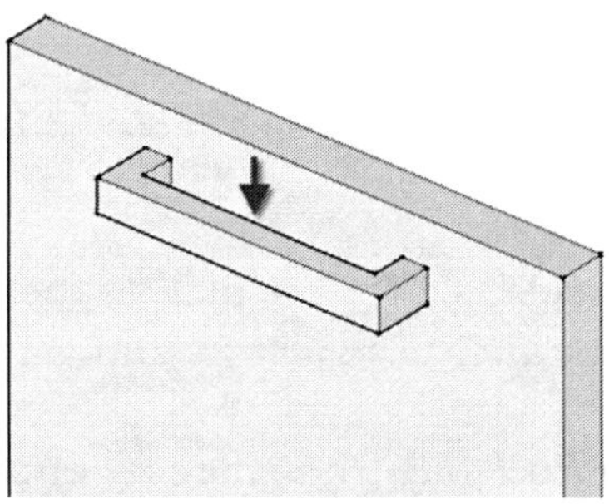

FIGURE 8.18 Pull completed

Next, you will group all the lines and surfaces that make up the pull into a single entity called a *Component*. As mentioned previously in this book, using *Components* is more efficient and makes the file smaller when the item will be used many times.

42. In the 3D view, *Zoom* in on the pull and select a window picking from left to right.
    a. Be sure to **pick from left to right** and adjust the view so you are only selecting the pull and nothing else behind it.

43. With the pull selected, click the **Make Component** icon.

44. Fill out the dialog as shown in Figure 8.19.

45. Click **Create**.

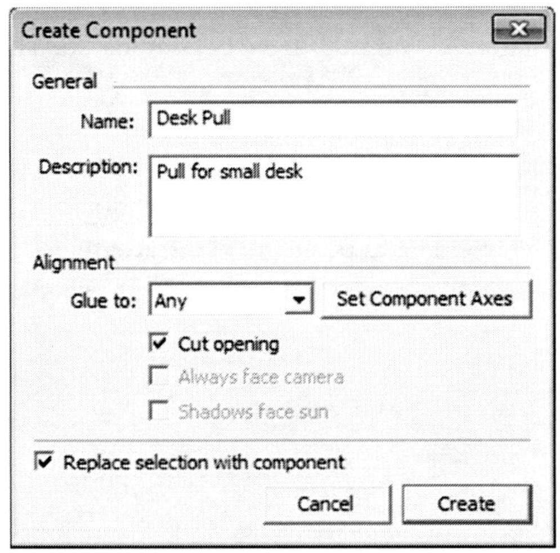

FIGURE 8.19 Create Component dialog

You now have a *Component* created in the model of your pull. Because the "Replace selection with component" was selected, the original lines and surfaces have been replaced with a copy of the new *Component.*

Next you will copy the *Component* down to the other drawer.

46. Select the *Component* and use the **Move + Ctrl** key to copy the pull down to the other drawer. Use the pick points shown in Figure 8.20.

Now that the pull is a *Component* you can edit one and the other will instantly update. You will try editing a *Component* next.

47. **Right-click** on one of the pulls and then select **Edit Component** from the pop-up menu.

48. Make a change to the pull, something simple such as using ***Push/Pull*** to make the extrusion taller (i.e., thicker) or something more detailed like making the pull curved (Figure 8.21).

49. When finished editing the *Component*, click away from it and the edit mode is finished.

Notice both pulls have been updated. This can save a lot of time!

Another right-click option is *Explode*. This allows you to reduce a *Component* back down to its basic elements and be changed differently from the other *Components*. *Explode* only affects the selected elements.

50. **Save** your model.

Before leaving the small desk, you will take a look at one more thing. As SketchUp models get more complicated, they become harder to modify. However, the process follows the same general steps as with the 2D shapes.

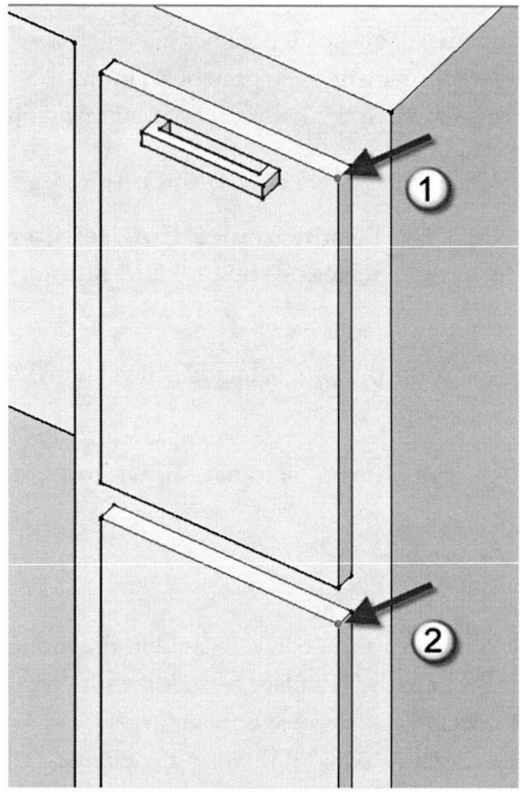

FIGURE 8.20 Copying component

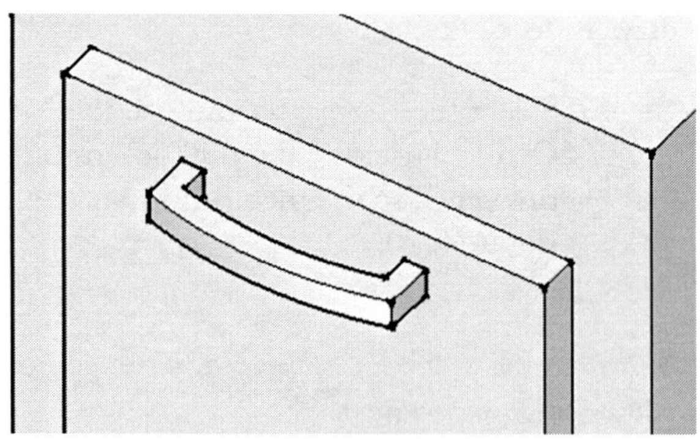

FIGURE 8.21 Editing a component

Next, you will make the desk 8″ wider because the drawers are too narrow.

51. Switch to the front view.

52. Drag a selection window, going from left to right (Figure 8.22).

    a. This will not work properly if you pick in the opposite direction.

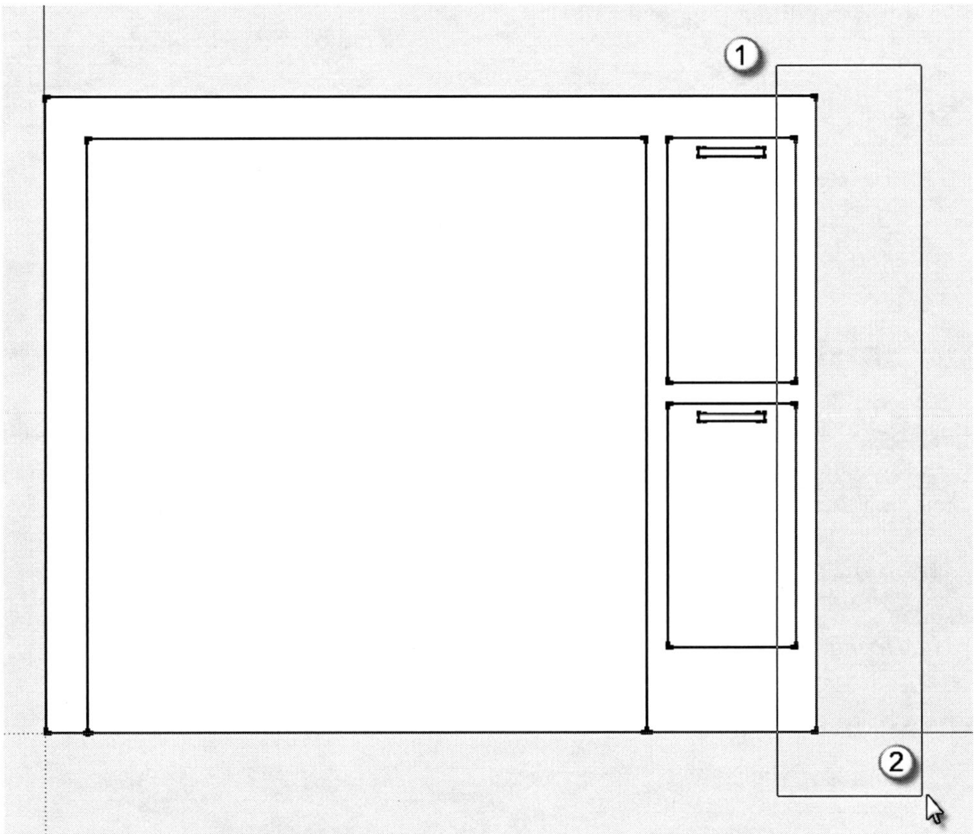

FIGURE 8.22 Selection window

53. **Move** the selected entities **8″** to the right.

54. Select the two pulls and move them **4″** to the right.

55. Switch to the **3D view**.

The model is now modified (Figure 8.23)!

56. **Save**.

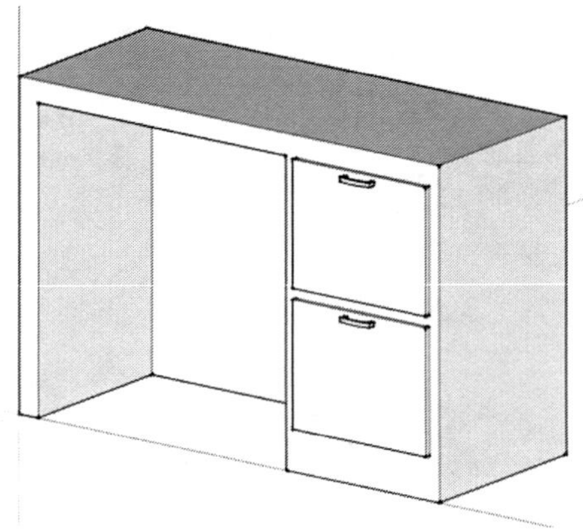

FIGURE 8.23 Complete

file name: Small Dresser – 3D

Often, it is ideal to add *Guides* to define an area rather than starting with lines. This is because lines can divide other lines and surfaces. You will use *Guides* to define the location of the drawer panels before sketching them.

57. **Open** the small dresser file and **Save As** to **Small Dresser – 3D**.

58. Use ***Push/Pull*** to make the dresser **4′-6″** tall.

59. Switch to the **Front** view.

60. Add the ten ***Guides*** shown in Figure 8.24.

    a. To add a *Guide*: click and drag on an edge using the *Tape Measure* tool; and then type a distance for accuracy.

    b. The bottom *Guide* is **4″** up from the floor.

    c. All remaining spacing is **1″** and the drawer panels are equal in height.

    d. Do the math first, to determine what the panel height should be.

FIGURE 8.24 Guides added

It is worth pointing out that SketchUp has a ***Divide*** tool, but it will not work in this case. To use it, you draw a line and then right-click on it, select **Divide** and then type in a value and press **Enter**, but this does not take into account the spacing between the drawer panels

With the guides in place, you can quickly sketch the rectangles to define the edges of the drawer panels.

61. Use the ***Rectangle*** tool to define the perimeter of the drawer panels; simply snap to the intersections of the *Guides.*

62. Switch to the **3D view**.

Your model should look like Figure 8.25. Note that the *Guides* were created on the plane related to the edge used to define it. Thus, picking the grid intersections causes the rectangles to be created on the correct plane – which subsequently divides the surface. You are now ready to *Pull* the panels.

63. Use ***Push/Pull*** to extrude the panels ½" out from the surface.

You could leave the *Guides*, and even turn them off so they are not in the way. However, you will just delete them as they are no longer needed.

64. Select the **Eraser** tool and erase each of the *Guides* (by picking them).

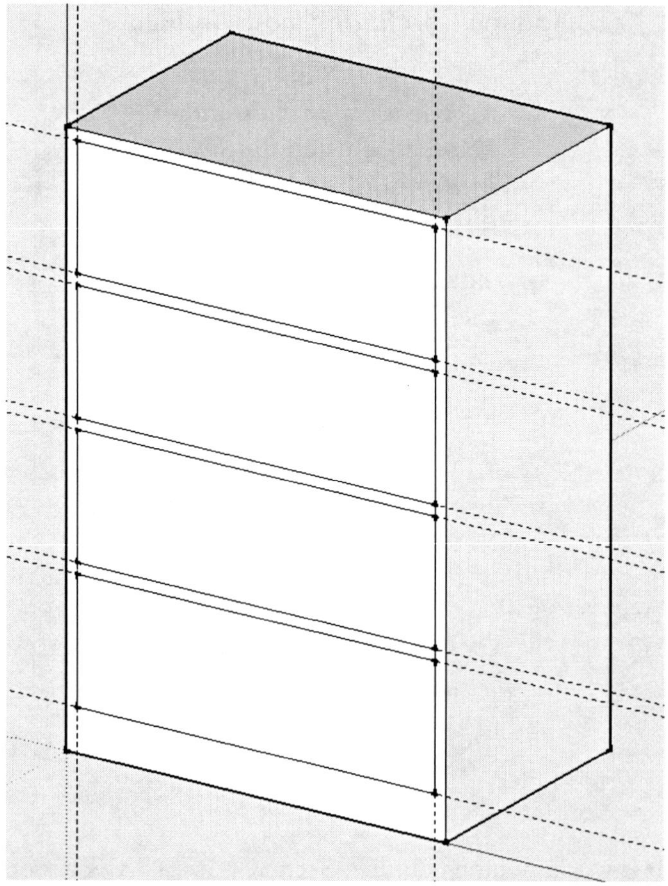

FIGURE 8.25 Rectangles added

The last step in completing the dresser is to add the pulls. You could recreate them from scratch, following the previous steps covered. However, it would be much faster to open the Small Desk – 3D file and copy one of the pulls to the *Clipboard*, and then *Paste* it into the dresser model. You will see that the pull will want to automatically "snap" to a surface due to the "glue to" setting when the *Component* was created.

65. **Open** the **Small Desk – 3D** file

    a. If you browse to the file, using *Windows Explorer*, and then double-click the file, it will open another session of SketchUp. This will allow you to keep the dresser file open.

66. Select one of the pulls and press **Ctrl + C** to *Copy* it to the *Clipboard.*

67. Switch back to the dresser model and press **Ctrl + V** to *Paste* the pull into the current model.

Notice as you move your cursor around the screen, the pull follows the surface below your cursor. It wants to stick to a surface due to the "glue to" option setting when it was first created.

68. Place the pulls approximately as shown in Figure 8.26.

You may want to switch to a "front" view and then add *Guides* to get the first drawer set up. Once you have one drawer set, you can copy it from one drawer to the next until they all have pulls.

69. **Save** your model.

The dresser is done for now.

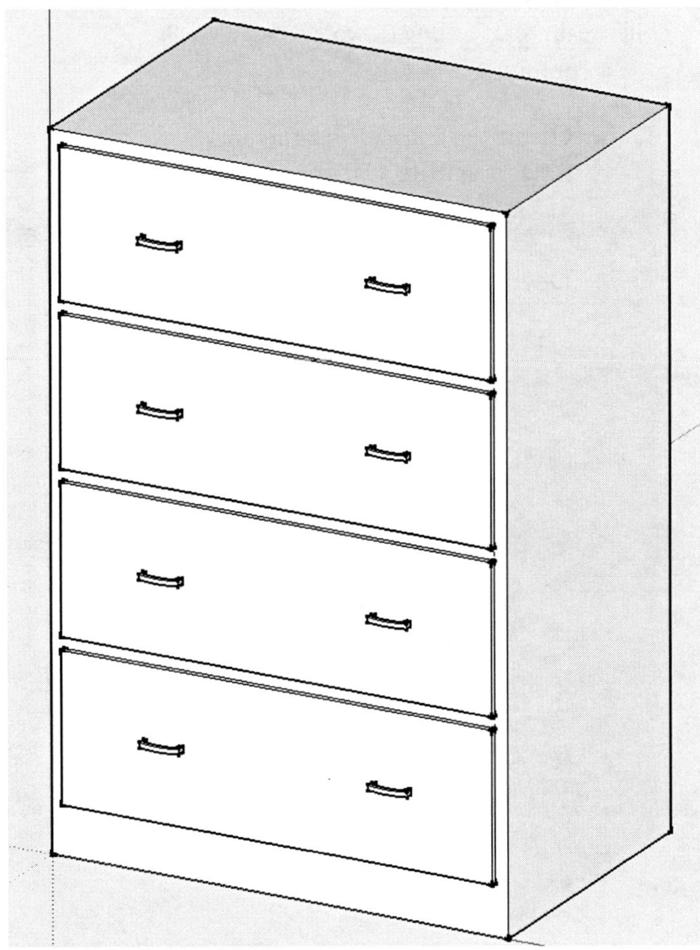

FIGURE 8.26 Pulls added

file name: **File Cabinet – 3D**

It is not always necessary to use the *Push/Pull* tool to create an extruded 3D element to represent something. In the case of this file cabinet it is easier to simply sketch the lines on the face of the cabinet which nicely defines the two drawers. This model can be developed more quickly and is less of a burden on the overall model due the less complex geometry and fewer faces and surfaces.

Worrying about the complexity of this file cabinet may seem trivial now, but in a large model with several chairs, desks, file cabinets, etc., you can see how the overall number of faces and edges could really start to bog down even the fastest computer.

70. **Open** the *File Cabinet* file and **Save** it as **File Cabinet – 3D.skp**.

71. Develop the cabinet:

    a. **27″** high

    b. Pulls ***Copy/Pasted*** from previous file.

    c. Use the ***Line*** tool to sketch the drawers:

        i. 1″ space on sides and top;
        ii. 4″ space from bottom;
        iii. Drawers are equal height.

FIGURE 8.27 File cabinet

Your file cabinet should look like Figure 8.27. Even though new surfaces were made within the perimeter of the drawers, they do not need to be extruded into a 3D element.

72. **Save**.

At this point you have learned to use a majority of the tools typically used on a regular basis by the average SketchUp user. There certainly is more to learn, but you are well on your way!

file name: Square Chair – 3D

In this exercise you will learn to modify geometry once it is 3D; making the backrest higher than the armrests.

73. **Open** the *Square Chair* file and **Save** it as **Square Chair – 3D.skp**.

74. Use ***Push/Pull*** to make the armrest and backrest **26″** high (Figure 8.28).

75. Make the seat area **16″** high (Figure 8.29).

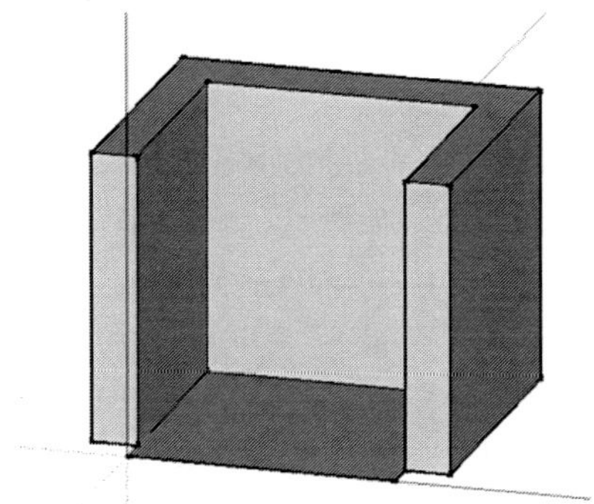

FIGURE 8.28 First extrusion

You now have the basic chair defined. However, you decide you would like to have a higher backrest and have the armrests curve down towards the front.

76. *Orbit*, *Pan* and *Zoom* in as needed, and then use the ***Line*** tool to add the two lines shown in Fig. 8.30.

77. Use ***Push/Pull*** to make the back rest **4″** higher.

78. Select and erase the extraneous lines highlighted in Figure 8.31.

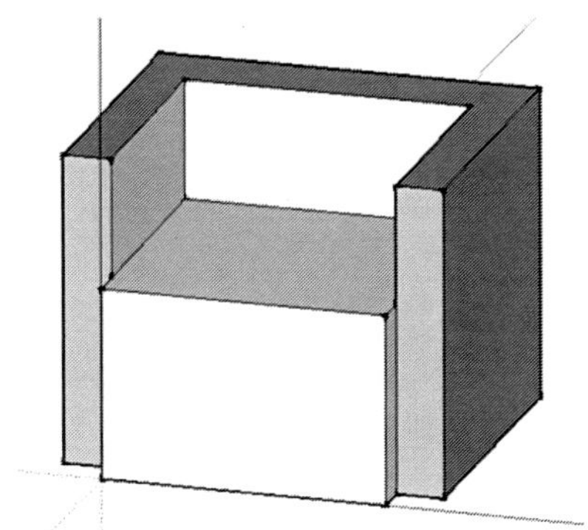

FIGURE 8.29 Second extrusion

Notice how the surface automatically heals itself when the lines are deleted.

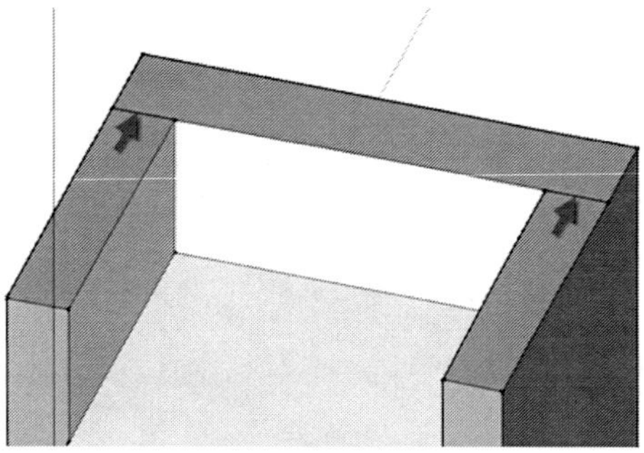

FIGURE 8.30 Lines added at backrest

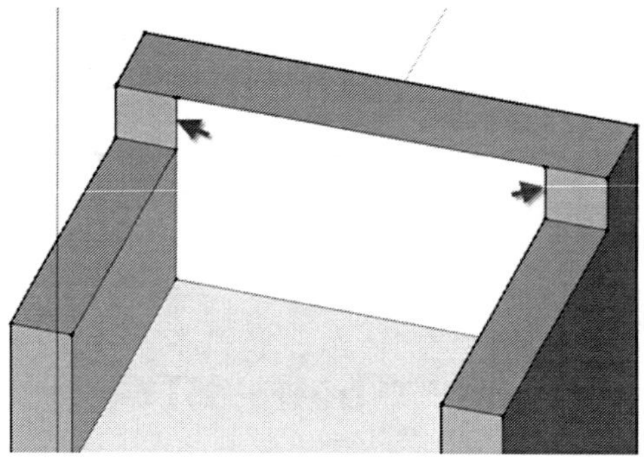

FIGURE 8.31 Lines to be erased

Now you will carve out a portion of the arm rests to make them curve down and toward the front of the chair. You will switch to a side view (this can also be done in a 3D view). In the side view you will sketch the profile of the portion you wish to exclude. The *Push/Pull* tool will be used to carve out the portion not needed, just like you did with the coffee table. But, before you use the *Push/Pull* tool you will want to copy the profile over to the other armrest so you do not have to recreate it.

79. Switch to a side view and sketch an **Arc** similar to that shown in Figure 8.32.

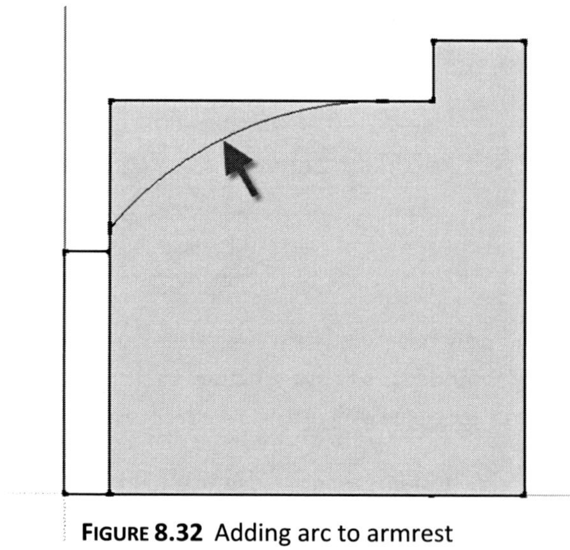

FIGURE 8.32 Adding arc to armrest

80. Switch back to the **3D view** and ***Copy*** the arc to the other armrest (Figure 8.33).

81. Use ***Push/Pull*** to drag the new surface over to align with the other side of the armrest – this will cause the entire extrusion to be deleted; repeat for other side.

As you can imagine, these types of modifications could continue to be made on this chair until it was exactly the way you want it. You may want to do a **Save As** once in a while to make it easy to go back to a previous design state if you get to a point where you are not happy with the design and want to go back.

Keep in mind that edges are required anytime there is a change in direction of adjacent surfaces, but not when surfaces are coplanar. So, the line at the top of the curved armrest is required in Figure 8.34, but the lines you deleted in Figure 8.31 were not.

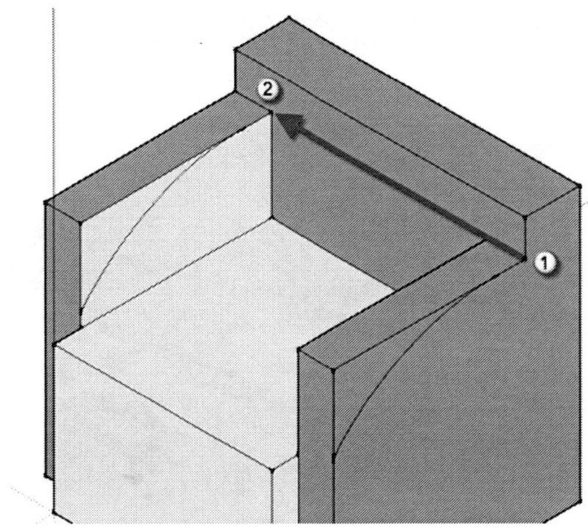

FIGURE 8.33 Copy arc to other armrest

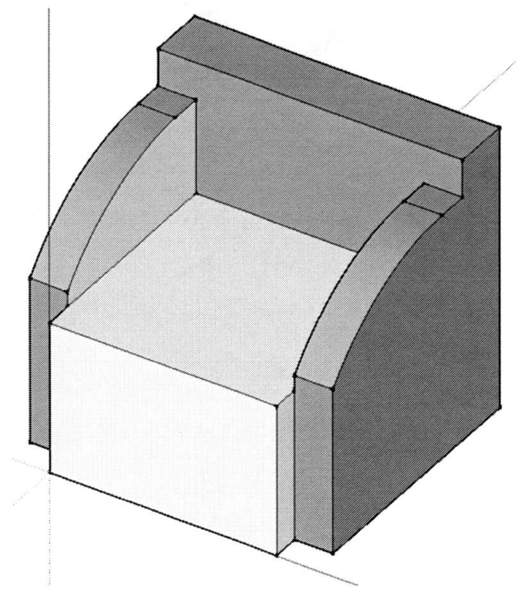

FIGURE 8.34 Use Push/Pull on armrest

Project Example: Custom Furniture. *Image courtesy of LHB; www.LHBcorp.com*

Section 9
Adding Materials

Now that you know how to develop simple geometry, you will make the models look a little more realistic and add materials to them. SketchUp comes with a nice selection of materials from which to choose. It is also possible to scan a material and use it on your model!

Materials Dialog

The *Materials* dialog is used to select and add *Materials* to your model.

1. **Open** your SketchUp model: **Bookcase – 3D.skp**.

2. Select the **Paint Bucket** icon from the toolbar.

You are now in the *Paint Bucket* tool, and if it was not already open, the ***Materials*** dialog box pops up.

3. Pick **Wood** from the drop-down list in the *Materials* dialog box (Figure 9.1b).

At this point you have ten wood materials from which to choose. Most of these are flooring materials (thus, they have lines in them to represent floor boards) and one material is OSB (Orientated Strand Board) which is not a finish material.

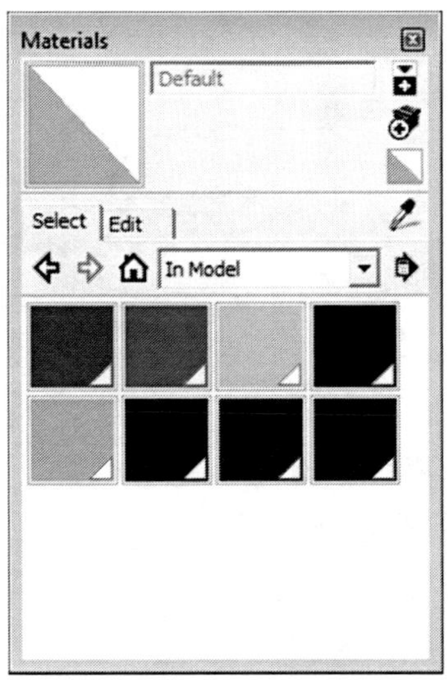

FIGURE 9.1A Materials

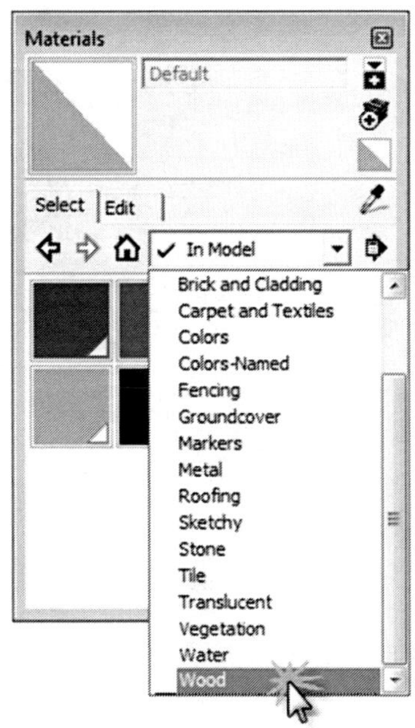

FIGURE 9.1B Materials list

4. Select **Wood_Cherry_Original** from the options listed under *Wood.*

5. Move your cursor into the model area and click on 2 different surfaces to apply the material (only click on two for now).

As you can see, the material is added to each surface as you click on it using the *Paint Bucket* tool. This is handy if you want to have the shelves be a different material than the frame of the unit. Similarly, if you need to add more refined materials you can sketch additional lines to divide the surfaces into separate areas.

However, clicking each surface would take a bit of time. So the next steps will show you how to quickly add the material to the entire bookcase at once.

6. With the *Paint Bucket* tool still active, right-click on one of the surfaces and pick **Select → All Connected**; the same *Layer* would also work in this case (Figure 9.2).

Project Example: Waiting Room. *Image courtesy of LHB; www.LHBcorp.com*

7. Click on one of the surfaces to apply the material to all faces.

> ***TIP:*** *You can also press* CTRL *or* SHIFT, *while painting a surface, to…*
> ***CTRL:*** *Paint all connected faces with matching paint*
> ***SHIFT:*** *Paint all faces in model with matching paint*

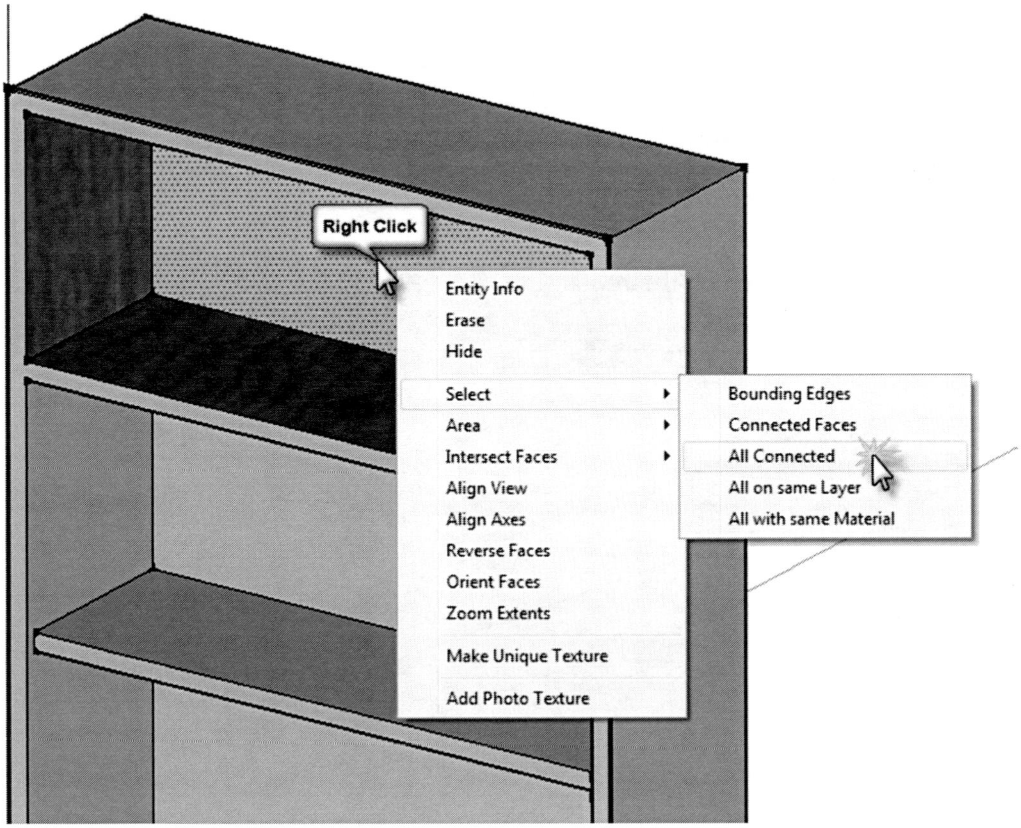

FIGURE 9.2 Adding materials

The wood material has now been added to the entire bookcase. The materials are designed to be real-world scale, so you need to model things the same size they would be in the real world. Otherwise, things such as bricks will not look right.

8. **Save** your **Bookcase – 3D** file before moving on.

In the next steps you will add a transparent material to give the appearance of glass. This will be a glass panel in the center of the coffee table.

9. **Open** the *Coffee Table – 3D* file.

The first thing you will do is carve out an area for the glass panel in the center of the table.

10. Switch to the **Top** view and ***Offset*** the outer edge inward **3″**.

11. Switch back to the **3D view** and use ***Push/Pull*** to remove the center of the table; click and drag the surface down until it aligns with the bottom edge of the table top.

12. Use the ***Select*** tool to pick the remaining surface and **Delete** it.

Your model should now look like Figure 9.3.

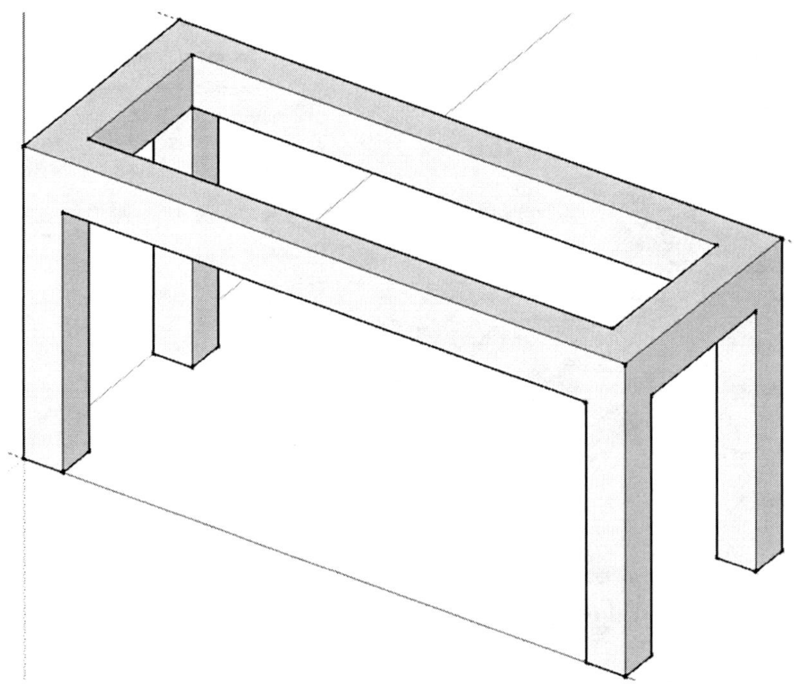

FIGURE 9.3 Center of table removed

Before modeling the glass, now is a good time to quickly make everything a wood material.

13. Using the steps recently covered, make all elements material: **Wood_Board_Cork**.

The material may not actually be cork, but the color might be the closest thing to what you are thinking, and that will work for now.

Next, you will create a surface at the top of the new opening to represent the glass. This can easily be done in the **3D view**.

14. Select the **Rectangle** tool and then pick two opposite corners of the opening in the center of the table (Figure 9.4).

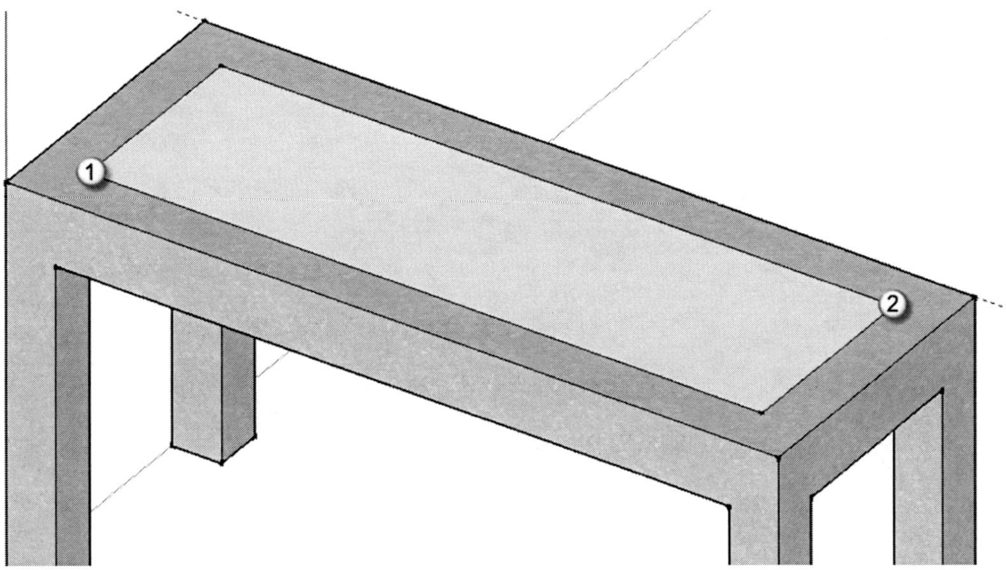

FIGURE 9.4 Adding surface at opening

As mentioned earlier, SketchUp does not allow lines to overlap. So the lines for the rectangle were immediately deleted, but they caused SketchUp to check and see if any enclosed areas need a surface.

15. Use the ***Paint Bucket*** tool to set the new surface to **Translucent \ Translucent_Glass_Corrugated**.

The glass material is now added to the coffee table (Figure 9.5). There are a number of things you could do at this point. You could select the surface and copy (via **Move + Ctrl**) the surface down ½″ inch to give the appearance of thickness.

You can also right-click on the glass surface, and select **Texture → Position**. This gives you the option to rotate and adjust the scale of the material.

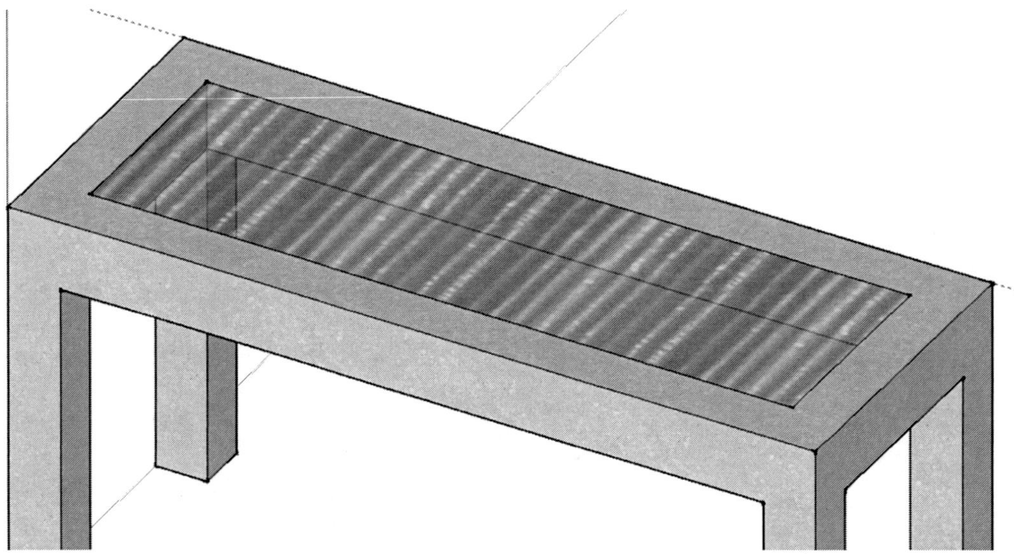

FIGURE 9.5 Glass material added to table

Just in case you changed something, the following needs to be set so your screen matches the screen shots in this book.

- View menu
    - Edge Style
        - Edges (checked)
        - Profiles (checked)
        - Extensions (checked)
    - Face Style
        - Shaded with Textures (checked)

Try ***X-ray*** and ***Back Edges*** before moving on, and then set things back to the defaults listed above.

As you did with the desk, try adjusting the overall length and width of the table. You have to use very specific selection windows to make this type of modification.

16. **Save** your model.

This concludes the basic introduction to SketchUp. You will learn a few new things later in the book, when you start the design of the interior fit out. However, you are already off to a good start.

Many SketchUp users buy a book just on SketchUp and read a portion of material equivalent to that which has been covered thus far and just learn the rest on their own – using trial and error plus the *Help* system. Of course, some would benefit from a more advanced book, but what you have learned thus far is almost everything you need to know for basic modeling.

17. Use the techniques learned here to create the remaining 3D models; based on the 2D sketches created in the previous chapter.

18. Apply materials to all remaining models. Try adding multiple materials to one or two of them.

19. **Save** all files before moving on.

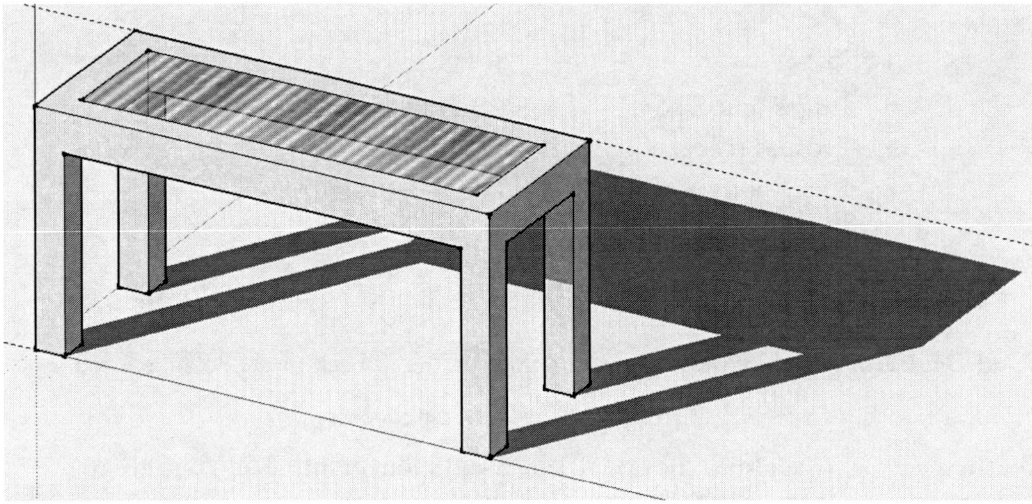

FIGURE 9.6 Shadows turned on via the View menu

Creating Custom Materials

Creating a custom *Material* is fairly easy in SketchUp. The most difficult part is finding, or creating, a good repeating image; these are images which are seamless and don't reveal an edge when painted on a surface (Figure 9.7). There are a number of sources for tileable (or repeating) images online. Some are free and some are not. Also, if you have other graphics, CAD or rendering packages such as Autodesk Revit or AutoCAD installed on your computer (which is common in a school lab), you have access to a number of images which are installed with that software. The Autodesk textures, for example, can be found here: C:\Program Files (x86)\Common Files\Autodesk Shared\Materials\Textures.

FIGURE 9.7 Example of repeating image

The next few steps will walk you through the process of creating a new material. We will look at a real-world example by downloading an image file from a carpet manufacturer. This image will then be used by the new material, which can then be painted on any surface.

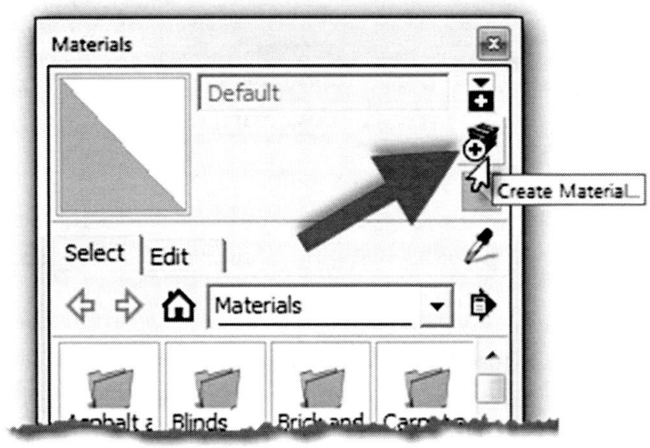

FIGURE 9.8 Create a new material icon

20. Open the **Materials** window if necessary.

21. Click the **Create Material** icon in the upper right (Figure 9.8).

You are now presented with the *Create Material* dialog shown in Figure 9.9. First you will give the material a name; if you don't, the default name provided will be used, which is *Material1* in this example.

A material consists of either a **solid color** or a **texture**, i.e. a raster image file. There is a third option, which is a combination of the color and texture, when *Opacity* less than 100% is specified. This option will show some of the color through the texture depending on the *Opacity* setting.

All of these options are pretty straightforward. One thing to note about selecting a color is the ***Picker*** drop-down. Here you can change from selecting a color visually to entering specific values. This is great when you are, for example, specifying paint from a manufacturer who provides the **RGB** values for all their colors (e.g., *Sherwin-Williams*).

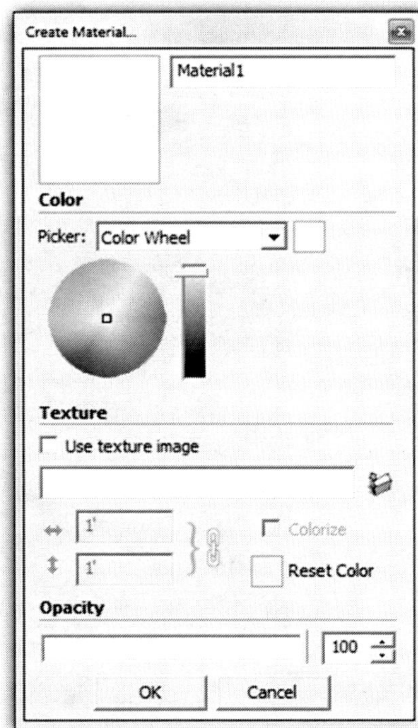

FIGURE 9.9 Create material dialog

Next you will use your internet browser to access the *Shaw* website.

22. Browse to the following URL: **http://www.shawcontractgroup.com/ProductSpec/Show/59483**

Notice that the last number is the model number for the *Shaw* carpet we are using. This can be changed to another known model number to quickly access similar information for another *Shaw* product.

23. Follow the steps shown in Figure 9.10 to download an image file for the specified carpet; select a location on your hard drive to save the file.

FIGURE 9.10 Downloading Shaw carpet image file

If you open the file you downloaded it should look similar to what is shown in Figure 9.11. Notice the text across the bottom gives a disclaimer and information about the carpet in the image. In our case we need to crop this image down from a 9x9 tile pattern to 8x8 to get rid of the text. We will select our pattern from the upper left corner to get a pattern which will repeat properly in SketchUp.

FIGURE 9.11 Downloaded image file

24. Open the image file in an image editing program such as Adobe Photoshop and crop the image down as shown in Figure 9.12.

Next you will switch back to SketchUp and associate the new image with your material.

FIGURE 9.12 Cropped Shaw carpet image file

Now you will modify the new material to represent a tile carpet from the *Shaw Flooring* image you just downloaded.

25. Change the name to **Shaw Carpet**.

26. Check the **Use texture image** option (Figure 9.13).

As soon as you do this, a *Choose Image* dialog will appear. If you need to select another image later, you can click the icon to the right of the image file name.

27. **Browse** to the carpet image you just downloaded and cropped.

    a. If you do not have this file, you can download it from the internet at SDCpublications.com.

    b. Once you have selected the image, click **Open**.

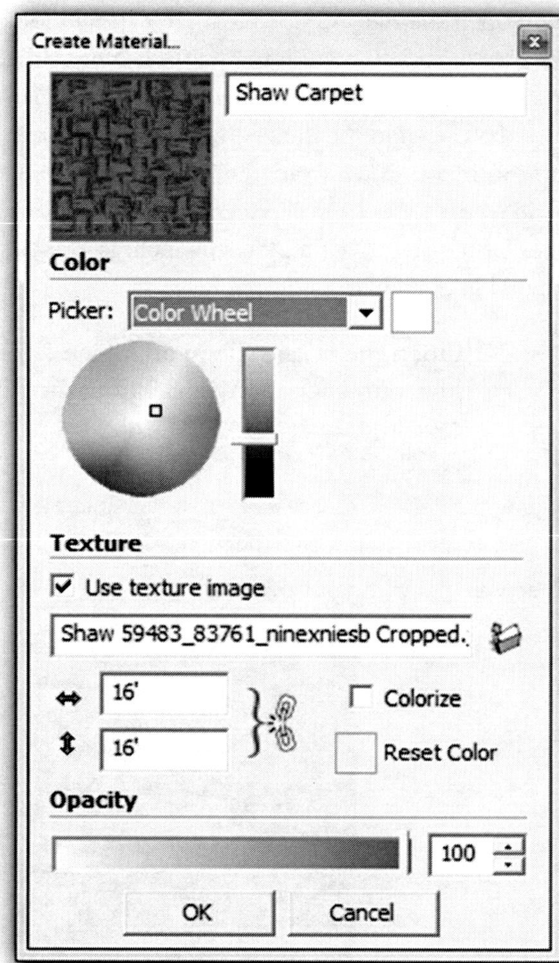

FIGURE 9.13 Custom material creation

We happen to know that these carpet tiles are two foot square, so eight tiles would be sixteen feet. We need to tell SketchUp our image, which represents an 8 tile x 8 tile area, is sixteen feet in each direction.

28. Change the *Width* and *Height* to **16′** as shown in Figure 9.13.

    Click **OK** to finish creating the new material.

29. In a new file, sketch a **rectangle** on the floor. Make it large enough to show 3 or 4 tiles in each direction.

30. **Paint** the face with your new material.

You should now see the carpet squares in the model. The image to the right shows a larger area covered with the carpet tiles. This is fairly realistic because the tiles are often rotated when they are installed. So downloading a larger sample area, as we were able to do, really helped. Not all product manufacturers provide this option. This would also include stone or ceramic floor and wall tiles, ceiling tiles and more.

Sometimes you need to download, scan or photograph what you can and then use an image editing program to make a workable image. In our carpet example, if you could only download one 2′x2′ image, you could create a larger image, in Photoshop for example, and copy plus rotate to create a similar result. For some materials, such as tile, it is a little trickier as you have to make sure the grout lines work when tiled.

Knowing how to use a good image editing program really helps!

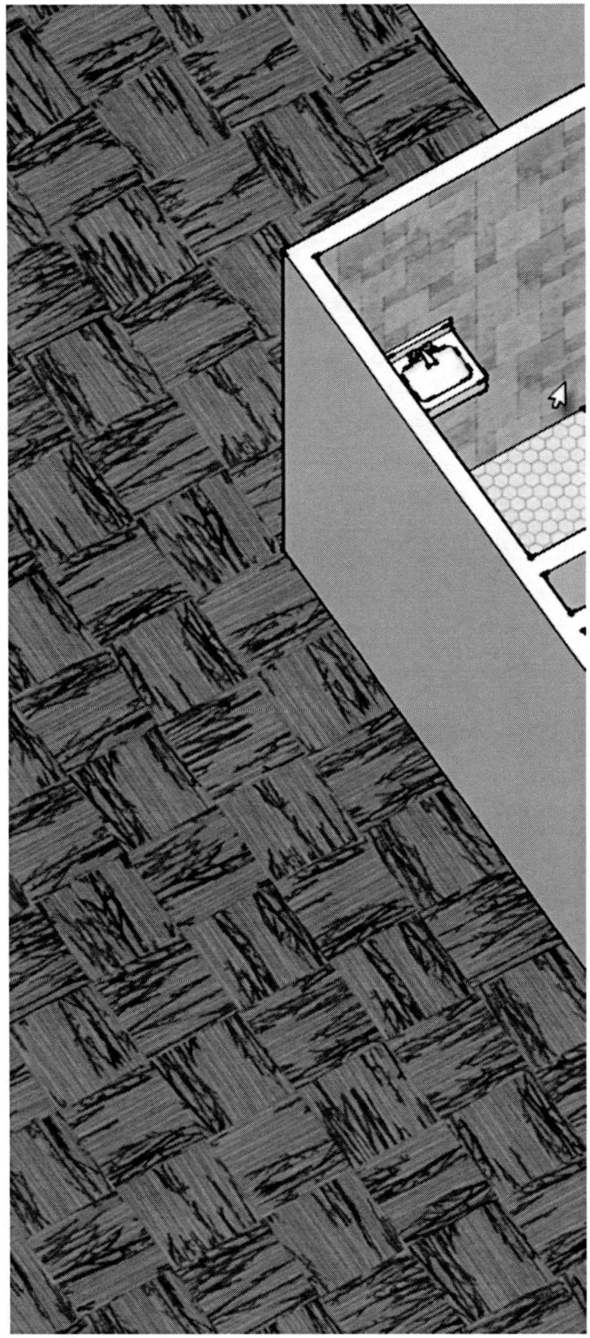

FIGURE 9.14 Custom material creation

Calculating the Area of a Material

SketchUp has the ability to report the area for a material used in the model. Follow these simple steps to derive the square feet of any material:

- Open the **Materials** window
- Switch to view the **In Model** materials
- **Right-click** on the desired material
- Select **Area**

You will the see the result as shown in Figure 9.15 below. If you plan on using this information, say to estimate material cost, you will want to use extra care when placing, i.e., painting, the material in your model. Applying materials by layer or to multiple faces at once might allow "extra" faces to be included in the final number.

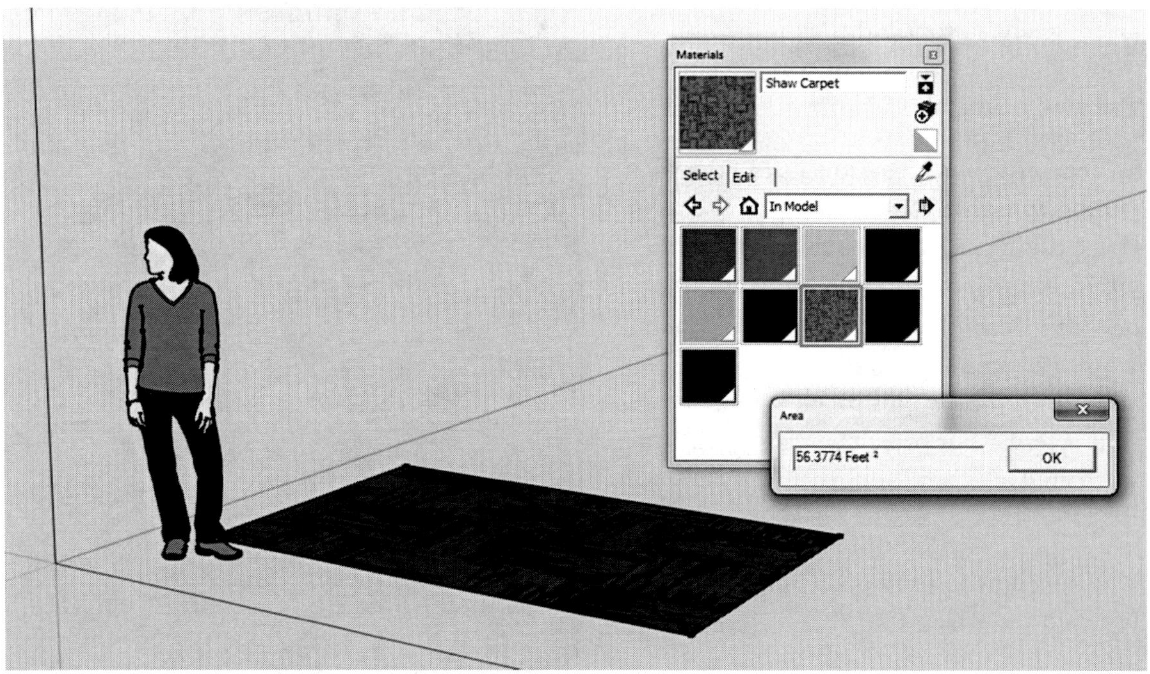

FIGURE 9.15 Calculating area of a material

Once a custom texture has been assigned to a material, the texture representation is saved in the SketchUp model. You do not have to maintain the original texture file with the same name and in the same location on your computer's hard drive.

Creating a Custom Collection

When you initially create a material, it only exists in the current model. If you want to access your custom materials in other SketchUp models you will have to create a special location to store them called a *collection*. A collection is basically a folder on your hard drive where you save each material as an individual file with the extension SKM.

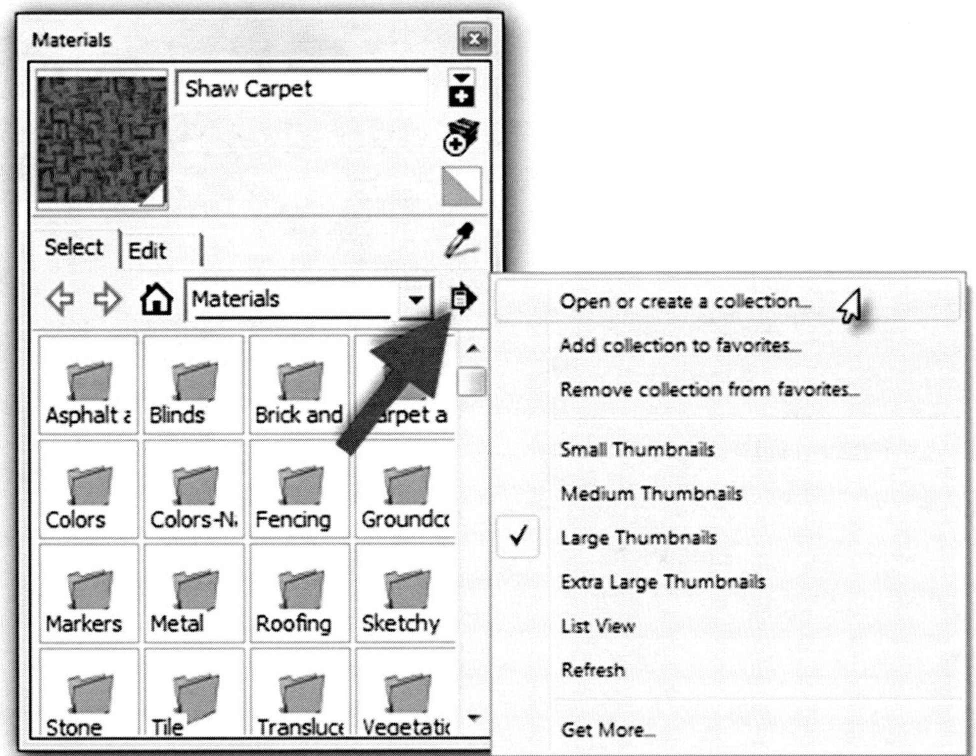

FIGURE 9.16 Creating a material collection

Before you point SketchUp to a place to store your custom collections on your computer, you need to create a custom folder. This way you can keep your materials separate from other files on your computer.

31. Using *Windows Explorer*, create a folder called **Custom Materials**.

FYI: *You can create this folder anywhere on your computer. If these materials need to be shared with others, in your class or office, you can create this folder on a server. You could also save it in the Cloud; maybe in Dropbox, for example.*

32. Click the **Details** icon, which is pointed out in Figure 9.16.

33. Select the **Open or create a collection** option from the fly-out menu.

34. **Browse** to the folder you create in Step 31 and then click **OK**.

Now you need to save one of your *In Model* materials to the collection folder.

35. Switch to the **In Model** materials.

36. **Right-click** on the "Shaw Carpet" material and select **Save As** from the pop-up menu (Figure 9.17).

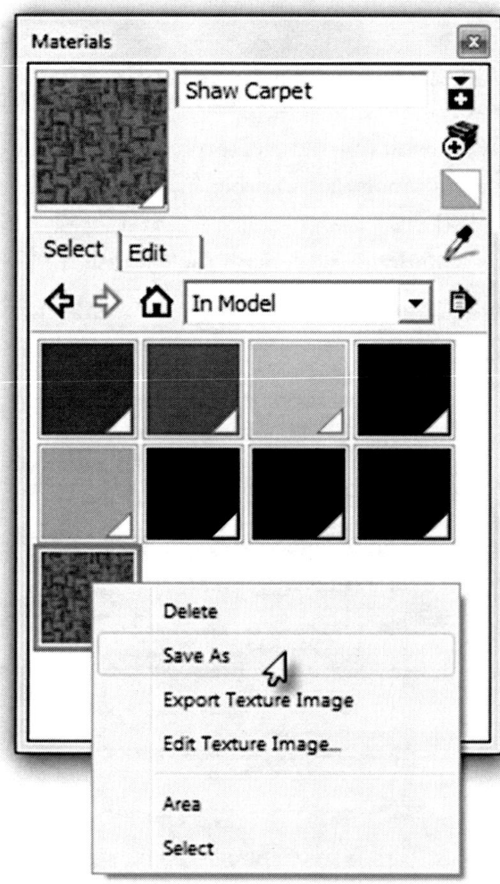

FIGURE 9.17 Saving material

37. **Browse** to the *Custom Materials* folder and click **OK**.

You can now see the custom material, and any others, from any SketchUp model, which have been saved there.

If you want to see these materials all the time, you need to add it to the favorites list. Here is how you do that:

38. Select the **Details** icon again, and then select **Add collection to favorites.**

39. Browse to the *Custom Materials* folder again, and then click **OK**.

You now have the basics of how to use and manage materials in SketchUp.

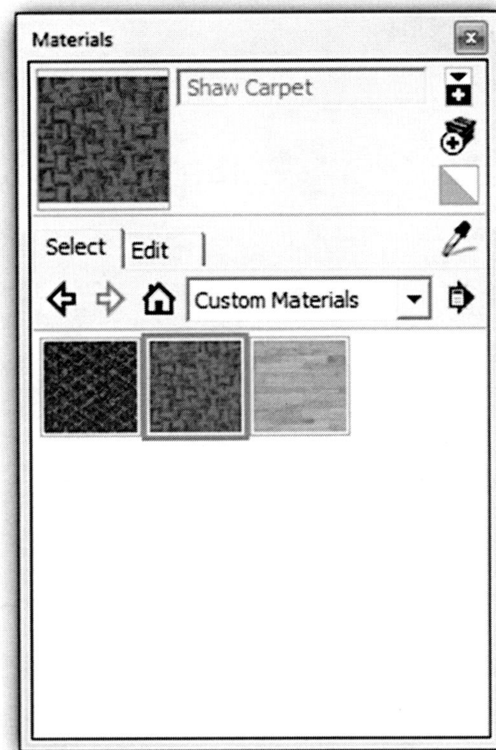

FIGURE 9.18 Saving material

NOTES:

Section 10
Detailed SketchUp Model

It may be helpful at times to create a more detailed SketchUp model. Some do this for an entire project; others just use it to focus on small custom portions of the project. This section will focus on the latter, and walk through the process of modeling a reception desk. This could also be done for built-in casework, such as cabinets or bookshelves, custom furniture, etc.

You will learn a few new concepts here, such as how to cut a section through your model. However, you already know most of the steps necessary to create the reception desk model. This tutorial will just help you learn to think about what you are trying to model and the various ways in which you can approach the problem given SketchUp's toolset.

For this tutorial you will start a new SketchUp model. You could work within a project model if you wanted. However, for something detailed like this reception desk, it is easier to work in a separate model and then load it into the project.

1. Start a new SketchUp model.

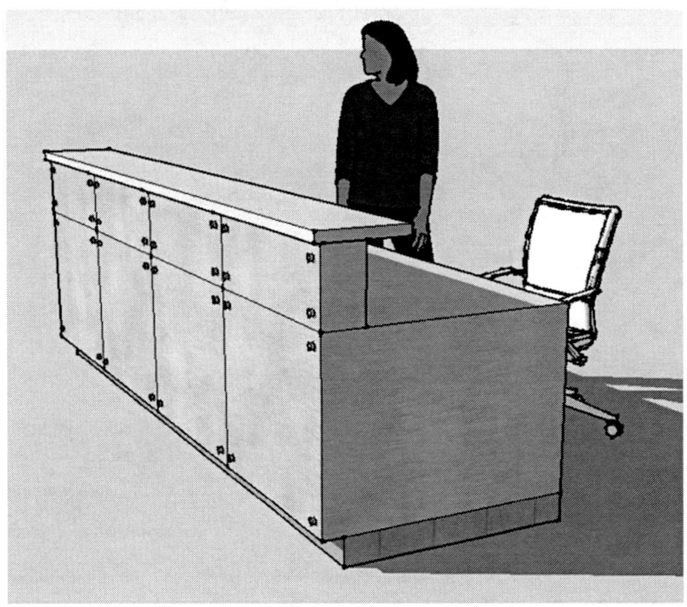

2. Create a rectangular box (Figure 10.1):

    a. Sketch a 10′-0″ x 3′-0″ rectangle on the ground/floor.

    b. Use ***Push/Pull*** to extrude the rectangle 3′-6″ upward.

The rectangle represents the outer extents of what we think the desk will be. The 3′-6″ high is based on the desire to have a 42″ high transaction surface; this is a surface for customers to write on and look at paperwork provided by the receptionist. The final desk may extend outside of this box. But, we will use this as a starting point. Think of it as a piece of wood you will carve portions away from.

The default person can remain and be used as a scale reference.

FIGURE 10.1 Start with a rectangular box

3. Sketch an outline as shown in Figure 10.2):

   a. The three dimensions shown are:

      i. **1′-0″** – transaction surface (1½″ thick)

      ii. **2′-6″** – typical desk height

      iii. **6″** – thickness of wall supporting transaction surface.

      iv. See Figure 10.3 for intended goal

FIGURE 10.2 Sketch outline of areas to be carved out of the box

4. Use the ***Push/Pull*** tool to carve out a portion of the box behind the transaction counter (Figure 10.3):

    a. Pull the surface until it snaps to the opposite end of the box so the section being pulled completely disappears once you let go of the mouse button.

This step also defined the height of the work surface (30″ high).

The next step will be to carve out a portion of the box to define the knee space below the work surface. This often requires brackets to support the work surface, but that will be ignored here – we will save that for the *Construction Documents* phase.

FIGURE 10.3 Using Push/Pull to remove a portion of the box

5. Sketch the **lines** shown in Figure 10.4 on the back face of the desk:

    a. 1½″ thick work surface

    b. 6″ side walls

6. Use ***Push/Pull*** to "push" the face back 2′-6″.

This modification leaves a 6″ wall to support the transaction counter (3′-0″ – 2′-6″).

FIGURE 10.4 Sketch outline for open space below work surface

FIGURE 10.5 Use Push/Pull to carve out leg space

7. Using similar steps, define a 3″ deep and 4″ tall **toe space** on the front side (or public side) of the reception desk (Figure 10.6).

8. Sketch the **lines**, equally spacing the vertical lines, as shown in Figure 10.6:

    a. Draw one centered and then copy that line 2′-6″ each way

    b. Copy via the *Move* tool while holding down the Ctrl key

FIGURE 10.6 Toe space and line work added

The lines sketched in the previous step will be used to define metal panels. If the desire were to have a more exaggerated reveal, you could sketch the reveal profile and then use *Push/Pull* to create it. However, in most cases a line can adequately suggest a reveal without the extra work.

The next step is to start adding materials. You will have to use *Orbit* to apply materials to all sides of the desk.

9. Use the ***Paint*** tool to add **Metal Aluminum Anodized** to the front and sides of the desk (Figure 10.7).

10. Add the horizontal line at each side, aligned with the top of the top space. This will define the base material.

FIGURE 10.7 Adding materials

11. Add more materials using the ***Paint*** tool:

    a. Markers\Yellow Green – work surfaces

    b. Tile\Tile Ceramic Natural – base

12. Sketch additional *lines* and use ***Push/Pull*** to refine the transaction surface as shown in Figure 10.8:

    a. Make the front edge extend 1″ out

    b. Make the sides extend ½″ out

    c. Adjust the painted faces as necessary

FIGURE 10.8 Defining transaction counter

Next you will be adding decorative fasteners at the corner of the panels. To help locate them, you will add guides and then use the intersection of these guides to locate the fastener. The fastener will be created as a *Component* so they can all be changed at once, if need be later.

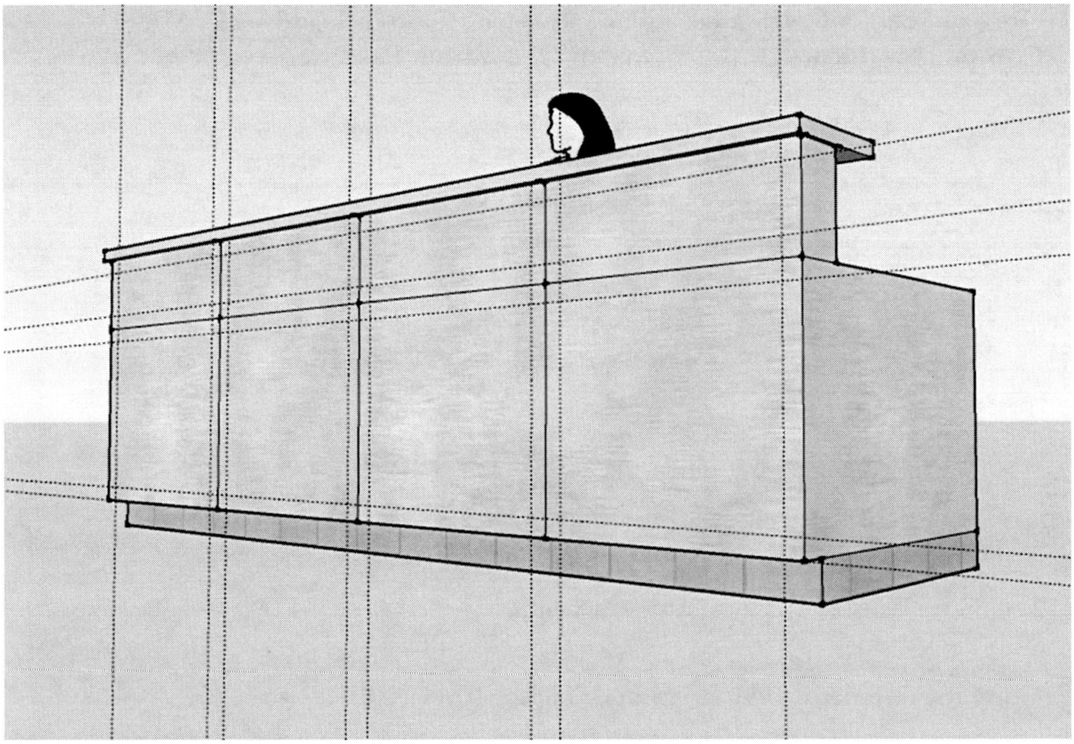

FIGURE 10.9 Adding guides to define decorative fastener location

13. Add **Guides** 2″ from the edge of the panels as shown in Figure 10.10.

    REMINDER: *Use the* Tape Measure *tool.*

14. Make a **2″** diameter and ½″ thick disk.

    a. Create the first fastener off to one side, in mid-air, so it does not modify the faces of the panels.

    b. The view needs to be almost directly beside you to get the circle aligned with the vertical plane.

    c. **Paint** with the same material as the work surface: Yellow Green.

15. Once finished, select disk (all edges and faces), right-click and select **Make Component** (Figure 10.10). Name it: **Decorative Fastener**.

FIGURE 10.10 Create fastening and turn into component

16. **Copy** the fastener *Component* around (Figure 10.11).

FIGURE 10.11 Decorative fasteners added

It is often helpful to use the ***Section Plane*** tool to look at your model in section. This can be done vertically or horizontally. In this exercise you will look at a vertical application. This could also be applied horizontally to a floor plan (i.e., top) view of a more detailed floor plan model.

17. Select **Tools → Section Plane** from the menu.

18. Hover your cursor over the side of the desk, until the *Section Plane* appears as shown in Figure 10.12, and then click.

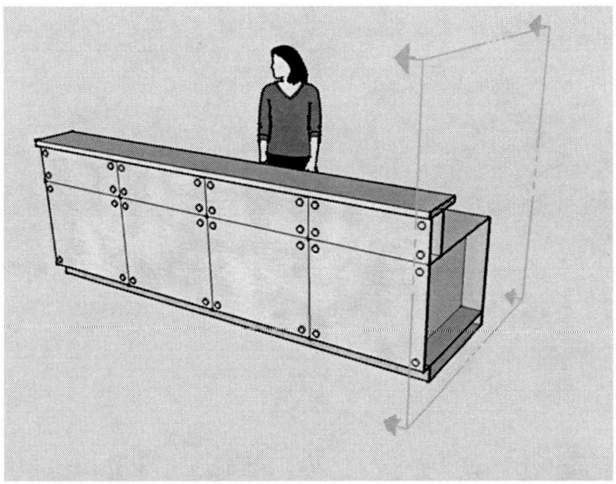

FIGURE 10.12 Adding section plane

19. Select the *Section Plane*, and then use the **Move** tool to reposition it so you see the desk in section as shown in Figure 10.13.

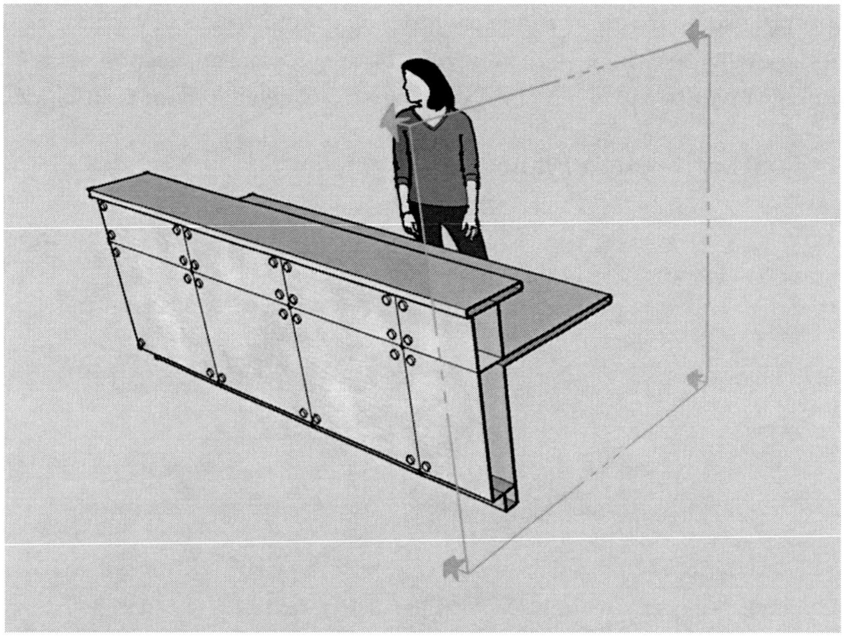

FIGURE 10.13 Adjusting section plane location

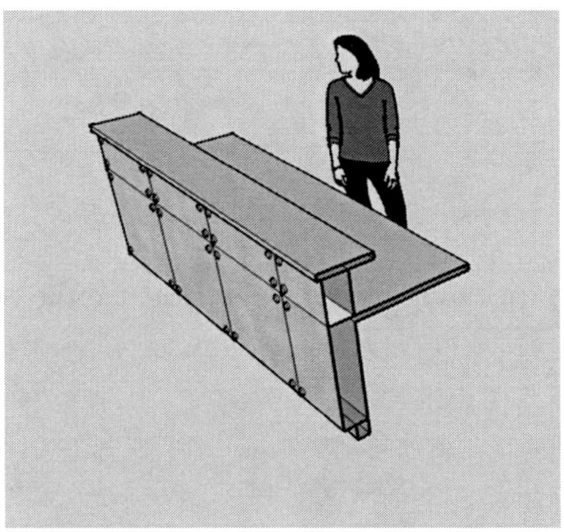

FIGURE 10.14 Section plane visibility turned off

20. From the *View* menu, toggle off **Section Planes**.

Notice how the *Section Plane* element is no longer visible but the model is still in section. This can create a nice presentation drawing. Additionally, toggling off the **Section Cuts** item in the *View* menu restores the entire model.

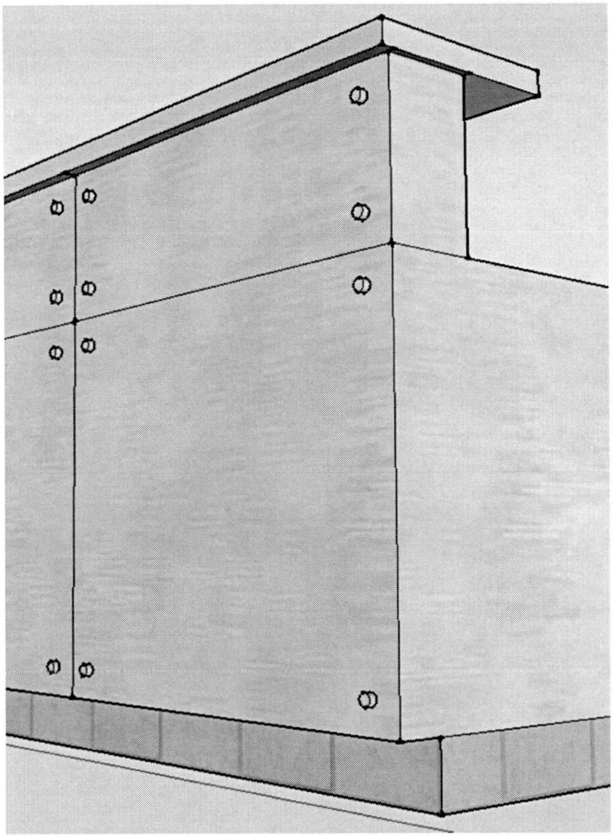

FIGURE 10.15 Edit fastener component

It is decided that the 2″ diameter fasteners do not look good aesthetically. Therefore, you decide to change them to 1″ diameter. Changing one *Component* changes them all!

21. Edit the *Component*; double-click on it.

22. Use the **Scale** tool from the *Tools* menu.

Another option, rather than copy, is to delete the edges and faces within the *Component* and create the geometry from scratch. When finished with the *Component* edit, all instances will be updated.

This may take a little trial and error to get it right.

This last step will cover placing furniture in your model.

23. Select **Window → Components**.

24. Type **Haworth** and press **Enter**.

25. Select one of the chairs listed, that are created by *Haworth*. Place it in your model (Figure 10.16).

If you open the **Layers** dialog, you will see new *Layers* created for the chair. The arm rests have their own layer. Therefore, the arms can be turned off if needed.

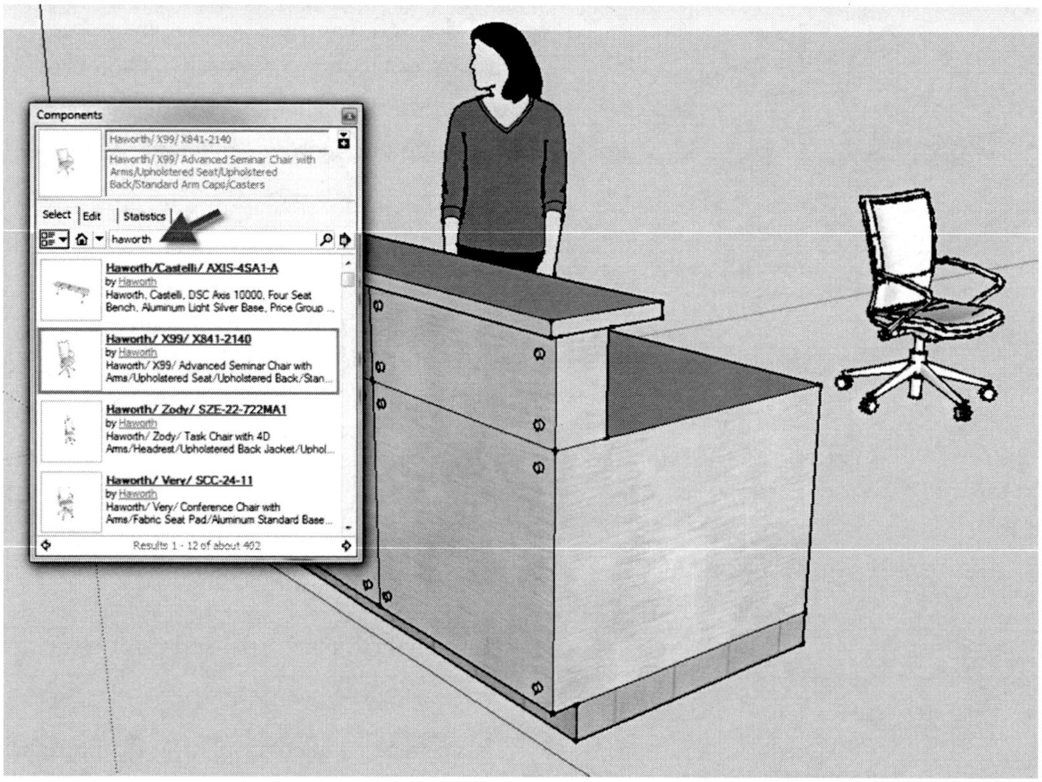

FIGURE 10.16 Placing components

It is good to remember that some manufacturers have created SketchUp content and made it available on the internet. This can save a lot of time and help to quickly make your models look really great!

This model can now be printed and added to a presentation board. You can use File → Export → 2D Graphic to create a raster image file on your hard drive for use in Adobe Photoshop or InDesign and Microsoft Word. This export feature prompts you for a file name and location.

Section 11
Working with Styles

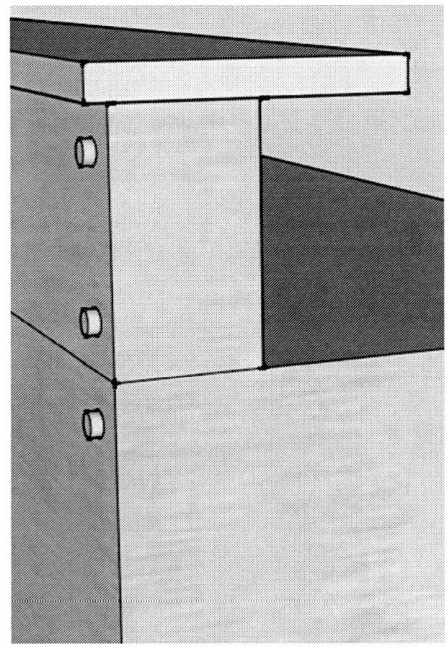

FIGURE 11.1 Default style settings

In addition to SketchUp's ease of use, another great attraction for a designer is the aesthetic quality of the images which can be produced. With very little effort, images can be created with "styles" ranging from technical to hand drawn. This can affect all aspects of the model, including the background. As you will soon discover, you have a number of options to control the graphic styles.

The template you started from automatically has a few *Style* related items set (Figure 11.1). For example, the **Edge Extensions** feature causes the line ends to extend and overlap slightly to accentuate the beginning and end of each line. This is something many designers do when sketching by hand. Another setting from the typical architectural template is **Profile**. This feature thickens lines at outside edges and plane changes to help with edge and depth perception. We will explore how to control these options and more in this chapter.

There are three main ways in which we can work with *Styles* in SketchUp.

- View menu toggles
- Styles toolbar
- Styles browser

We will use the reception desk model created in the previous chapter as the "sandbox" to experiment with the *Style* tools. Maybe we are preparing presentation images of this new desk design for a client.

1. Open your **Reception Desk.skp** model.

Next you will create a copy of the file so you don't have to worry about messing up the original.

2. From the **File** menu, select **Save As**.
3. Name the new file: **Reception Desk – Styles.skp**.

View Menu Toggles

First we will take a look at the toggles related to *Styles*. These allow you to control which *Style* settings are applied to the model, if any.

First we will turn off *Profiles*.

4. Select View → Edge Style → Profiles (Figure 11.2).

Notice all the lines, or edges, are now the same thickness. Next you will turn off all the *Edge Styles* to see the stripped-down basic model.

5. From the ***View*** menu, uncheck all the options under **Edge Style**.

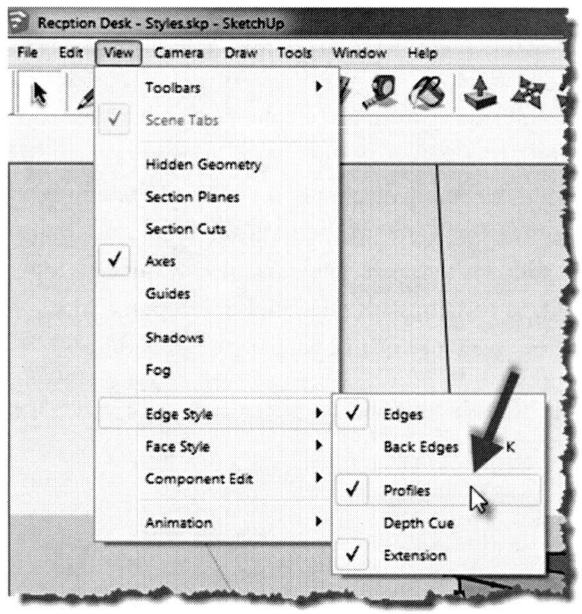

FIGURE 11.2 Style toggles

Notice the model is very simple looking, and does not have much definition (Figure 11.3). The only style still applied now is the *Face Style*: **Shaded with Textures**. This toggle can also be seen from the *View* menu (Figure 11.4). At least one *Face Style* must be selected, so this is a toggle between options shown in the menu fly-out. Don't change these settings back yet.

FIGURE 11.3 Result of turning off all Edge Styles

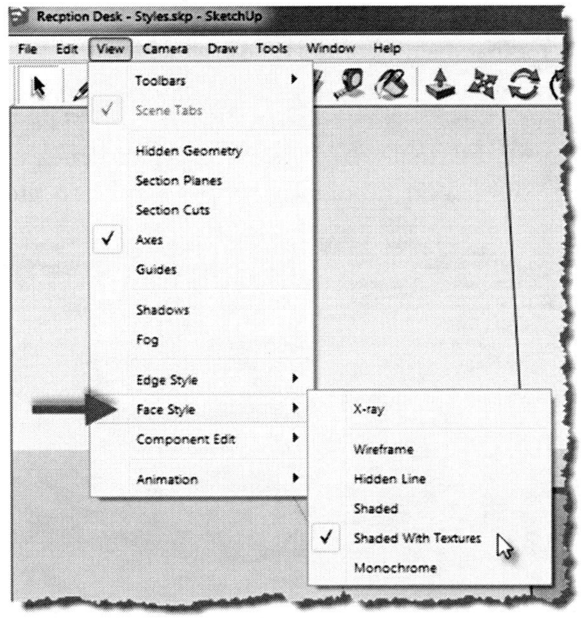

FIGURE 11.4 Face Style toggles

Styles Toolbar

SketchUp provides a *Styles* toolbar which allows the designer the opportunity to quickly adjust the active *Style*. The first thing you need to do is make sure the toolbar is turned on.

6. To turn on the toolbar, select **View → Toolbars → Styles**.

You now have a toolbar open, which can be docked (i.e., attached to the top edge of the screen).

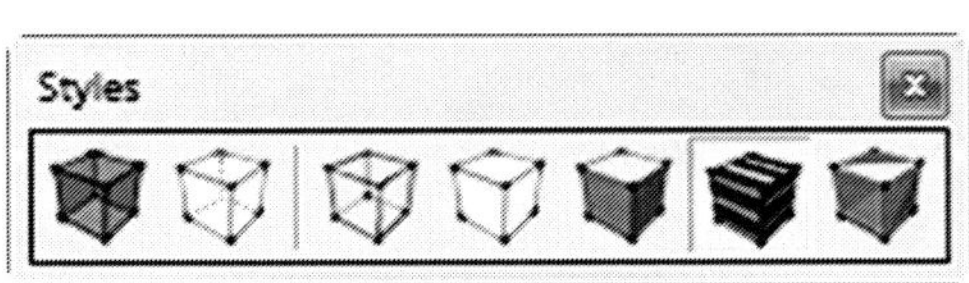

From left to right, these commands are:
X-Ray, Back Edges, Wireframe, Hidden line, Shaded, Shaded with Textures, Monochrome.

The first two icons are toggles which can be on or off in addition to one of the remaining five icons. This toolbar mainly controls the toggle between *Face Styles*. Only the *Back Edges* tool is an *Edge Style* setting.

7. Ignore the first two icons for now, and click on the last five icons to see what each one does. You should see results similar to those shown below.

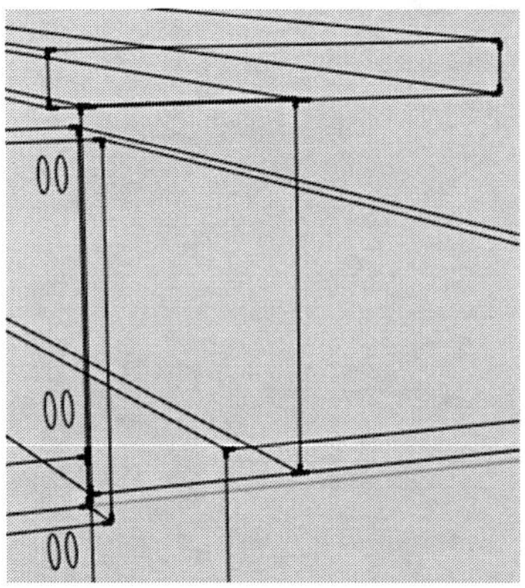

Wireframe

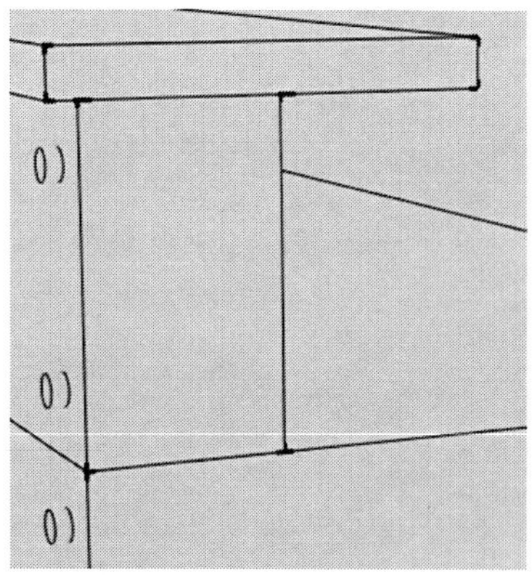

Hidden Line

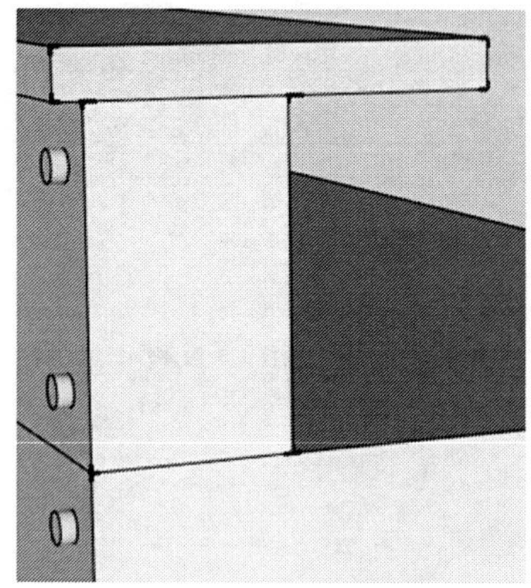

Shaded

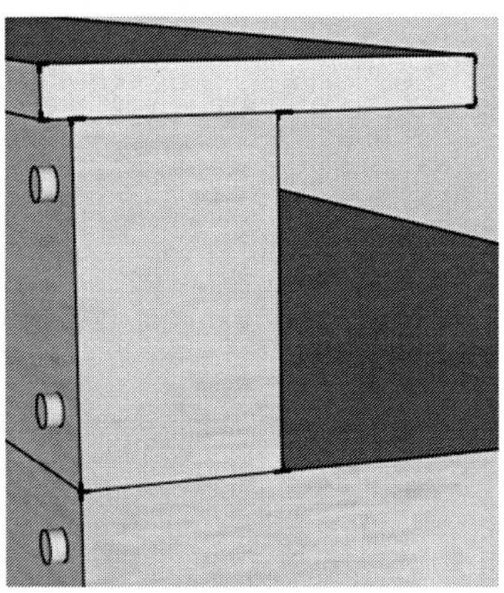

Shaded with Textures

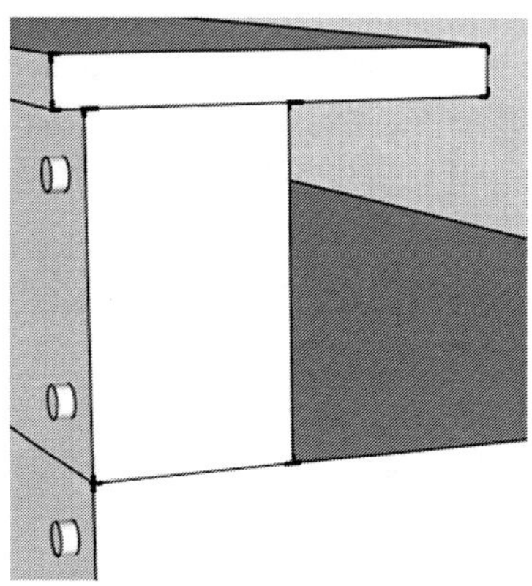

Monochrome

As soon as you click on *Wireframe* or *Hidden Line* you should notice that *Edges* (an *Edge Style*) are toggled back on. Those *Face Styles* require *Edges* be on.

Next you will review the effect that *X-Ray* and *Back Edges* have on the model – these are the first two icons on the *Styles* toolbar. For these two icons, they can both be "off" or just one of them can be "on".

8. With *Monochrome* still selected, click on the **X-Ray** icon, the first icon on the *Styles* toolbar.

As the name implies, you can see through everything, but without the radiation exposure (Figure 11.5). This allows you to get a better look at your model without the need to be continually orbiting around the model. This is usually used more as a "working" mode rather than a presentation technique. That's not to say there is not a situation in which this would be a great presentation style.

Take note that the **X-Ray** icon looks like it is pushed in, to indicate it is active. Let's switch to *Back Edges* next, and see what this does to our model.

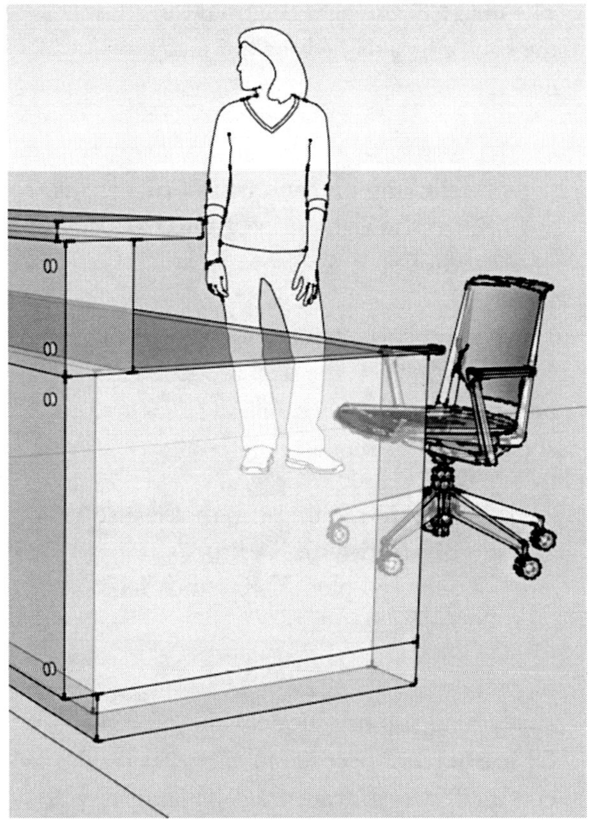

FIGURE 11.5 X-Ray mode toggled on

9. With *X-Ray* still selected, click on the **Back Edges** icon on the *Styles* toolbar.

Notice how the *X-Ray* mode is forced "off" and the *Back Edges* mode is now "on". This mode makes all edges, which are otherwise hidden on faces based on the direction you are viewing the model from, dashed. Put another way, this mode makes all "back edges" visible and dashed.

The image to the right (Figure 11.6) shows the back edges dashed for our reception desk.

10. With *Back Edges* active, try clicking on each of the five icons on the right side of the *Styles* toolbar.

You should have noticed, as soon as you selected *Wireframe*, the first two icons become grayed out because all edges are showing in this mode.

11. Before moving on, make sure **Shaded with Textures** is selected plus *X-Ray* and *Back Edges* are off.

Everything you have done with *Styles* thus far has been an override to whatever the current *Style* is for your model. Next you will look at how to apply, manage and create custom *Styles*.

FIGURE 11.6 Back Edges mode toggled on

Styles Browser

Now we will dig in and look at some really cool things we can do with *Styles*. Keep in mind that *Styles* do not actually change your model in any way. They just change how the edges and faces are presented, if at all. In this section we will look at how we can apply pre-created *Styles* and edit the current *Style*.

The first thing we need to do is open the *Styles Browser*, or dialog box.

12. Select **Window → Styles.**

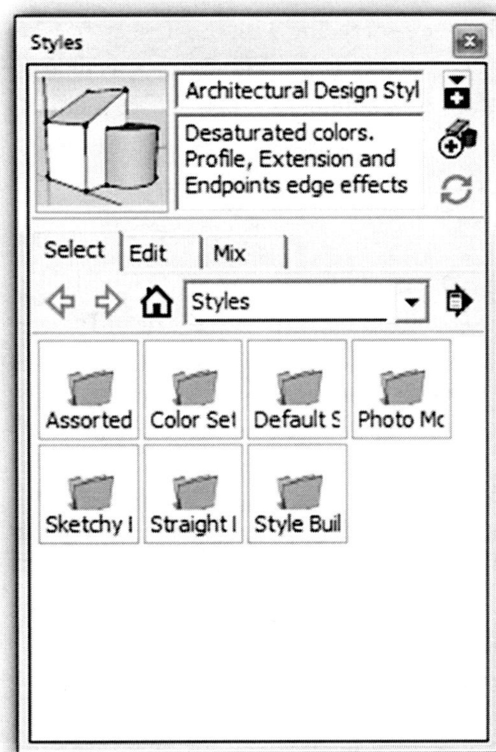

FIGURE 11.7 Styles browser

You now see the *Styles Browser* shown to the right (Figure 11.7). At the top you see a preview of the current style, the style name and a description. Below that are three tabs where you can **Select** (i.e., apply) a pre-baked *Style*, **Edit** the current *Style* and **Mix** various parts of the pre-baked *Styles* to get new results.

If you click on the title bar for this browser, it will collapse to maximize the visible portion of the canvas area (Figure 11.8). Clicking the title bar again expands it. You may close it by clicking the red X in the browser. You can also drag it to a second monitor if you have one.

We will start by applying pre-baked *Styles* to get some quick and amazing results.

13. On the **Edit** tab, open **Assorted Styles**.
    a. This can be done via the drop-down list directly below the tabs, or by clicking the "folder" image/ icon in the preview panel area below (Figure 11.7).

FIGURE 11.8 Styles browser collapsed

Notice, in Figure 11.9, that the drop-down list indicates the current collection/folder you are in and the preview panel below shows several previews. You will try several of these on you model.

Just before proceeding with the next step, take note that the *Section Cut* and *Guides* are currently off. You turned these off via the *View* menu previously in this chapter. These features will become visible again because these settings are saved in the *Styles*.

14. In the *Assorted Styles* folder, select the second item (pointed out in Figure 11.9). If you hover over the preview before clicking, you will see the *Style* name: **Brush Strokes on Canvas**.

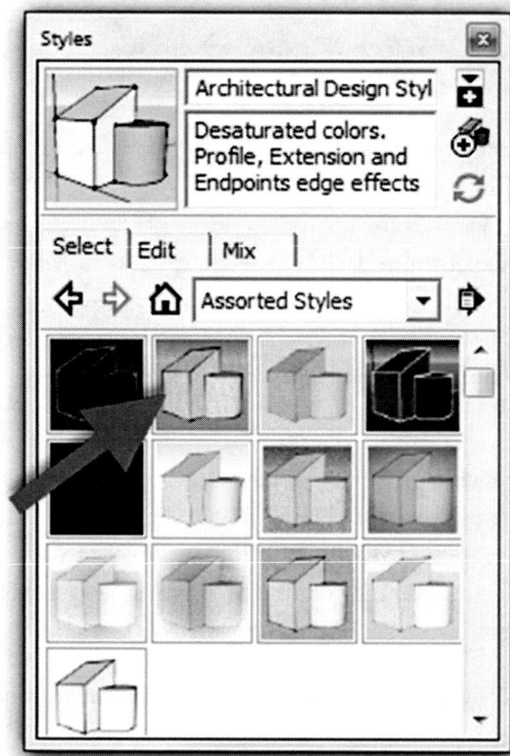

FIGURE 11.9 Styles browser collapsed

Notice the overall aesthetics of the entire model exhibition have changed drastically. As you will see, *Styles* control much more than you have seen so far. Next, you will turn off the *Section Cut* and *Guides* to clean up the image.

15. From the *View* menu, turn off the following:
    a. Section Planes
    b. Section Cuts
    c. Guides

Your model should now be presented as shown in Figure 11.10 on the next page. With just a couple clicks you have made a very compelling design presentation.

16. In the *Style Browser*, click on the same *Style* again: **Brush Strokes on Canvas**.

Notice the *Section Cut* and *Guides* came back. The changes made in Step 15 did not change the saved version of the *Style*. More on this in a moment.

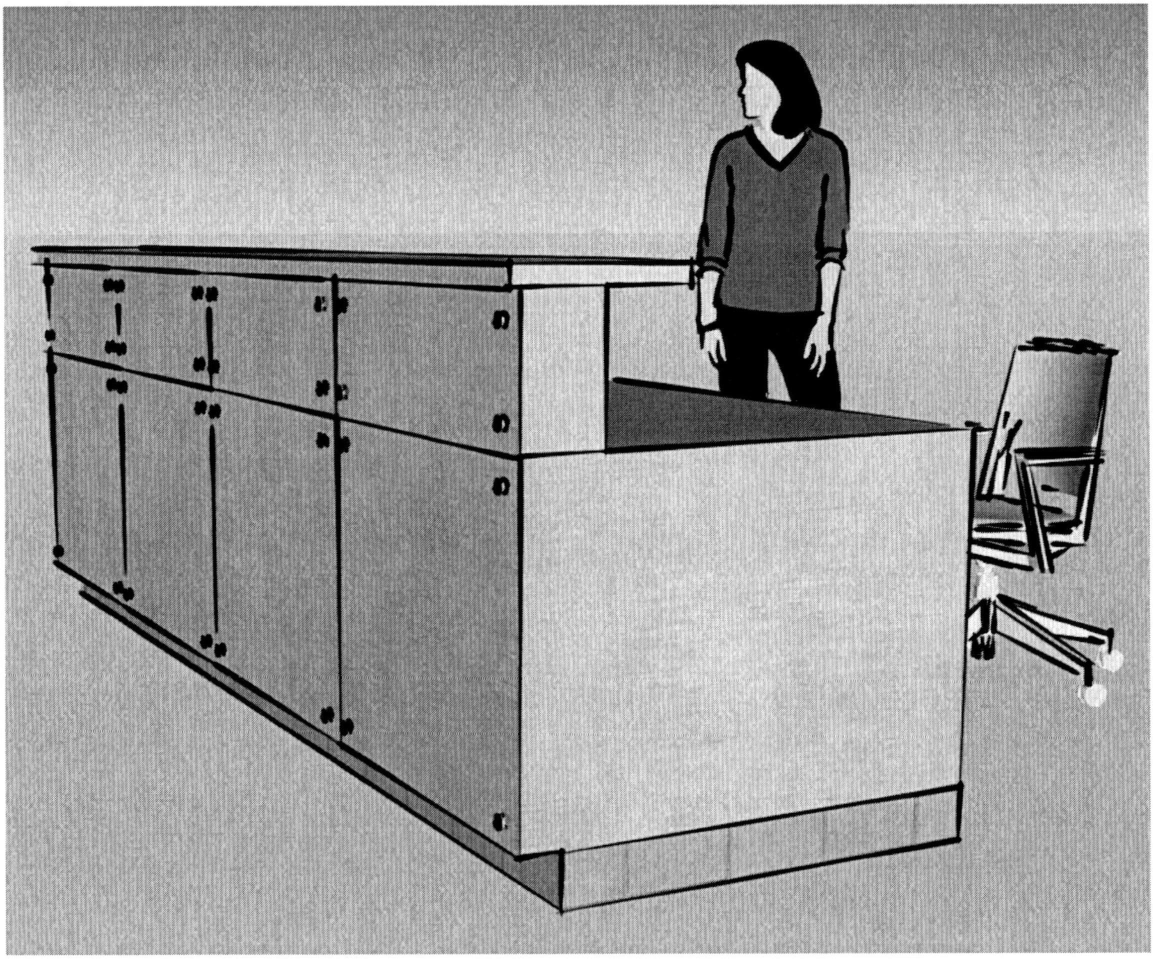

FIGURE 11.10 Brush Strokes on Canvas applied to model

17. Click on all the *Styles* listed under *Assorted Styles* to see how they look on your reception desk model.

FIGURE 11.11 Pencil on Tracing Paper applied to model

Notice that some styles change the background so that the horizon line is not shown and the outer edges of the screen are redefined.

In the example to the left, Figure 11.11, the *Style* **Pencil on Tracing Paper** applies a very whimsical line to the model edges. This makes the model look more hand drawn. This is great when you want to convey an initial design concept to a client, but don't want the model to look so polished and complete that they are afraid to suggest a change.

18. Set the current *Style* to **Pencil on Tracing Paper**.

19. Turn off the *Section* and *Guide* features again.

Notice, in the *Styles Browser*, that the preview in the upper left has two circular arrows superimposed on it (Figure 11.12). This indicates that the current *Style* has been overridden. You may either leave things as they are or click the update button to save the changes. If you don't save the changes, it will take more time to get back to this "style" if you, for example, try another *Style*.

In the next step you will update the *Style*. The one thing to be aware of is that you are only updating the COPY of the *Style* in your current model. This makes sense as you would probably not want to change a default, out of the box, *Style* that comes with the software for all future models.

20. Click the **Update Style** button pointed out in Figure 11-12.

Pencil on Tracing Paper is now updated, and when clicked on in the future, the *Section Cut* and *Guides* will not be visible. However, you have to click on the right version of the *Style*…

If you click on the *Pencil on Tracing Paper Style* shown to the right, under *Assorted Styles*, the *Guides* and *Section Cut* will actually appear.

21. Click on the *Style* **Pencil on Tracing Paper** again, under *Assorted Styles*.

You should see the *Guides* and *Section Cut*. This is the version of the *Style* which comes with the software. Anytime you apply a *Style*, a COPY of it is saved in your model. You will see this in the next step.

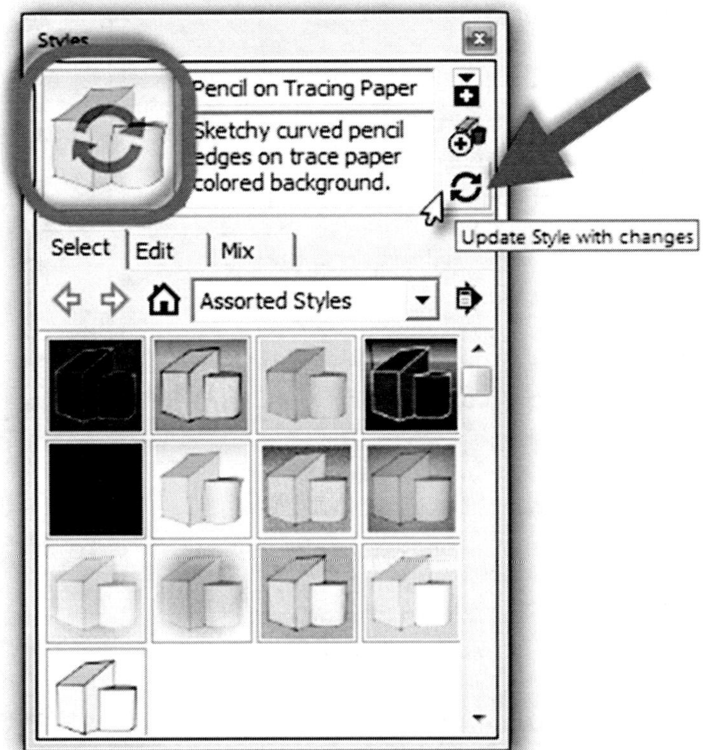

FIGURE 11.12 Updating the modified Style

22. Change the Collection/Folder from *Assorted Styles* to **In Model** from the drop-down list in the *Styles Browser* (Figure 11.13).

You should now see all the *Styles* you have applied (i.e., tried in this case) to your model (Figure 11.13). Just applying a *Style* one time, for just a moment, copies it into your model.

While several extra *Styles* in your model probably will not "break the bank" in terms of file size, it may be prudent to "clean house" and delete the extra unneeded *Styles*.

To remove a *Style*, simply right-click on the preview and select *Delete* from the pop-up menu.

23. Try several more *Styles* from other "collections" before moving on.

24. When finished, apply your copy of ***Architectural Design Style*** from the *In Model* area.

    a. This *Style* can also be found in the *Default Styles* collection.

    b. Turn off the *Section Cut* and *Guides* if they are on.

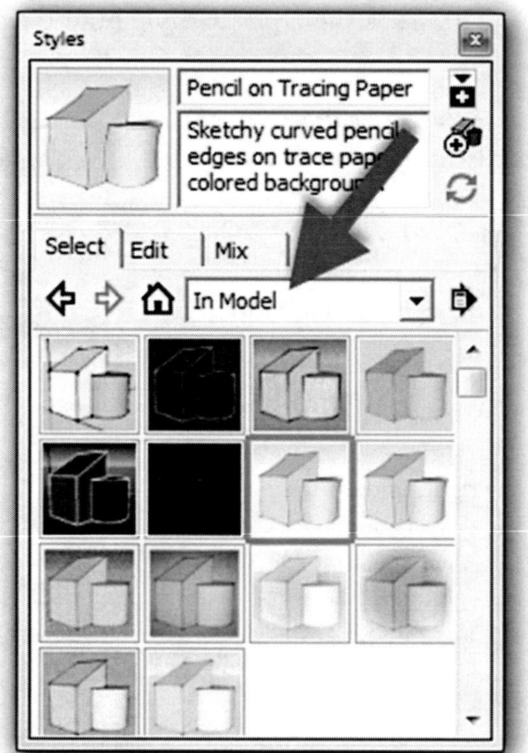

FIGURE 11.13 In Model styles listed

The next two images show two examples from the collection *Style Builder Competition Winners*. These styles have some pretty amazing techniques applied.

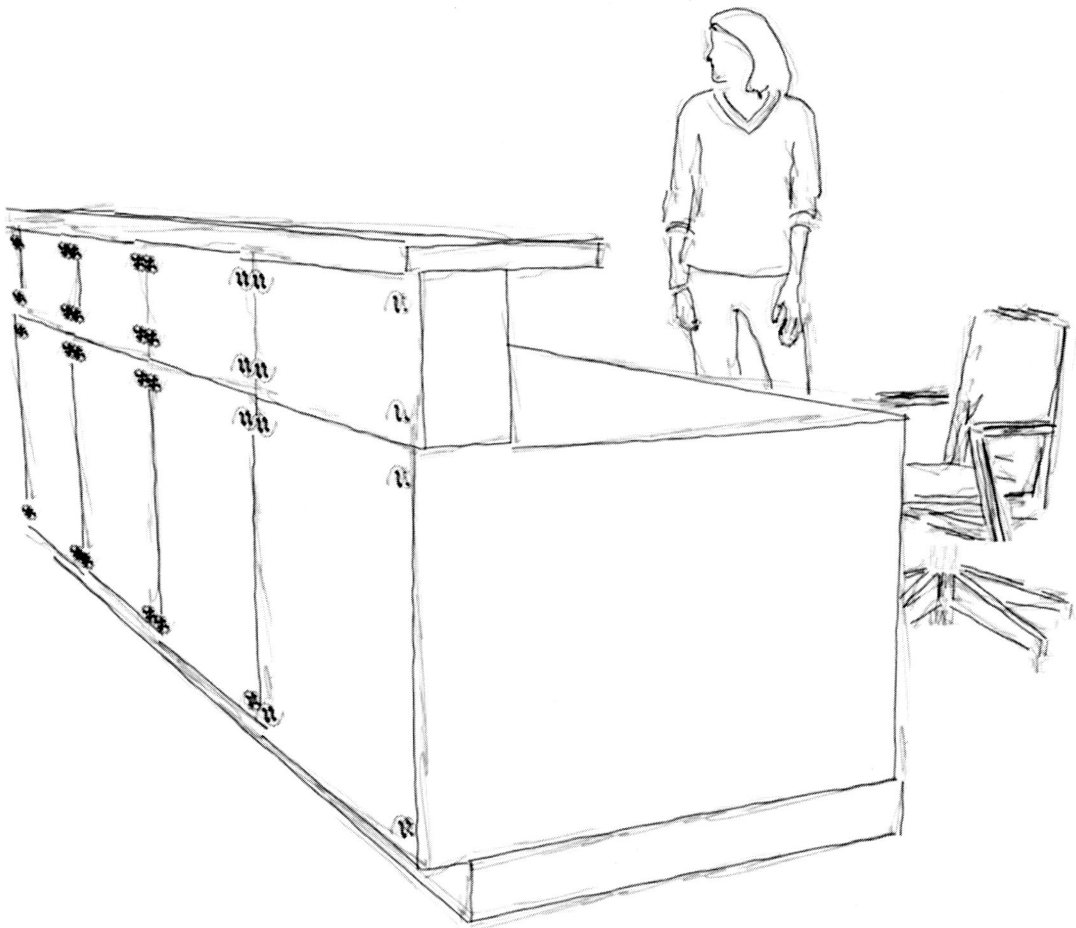

FIGURE 11.14 Style Builder Competition Winners: Pencil Sketch with Darker Traced Lines

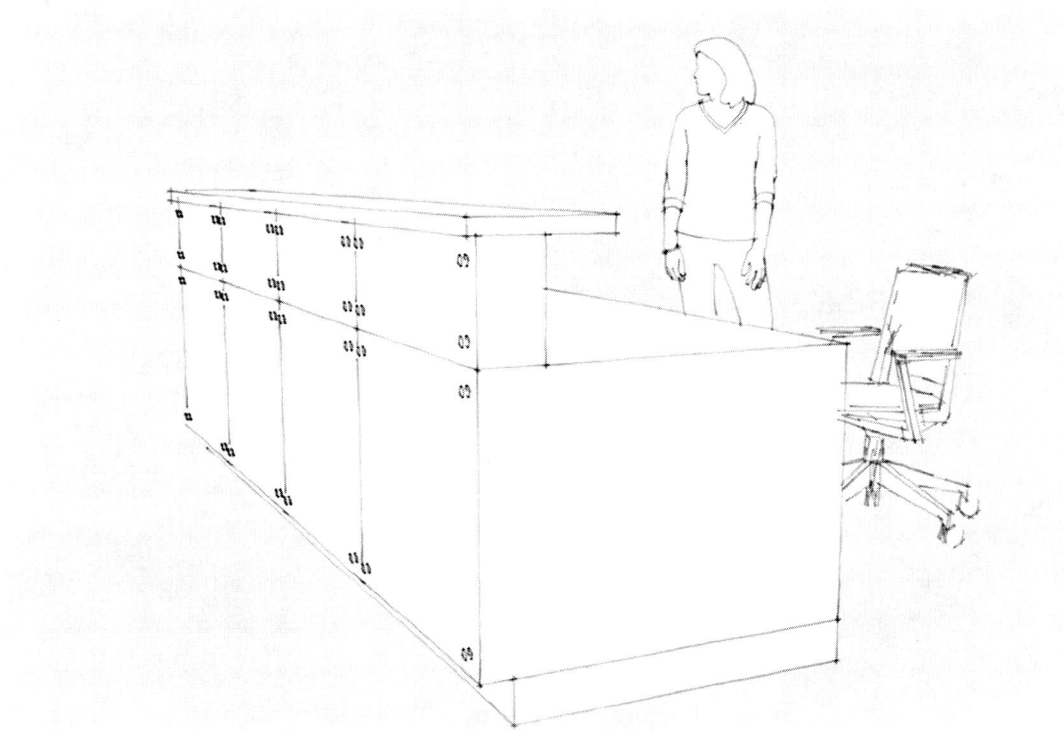

FIGURE 11.15 Style Builder Competition Winners: Pencil Edges with Whiteout Border

Styles Browser: Edit tab

To wrap up this chapter on *Styles*, you will take a look at the **Edit** tab in the *Styles Browser*. This is where you can control ALL the options related to how your model appears on the screen and prints.

25. If not already open, open **Styles** (aka *Style Browser*) from the *Window* menu.

26. Click on the **Edit** tab.

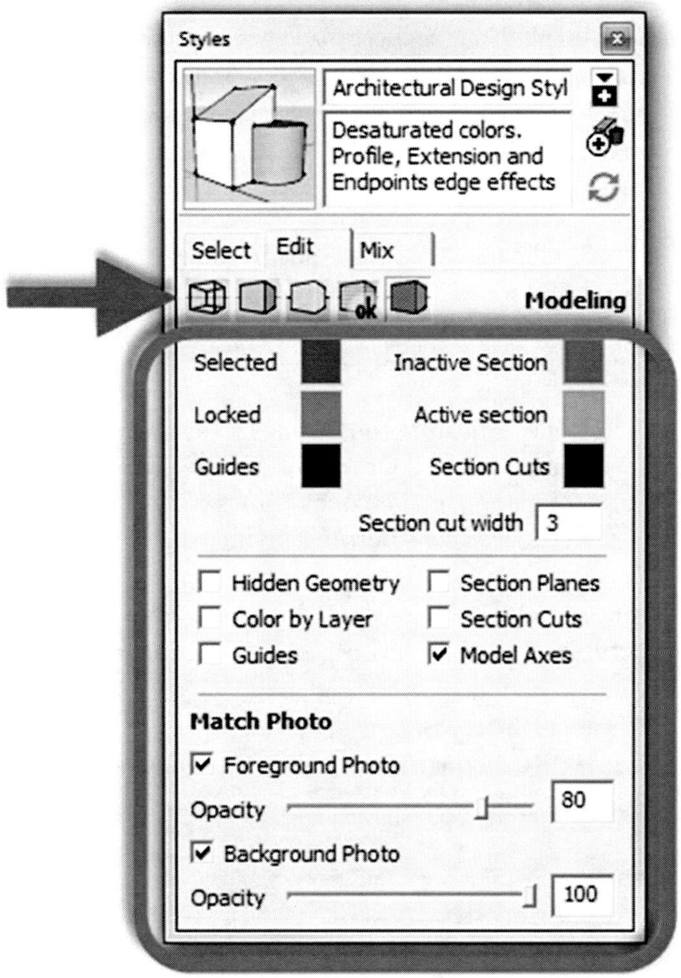

FIGURE 11.16 Style Browser; Edit tab

You should see something similar to Figure 11.16. Notice the FIVE icons highlighted by the added arrow. Clicking on each of these icons reveals different settings in the [windowed] area below. Currently in this image, the fifth, or last, icon is selected. You can tell, because the icon/button appears pushed in and the label to the right of the buttons changes depending on which one is selected.

From left to right, the icons are:

- Edge Settings
- Face Settings
- Background Settings
- Watermark Settings
- Modeling Settings

Edge Settings

Keep in mind, any changes made here directly affect the current *Style* listed above – and your model. Next you will make a few changes to the default *Architectural Design Style* to see what can be done here.

27. Click on the **Edge Settings** icon (Figure 11.17).

Notice the options change below.

28. Try adjusting the settings to see how they affect your model. When finished, make your settings match Figure 11.17 before moving on.

Your model should now look similar to Figure 11.19, shown on the next page. Notice the lines continue past their natural endpoint to exaggerate the corners. Also, the lines appear thicker closer to the viewer (i.e., you) to convey a sense of depth.

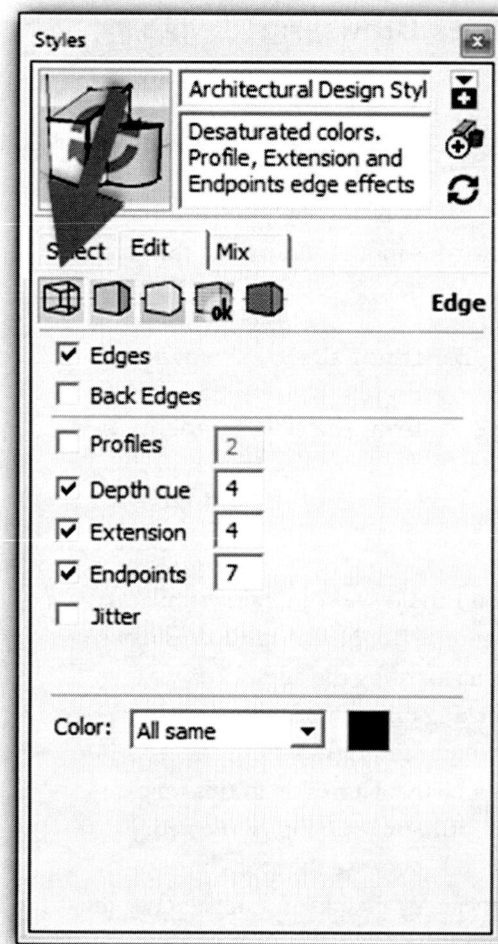

FIGURE 11.17 Style Browser; Edge settings

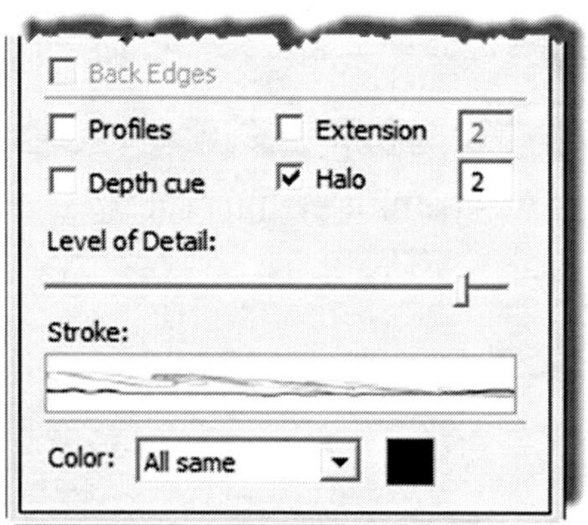

FIGURE 11.18 Style Browser; Edge settings

Some *Styles* utilize a newer feature called *Non-Photorealistic Rendering (NPR)* which presents different options (Figure 11.18). This feature allows you to scan in your own custom hand sketched line drawing and use it for your edges.

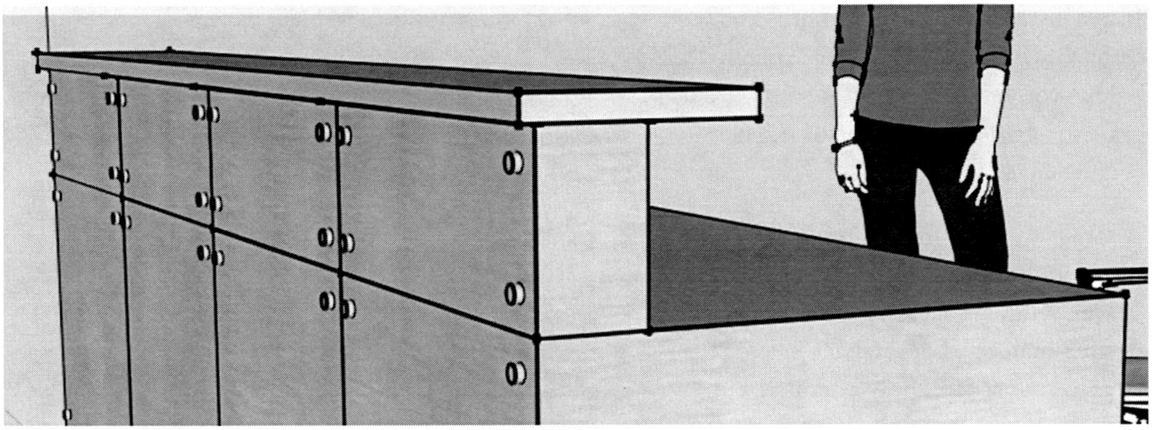

FIGURE 11.19 Changes to the edge settings

Face Settings

29. In the *Styles Browser*, under the **Edit** tab, Click on the **Face Settings** icon.

FIGURE 11.20 Style Browser; Face settings

You only have a few options here and you have already looked at several of them via the *Styles* toolbar (Figure 11.20).

An important concept to understand is that each face has two sides. Each side can receive a different material. When a face is initially created, the "front" side has a color applied, as does the "back" side. Those default colors are specified here. You can use the **Display shaded using all same** icon to verify face orientation. If a face is backwards, just select it, right-click and select *Reverse Faces.*

If you are modeling a grate floor, and want to see through it to the structure below, you have to apply the transparent grate material to both sides of the face (Figure 11.21).

Another way in which this concept could be leveraged is in visualizing small spaces. In the space, you would apply the desired material. On the back side of the faces of the space, apply a transparent material. This allows you to view the space from outside the space – seeing through only the walls directly in front of you!

FIGURE 11.21 Transparent material applied to both sides of face

The last thing to mention about *Face Settings* is the transparency options. In extremely large models you probably want to turn this off while working on the model. Otherwise the display can be very slow when panning and orbiting the model. The same applies to the quality setting. You might bump this up when printing or exporting images. Otherwise, keep it set at "faster" for optimal performance.

30. Click the **Display shaded using all same** option.

All the faces in your model should be white, which represents what SketchUp considers the "front" face. If you see any light blue faces, you will want to fix them. Keep in mind, you have to orbit the model and look at each face somewhat straight-on; otherwise you might see a surface that is shaded and just looks light blue.

31. **Orbit** your model and correct any backwards faces.
    a. Select the light blue face
    b. Right-click
    c. Select **Reverse Faces** from the pop-up menu

32. In the *Styles Browser*, switch back to **Display shaded using textures**.

Next we will take a look at the background settings.

Background Settings

33. In the *Styles Browser*, under the **Edit** tab, click on the **Background Settings** icon.

Here you see three color swatches (Figure 11.22): one for the *Background*, one for the *Sky* and another for the *Ground*.

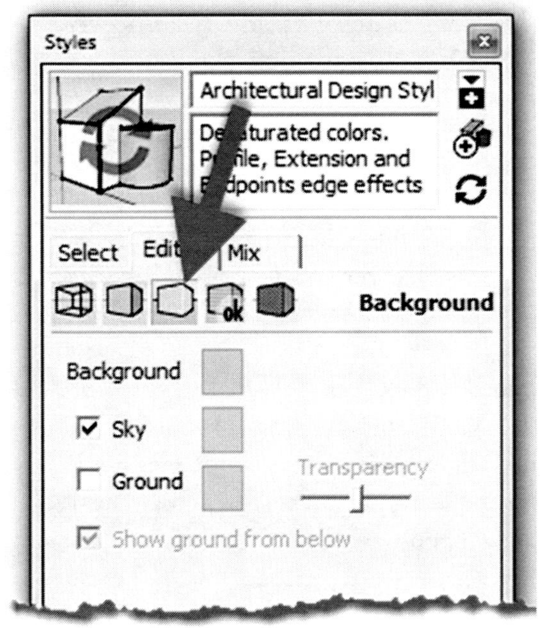

FIGURE 11.22 Style Browser: Background settings

Sometimes you just want the focus of your model to be the design, not the background or the horizon line, especially seeing as you never really see the horizon as a straight line unless you are looking at the ocean. In this case, you can uncheck (i.e., turn off) *Sky* and *Ground* and only see a solid color in the ***Background***.

As soon as you turn on the ***Sky***, you will see the horizon line even though the ground plane is not turned on. This is because the sky stops at the horizon. If you are looking up, you will only see *Sky*; if you are looking down, you would only see *Ground* or *Background*.

If you turn on the ***Ground*** you will not see the *Background* color unless the *Ground* plane is set to be transparent via the slider shown in Figure 11.22. You might want the *Ground* to be transparent if you need to show something below, such as structure.

In the world of interior design, you will likely want a solid colored background seeing as we are not typically dealing with the exterior of the building. You will make this change in the next step.

34. **Uncheck *Sky* and *Ground*,** if not already unchecked.

35. Click on the color swatch for ***Background***.

36. Set the color to an **off white** (or whatever you want) via the *Color Chooser* (Figure 11.23).

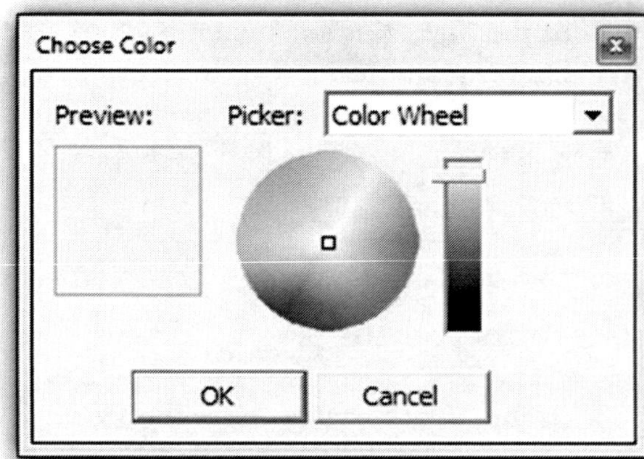

FIGURE 11.23 Choose Color dialog

Notice, in the *Choose Color* dialog, you can select RGB from the drop-down list in the upper right. This allows you to enter the *Red*, *Green*, and *Blue* numbers for a color. This is handy if you want to pick a color from a paint sample, such as from *Sherwin Williams* which provides the RGB numbers for all of their colors.

Shadows

We will digress for a minute and talk about shadows. Even though you do not have the *Ground* turned on, the shadows will still be cast upon the imaginary floor plane; which corresponds to the X and Y axes (the green and red lines).

37. From the *View* menu, click **Shadows** to turn them on.

Your view should look similar to Figure 11.24. Notice the solid colored background and the shadows on the imaginary ground plane.

The light source for the shadows is the sun, which is typically based on the geographic location of the building. For interior designers, shadows are used to convey depth and reveal form within the model (if used at all). The shadows can be thought of coming from an interior light source, but they are too directional for this to be the case. This is where we can take some artistic liberties with our presentation.

Before moving on, let's take a quick look at the *Shadow* settings.

FIGURE 11.24 Solid background color and shadows added

38. From the *Window* menu, select **Shadows**.

The *Shadow Settings* dialog appears. Adjusting the *Time* and *Day* controls where the sun is in the sky, which subsequently determines shadow locations. Notice the check box for "On ground" and "On Faces". Next you will adjust the Light and Dark values to give your model a deeper toned, more realistic feel.

39. Make the adjustments shown in Figure 11.25:

    a. Check the **On faces** option

    b. Adjust the **Light** and **Dark** values

Notice the richer color tones with more overall contrast (Figure 11.26). You can also see the shadow of the transaction surface on the work surface because the "On Surface" option was selected.

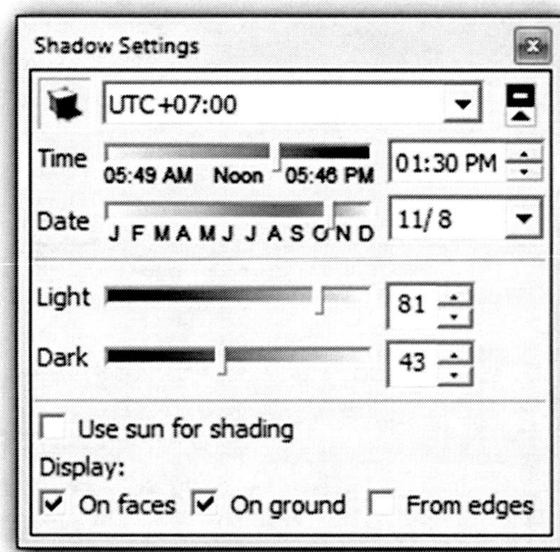

FIGURE 11.25 Shadow settings dialog

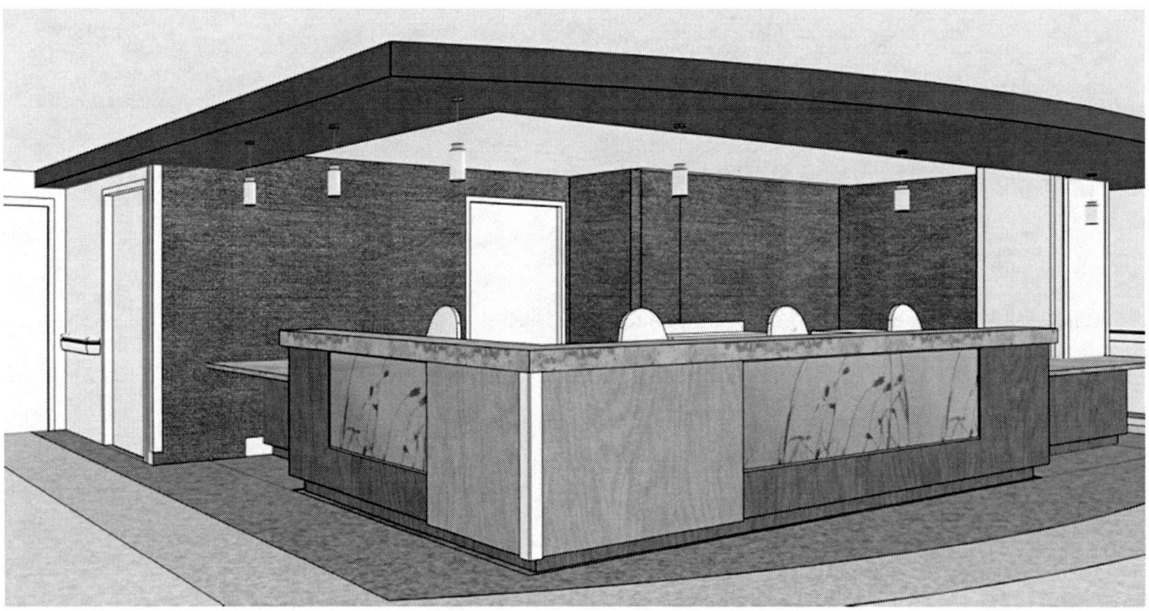

Project Example: Reception Desk. *Image courtesy of LHB; www.LHBcorp.com*

FIGURE 11.26 Shadow settings adjusted

One last thing about shadows… if you want to do **basic daylight** studies in SketchUp, you need to keep a few things in mind. First, your model needs to be fully enclosed. That is, it at least needs to have a ceiling and all the walls to prevent extra light from spilling in. You also need to tell SketchUp where your model is in the world, which can be done via **Window → Model Info → Geo-location**. Finally, you need to make sure your model is positioned according to True North (Solar North). We often use Plan North (or Project North) so all the geometry is orthogonal with the computer screen, which makes things easier to model and place on sheets. Keep in mind that SketchUp does not bounce light around or provide light level values, so this is just a basic investigation of daylight within the model. Now let's get back to talking about *Styles*…

Watermark Settings

In the *Styles Browser*, on the **Edit** tab, the **Watermark Settings** icon exposes the tools which allow you to add a watermark. A watermark can be a company logo which always appears in the lower right corner of the screen, or a background image which can also be faded into the background color. The watermark image can be tiled so it fills the entire background of the given view.

If you use an image of a fabric, you can set the image to be in the background, and fade-in to the background as in the example below.

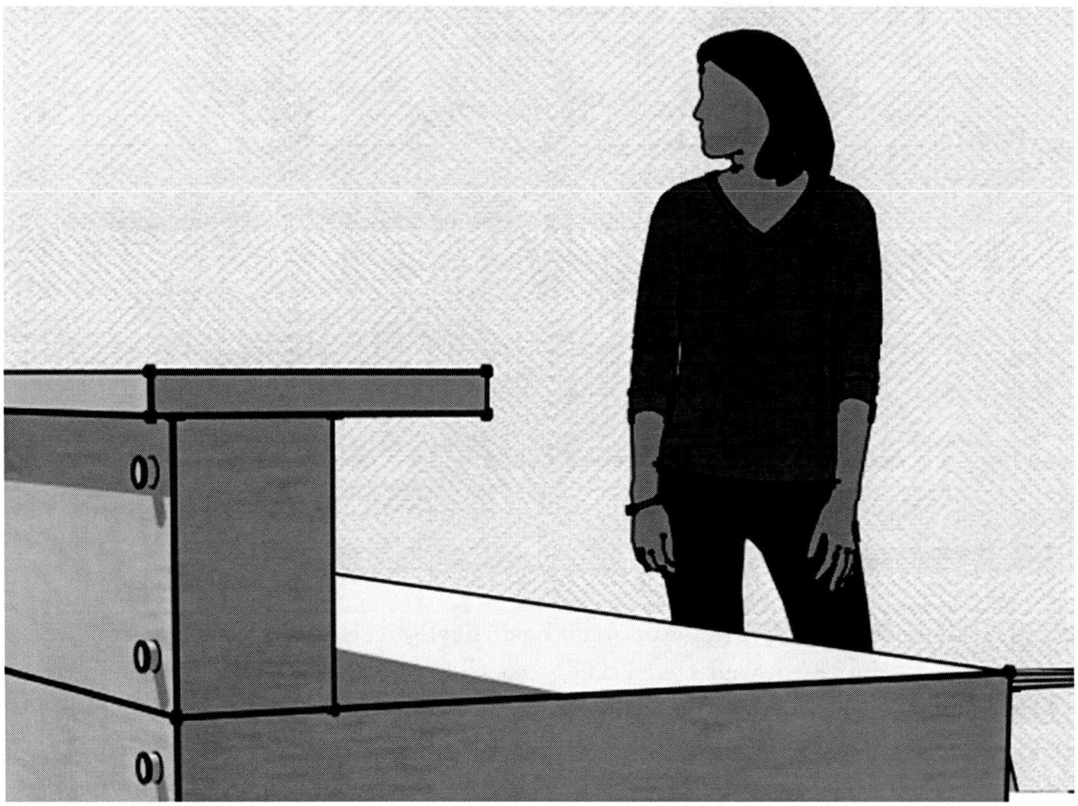

FIGURE 11.27 Background texture added using the Watermark feature

40. Add a fabric-type background per the following steps:

   a. Locate an image file

      i. Go to **www.pollackassociates.com**

      ii. Browse to a fabric you like

      iii. Right-click on it and select **Save picture as**

      iv. **Save** the file to your hard drive

   b. In the *Style Browser*, click the "+" icon to add a Watermark

      i. Browse to the image you just downloaded

      ii. Select **Background**, and then **Next**

      iii. Adjust the **Blend** to about the middle, and then click **Next**

      iv. Select **Tiled across the screen**

      v. Adjust the **Scale** as desired

      vi. Click **Finish**

Modeling Settings

The *Modeling Settings* control basic things related to the modeling environment. For example, does the *Section Plane* and *Cut* appear when this *Style* is active?

41. Uncheck **Model Axes** (all six boxes should be unchecked).

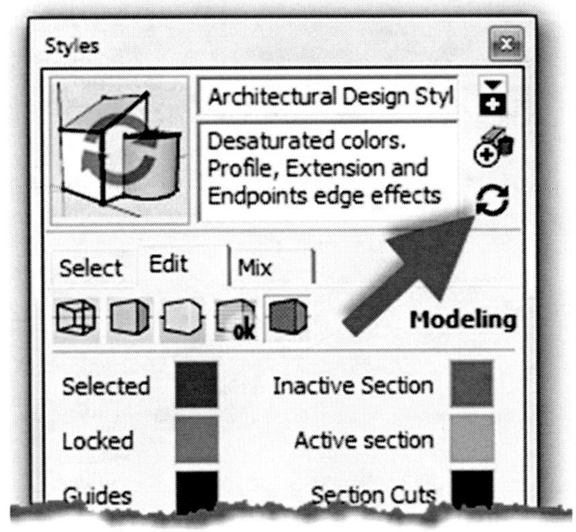

FIGURE 11.28 Style Browser: Modeling settings

Update Style with Changes

The last thing you want to make sure you do is save all these changes to the *Style*. If you don't save these changes, and then apply a different *Style* temporarily, you will not be able to get back to these exact changes without re-applying each change you made to this *Style*.

42. In the *Style Browser*, click the **Update Style with Changes** icon, which is pointed out in Figure 11.28.

43. **Save** your SketchUp model.

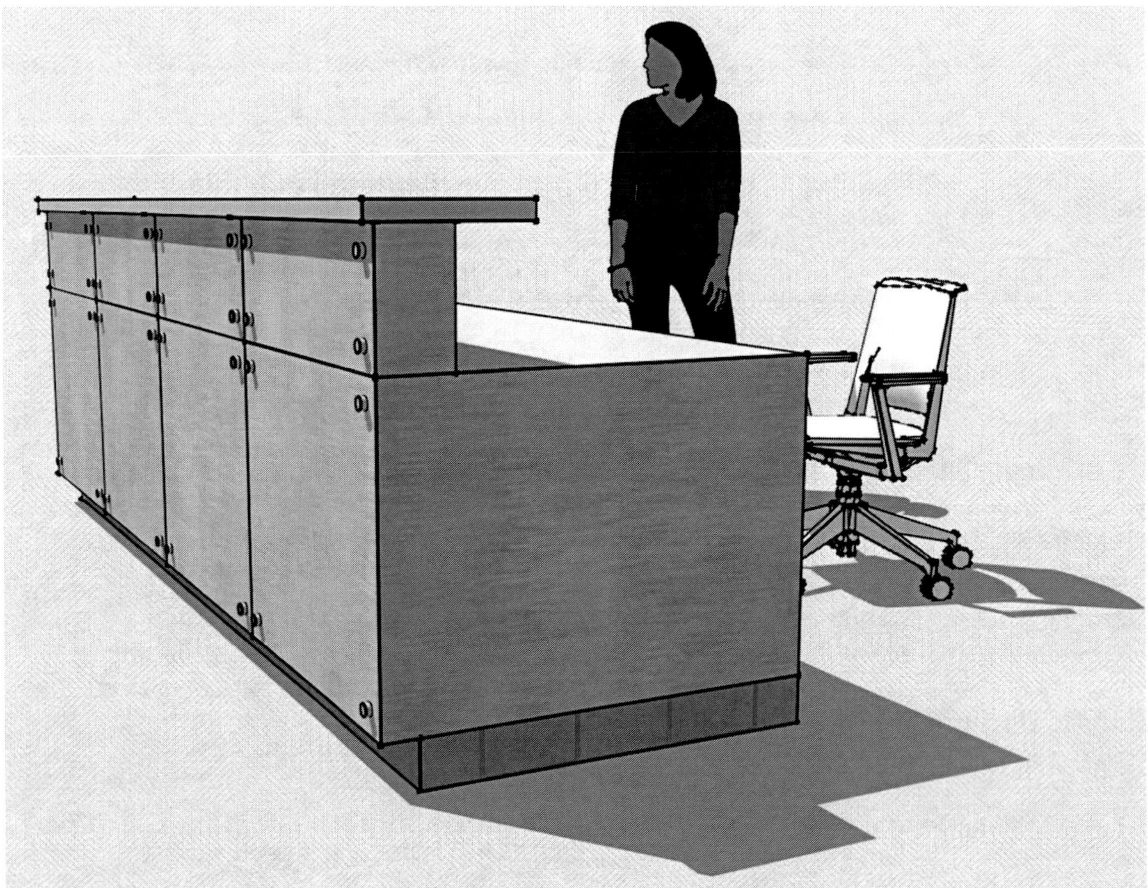

Section 12
Scenes and Animations

This chapter will teach you how to save different views of your model. You will also learn how to take those saved views and create an animation.

1. Open your **Reception Desk - Styles.skp** model.

Next you will create a copy of the file so you don't have to worry about messing up the original.

2. From the **File** menu, select **Save As**.
3. Name the new file: **Reception Desk – Scenes.skp**.

Creating a Scene

Creating a *Scene* is an essential part of the designer's workflow. This feature allows you to save multiple camera angles plus various options such as the *Style*. The *Scenes* are saved as "tabs" across the top of the *Drawing Window*. A single click on one of these tabs changes the view and, optionally, the *Style*, *Section Cut* and more. These tabs make it easy to jump around the model while you are working on it, or presenting it to a client.

4. Adjust your view of the reception desk to look similar to the last image in the previous chapter – if necessary.
5. From the *View* menu, select **Animation → Add Scene**.

You should now have a new tab, named **Scene 1**, near the top of your screen (Figure 12.1). The blank space to the right is where additional tabs will appear as new *Scenes* are created. Next, you will take a look at the *Scene Manager*, where you can rename the *Scene* to something more meaningful and to see what is saved with it.

6. Right-click on the tab named **Scene 1** (Figure 12.1).

7. Select **Scene Manager** from the pop-up menu.

Notice, in the pop-up menu, a few handy options, such as *Add*, *Update* and *Delete*.

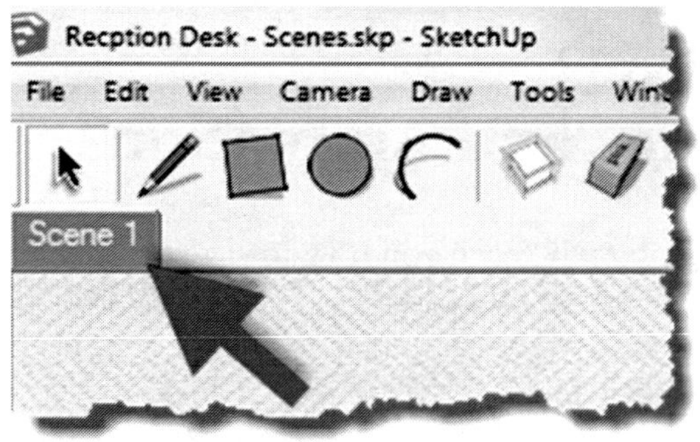

FIGURE 12.1 A scene tab added

8. Click the **Show Details** toggle in the upper right corner (a down-arrow with a plus symbol under it).

9. Change the name to **Desk - Front+Right** (Figure 12.3).

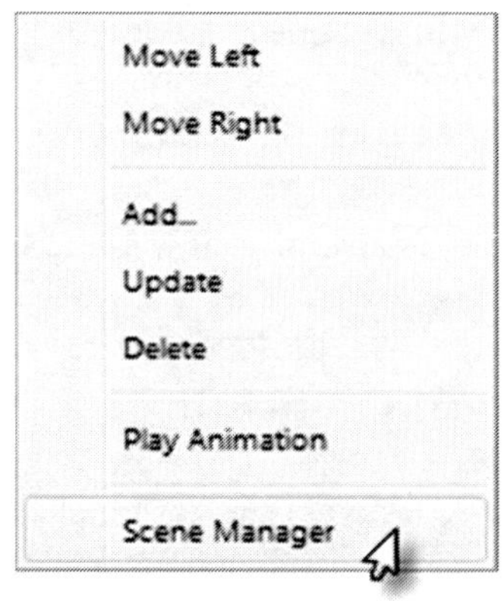

FIGURE 12.2 Scene tab right-click menu

Notice the various options associated with this saved scene (Figure 12.3). The first option determines whether or not this particular *Scene* will be included in an animation (if you decide to create one).

In the *Properties to save* section, a checked item means the settings for that item, for example *Style and Fog*, are saved when the *Scene* is saved, and then re-applied whenever this *Scene* is selected. If the box is not checked, the current values persist.

Next you will reposition the view of the desk such that we are looking more at the front, or what is often called the public side. Once we do this we can then save another *Scene*.

10. Adjust the current view of the model, using ***Orbit*** and ***Pan***, to look similar to Figure 12.4.

11. **Right-click** on the **Scene** tab, and select **Add**.

12. Create additional *Scenes*:

    a. In the order shown, adjust the view person images as shown on the next page.

    b. After each view is achieved, right-click on the last tab and click **Add**.

The new *Scene* is added directly to the right of the selected tab. This will be important if you plan on creating an animation – more on this later.

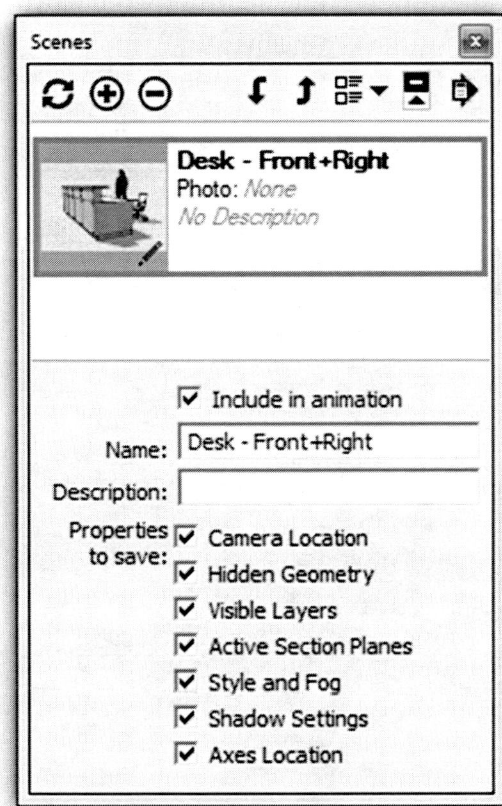

FIGURE 12.3 Scene Manager

FIGURE 12.4 Adjusted view of reception desk

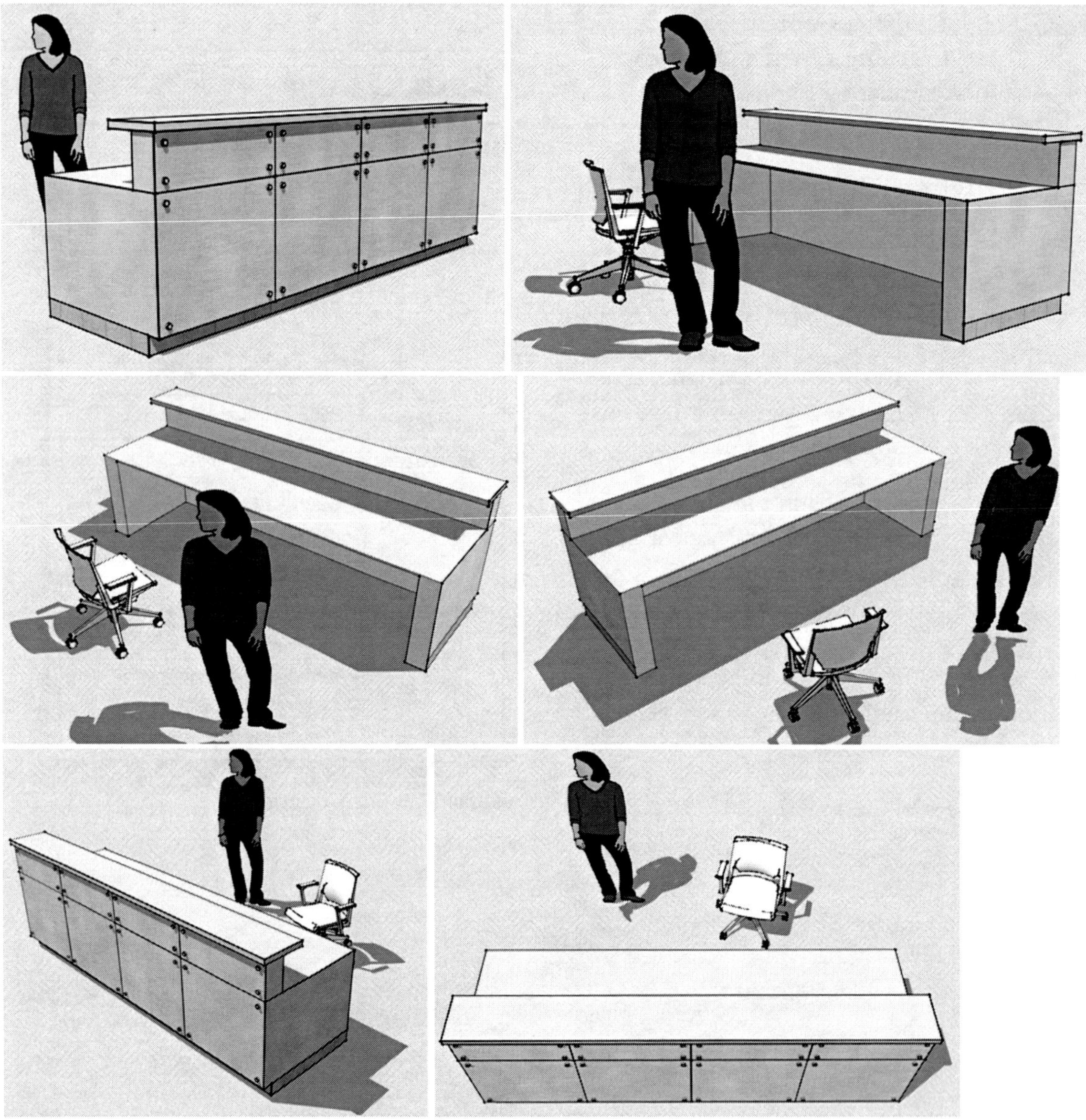

FIGURE 12.5 Scenes to be created in order shown

You should now have several *Scene* tabs as shown in the image below (Figure 12.6). As you will see in a moment, SketchUp creates a nice smooth transition between *Scenes.*

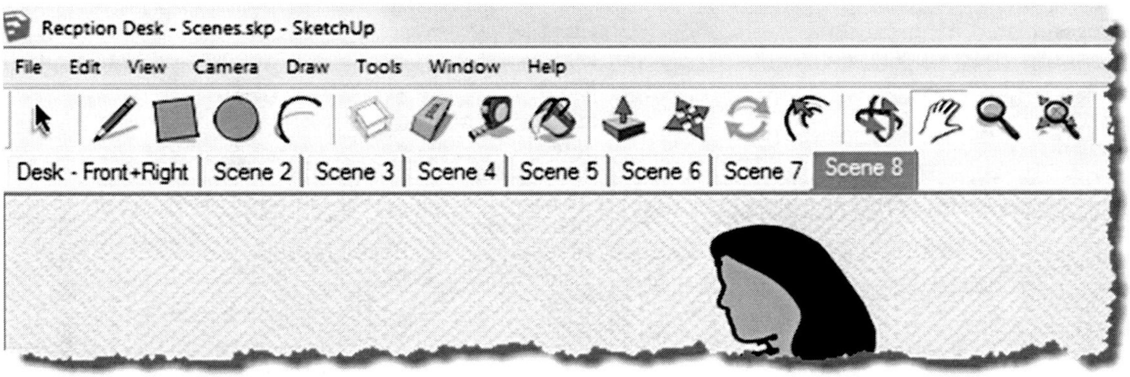

FIGURE 12.6 Scenes tabs added to the model

13. Click on each of the tabs, from left to right, to see how SketchUp transitions between tabs.

14. Now click on the tabs in a random order to see the transition results.

In both cases the transitions are nice and smooth. But, when we create the *Scenes* in a specific order we can better control the "path" for an animation. If required, we can use the *Scene Manager* to change the order of the scenes/tabs.

That is all you really need to know about saving scenes. Now let's talk about creating animations.

Creating an Animation

The first thing we will do is look at the settings related to animations.

15. Click on **View → Animation → Settings**.

This opens the *Model Info* dialog with the *Animation* category selected. Here you can specify how long it should take to get from one *Scene* to another.

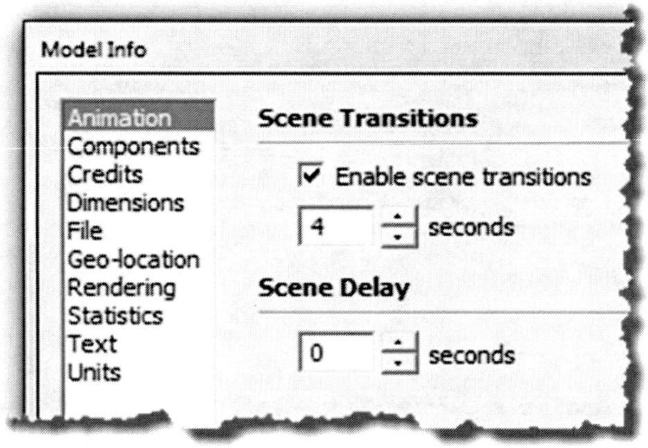

FIGURE 12.7 Model Info dialog

This value can vary depending on the size of your model and the distance between the created *Scenes*. If the transition time is too short or the space between the each *Scene* is too large, the animation can be way too fast. It takes practice to get everything just right so the animation looks good. This can be tricky because the transition time setting is for the entire animation. Sometimes you want to add additional *Scenes* to better control the path at corners or to stop and view an area – for example, looking from left to right without moving "your feet".

16. Change the *Scene Transition* time to **4 seconds**.

17. Change the *Scene Delay* to **0 seconds**.

    TIP: *This creates a smooth animation without a pause between each scene.*

18. **Close** the *Model Info* dialog.

19. Click on the first tab (named **Desk – Front+Right**).

SketchUp allows you to view the animation directly on the screen. We will try that first and then learn how to export the animation to a file which can be sent to a client or posted online for others to view.

20. To preview the animation, from the *View* menu, select **Animation → Play**.

21. Once you have seen the entire animation path, click the **Stop** button (Figure 12.8).

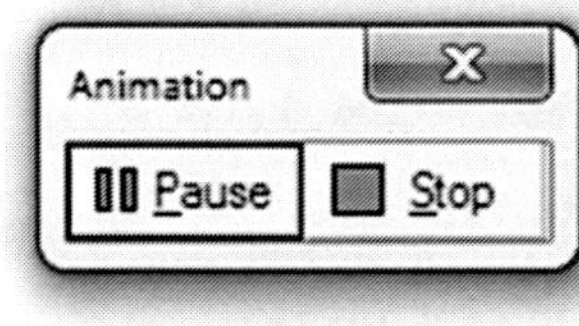

FIGURE 12.8 Animation controls

If you want to change anything, you either need to add new *Scenes* in the appropriate position or adjust an existing *Scene*. For the latter, you adjust the camera view as desired and then right-click on the *Scene* tab and click *Update*.

Now you will export the animation to an AVI file, which can be viewed by others using something like *Windows Media Player*. This way, the recipient does not need SketchUp installed, nor do they need to know how to use the software.

22. From the *File* menu, select **Export → Animation**.

23. Click the *Options* button.

Here is where you control the quality of the animation (Figure 12.9). The higher the settings, the longer it takes to create the animation.

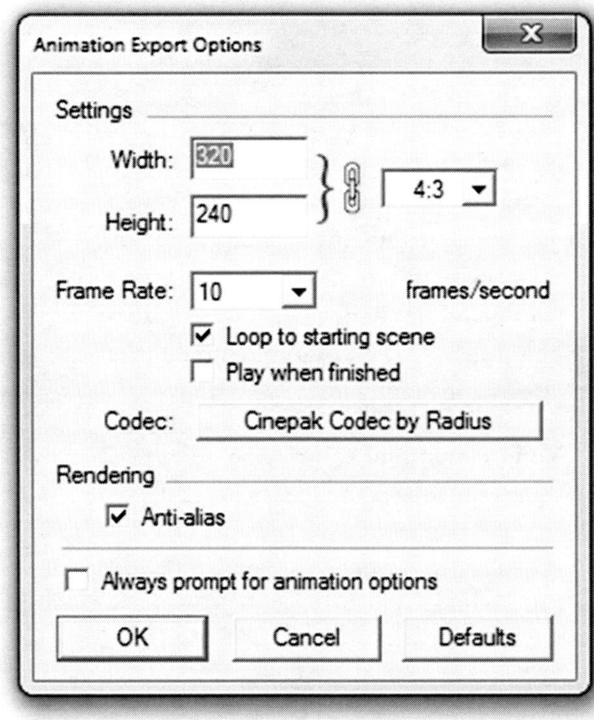

FIGURE 12.9 Animation export options

This author has worked on larger models/animations which have taken several hours for the export to complete. The **Width** and **Height** relate to screen resolution. You may have heard the team "HD" and "1080p" when talking about televisions. IF you set the height to 720 or 1080 you are making an animation equal to the quality of an HD movie. Setting the **Frame Rate** to 24 – 30 will also create a nicer animation. Finally, the **Anti-Alias** setting helps to smooth out angled lines.

For now, you will export the file with the default settings.

24. Click **OK** to close the *Options* dialog.

25. Browse to a location on your computer and click **Export**.

FYI: *Notice the suggested file name for the AVI is the same as your SketchUp model name.*

You now should see the *Exporting Animation* progress bar (Figure 12.10). Depending on the complexity of your model, the length of the animation path, the resolution settings and the quality of your computer hardware, your animation time will vary. This example should take less than five minutes.

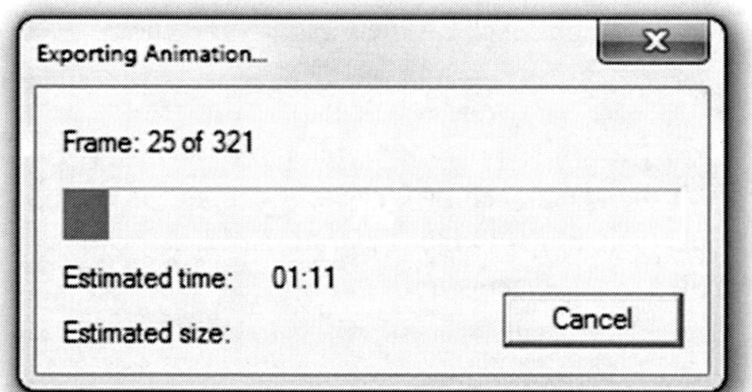

FIGURE 12.10 Exporting Animation progress bar

You can continue to work on other things on your computer as SketchUp is not utilizing all of your computer's resources to create the animation. You just cannot work on your SketchUp model.

26. Using *Windows Explorer*, browse to the location in which you saved your AVI animation file.

27. Double-click on it to open the file and play it using your default video viewing software; this is typically *Microsoft Windows Media Player* (Figure 12.11).

FIGURE 12.11 Viewing animation in Windows Media Player

The file should be about 6-7MB in size. This is getting a little large to email, but is no problem for FTP or a file sharing site such as DropBox.

Increasing the *Width* and *Height* values will make the initial view size larger on your screen.

One more thing about animations you should be aware of: you can really only set up one animation path in your model. This creates a challenge when you want to develop multiple animations in a larger project. To do this, you actually need to create a copy of the entire file, delete the *Scenes* and create new ones. The real problem arises when you need to make changes to the model. Now you have multiple copies to manage.

This concludes our investigation of *Scenes* and *Animations*!

Project Example: Custom Casework. *Image courtesy of LHB; www.LHBcorp.com*

Section 13
Floor Plans

You will start out drawing the line work for the walls and openings. You do not need to create all the detail such as the doors and windows themselves, or the stairs and elevators. Rather you can start out by just sketching the walls which define these spaces. Text may be added if needed to remind you that a space is an elevator or stair.

The dimensioned drawing on the next page is what you will work from. The dashed line work at the rear (north) of the building are existing items intended to be removed. The two toilet rooms (northwest corner) are not accessible so they will be removed and replaced. Keep in mind, when renovating an existing building, the space below (and sometimes above) often needs to be accessible to route piping and wires in the ceiling. This can be tricky when that space is actively occupied. Additionally, in multi-story buildings it is often necessary to align the toilet rooms from floor to floor to minimize piping, drainage and clearance issues. None of this will be assumed to be a problem for our project.

The second means of egress is a fire escape on the back side of the building (Figure 13.1). This, along with the doors, will be removed and a new stair shaft will be added by the building owner in conjunction with this project to bring the building up to code. Notice the windows have been filled in. It would be possible to open a few of them back up on the sixth floor if needed, except the northeast corner at the service elevator location (see the plan on the next page).

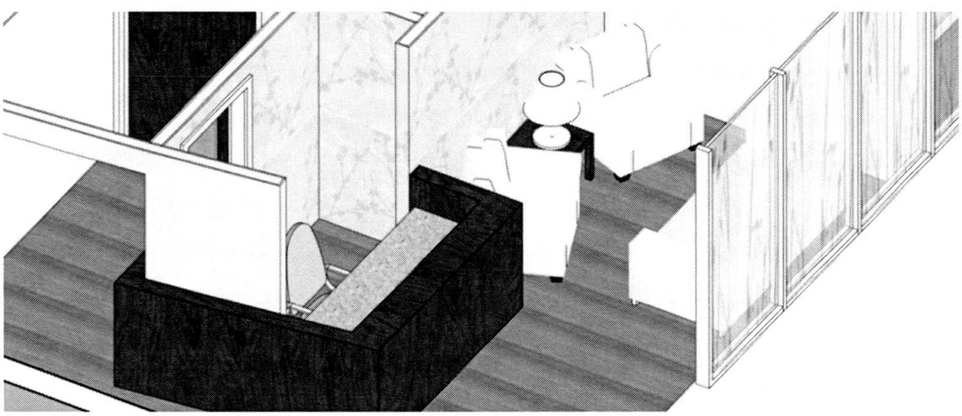

Project Example. *Image courtesy of LHB; www.LHBcorp.com*

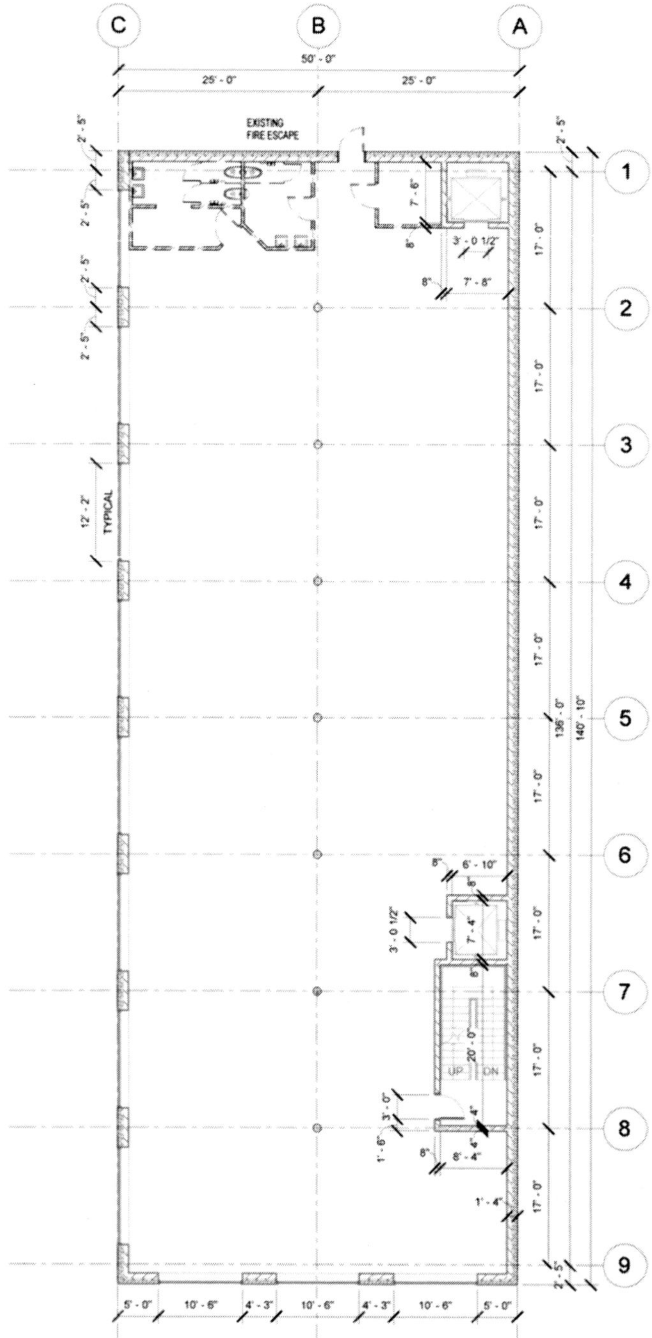

FIGURE 13.1 Existing conditions

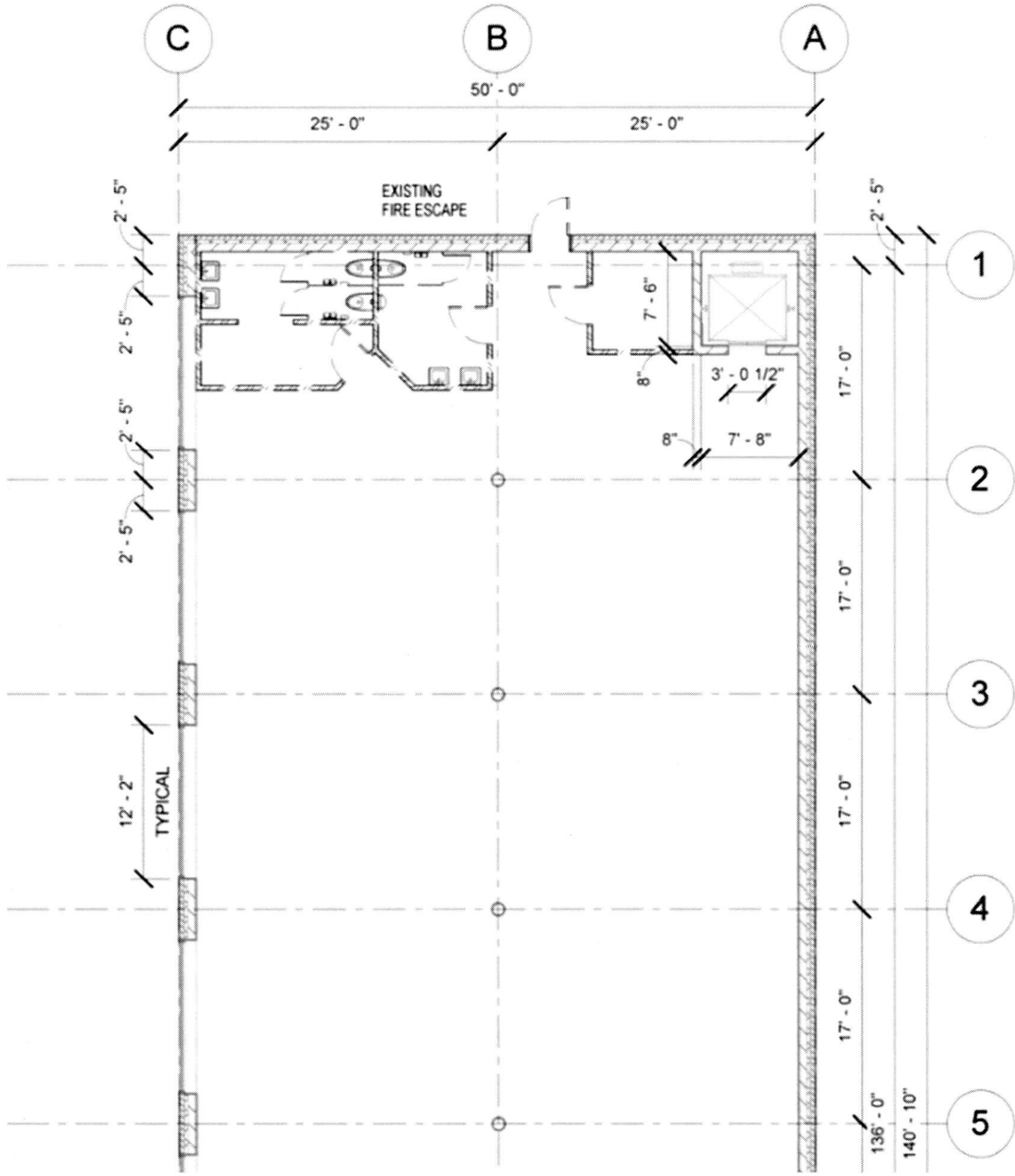

FIGURE 13.2 Existing conditions – enlarged plan - North

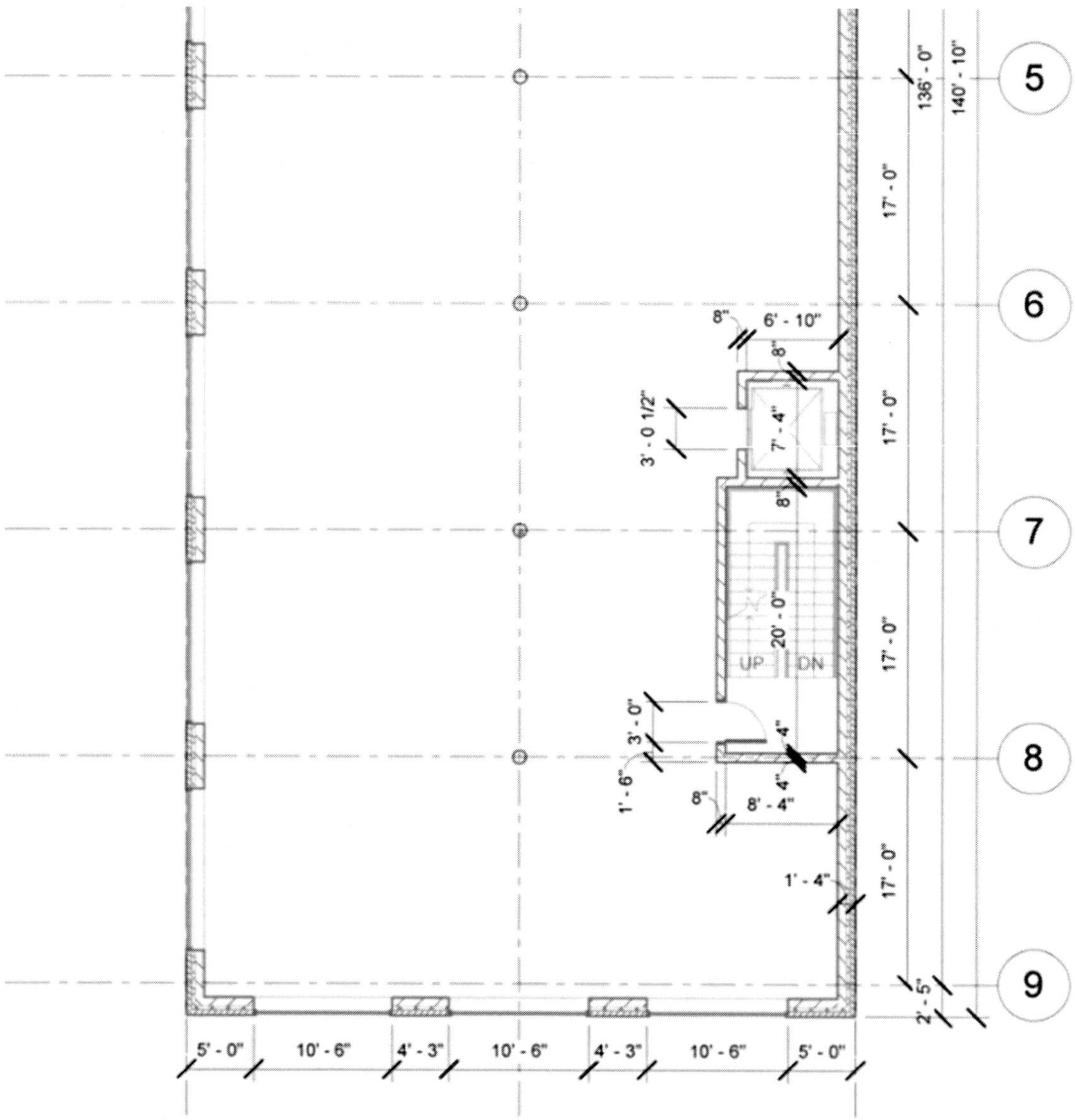

FIGURE 13.3 Existing conditions – enlarged plan - South

Now you will draw the existing plan, on the previous page, in SketchUp so you can print it out to scale on a plotter.

1. Using the steps previously covered in this book, create the **2D floor plan** in SketchUp:
    a. Follow the existing drawing on the previous pages (Figure 13.1 – 13.3).
    b. Set the **Camera** to **Parallel Projection** (see printing notes later).
    c. Switch to the top view (see printing note later in this chapter).
    d. All interior walls to remain are 8″ thick
    e. All exterior walls are 1′-4″ thick
    f. Only sketch the openings for the doors and windows.
    g. Do not draw the items to be demolished (shown dashed).
    h. Do not draw the lines for the stairs (i.e., handrails and steps).
    i. Do not draw the grids or dimensions.
    j. Add 12″ round columns.

When finished your SketchUp drawing should look similar to Figure 13.4.

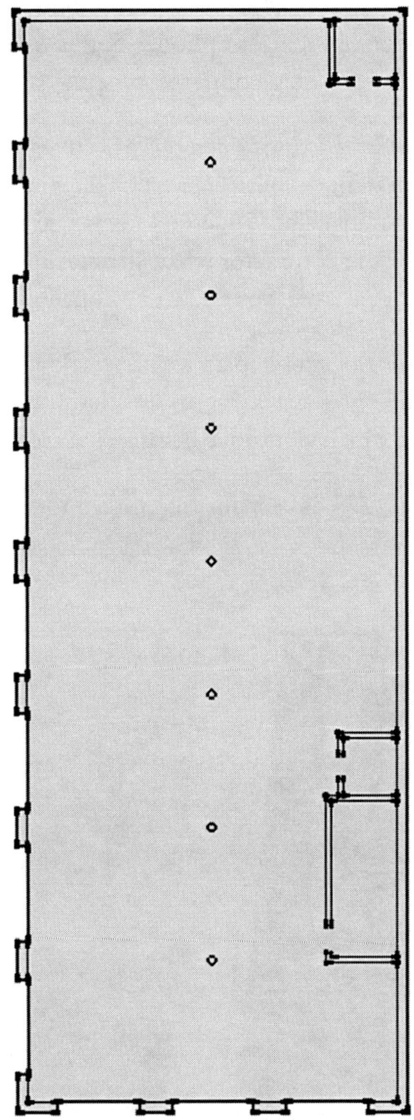

FIGURE 13.4 Initial SketchUp model

Notice the row of columns down the center of the building. These are a major component of the building's infrastructure and cannot be changed in anyway. They must be remembered and considered when working on design solutions.

In Figure 13.4, did you notice how the outside line of the exterior wall was omitted at each window opening? This is optional, and is used as a way to make all the window openings stand out more in this early stage of development.

All of the door openings are currently shown as simple openings in the walls. We have also left out anything we plan on demolishing: the existing toilet rooms and the door out the back of the building. These "demo" items will need to be drawn later in your CAD/BIM program to document for the contractor what, specifically, needs to be removed from the building. But for now that is not an issue we need to be concerned with.

For the simple plan we are working with here, it is not necessary to add any text. It is obvious that the two smaller rooms are elevators and the remaining set of walls defines the stair location, none of which can move because we are dealing with an existing building.

2. Save your SketchUp model as **Office Building Remodel.skp**.

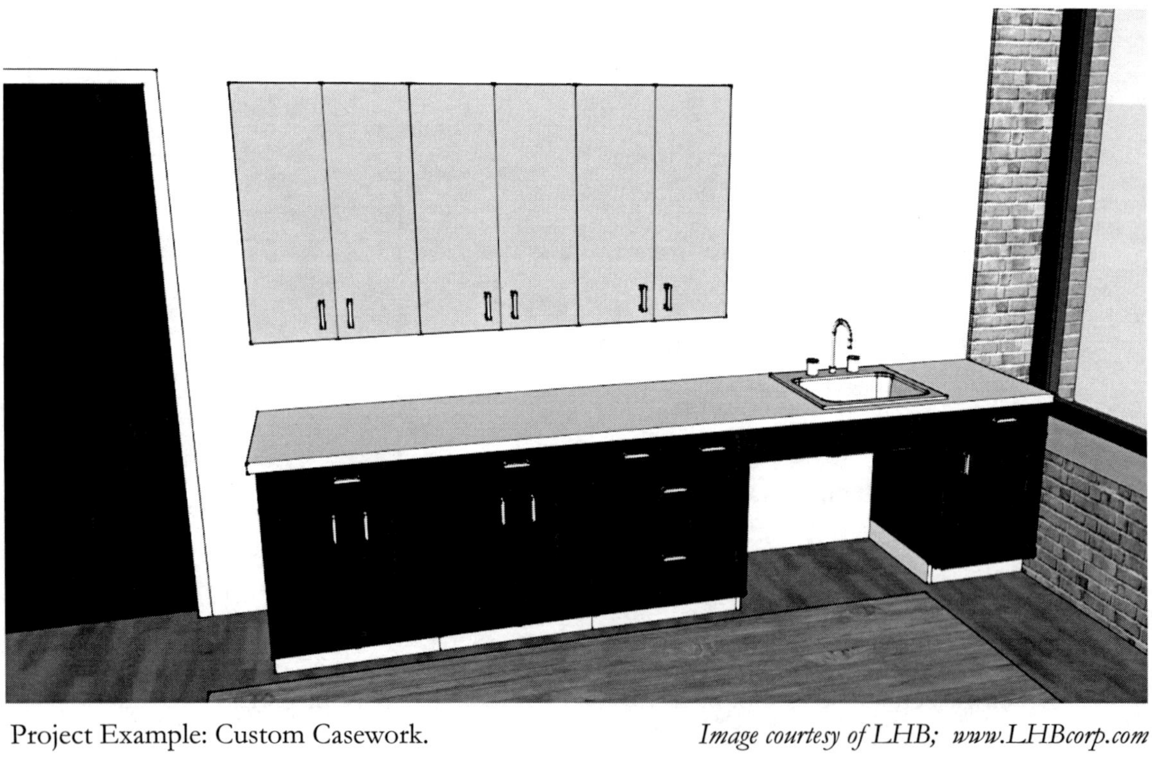

Project Example: Custom Casework. *Image courtesy of LHB; www.LHBcorp.com*

Section 14
Printing Your SketchUp Model

The next thing you will want to do is print the floor plan. You have two paths you can take at this point. Both end up at the same situation, that being a printed floor plan which is to scale.

One option is to print the floor plan on smaller paper, maybe not even to scale. This would allow you to do several quick sketch-overs by hand to start thinking about where spaces want to be and their adjacencies. An experienced designer can actually visually sketch pretty close to scale – picking up on known dimensions (e.g., the window width, stair width and depth, etc., are all known dimensions to the designer). Having a small printout is handy if you will be traveling or sitting somewhere and you have time to scribble a few ideas while you wait.

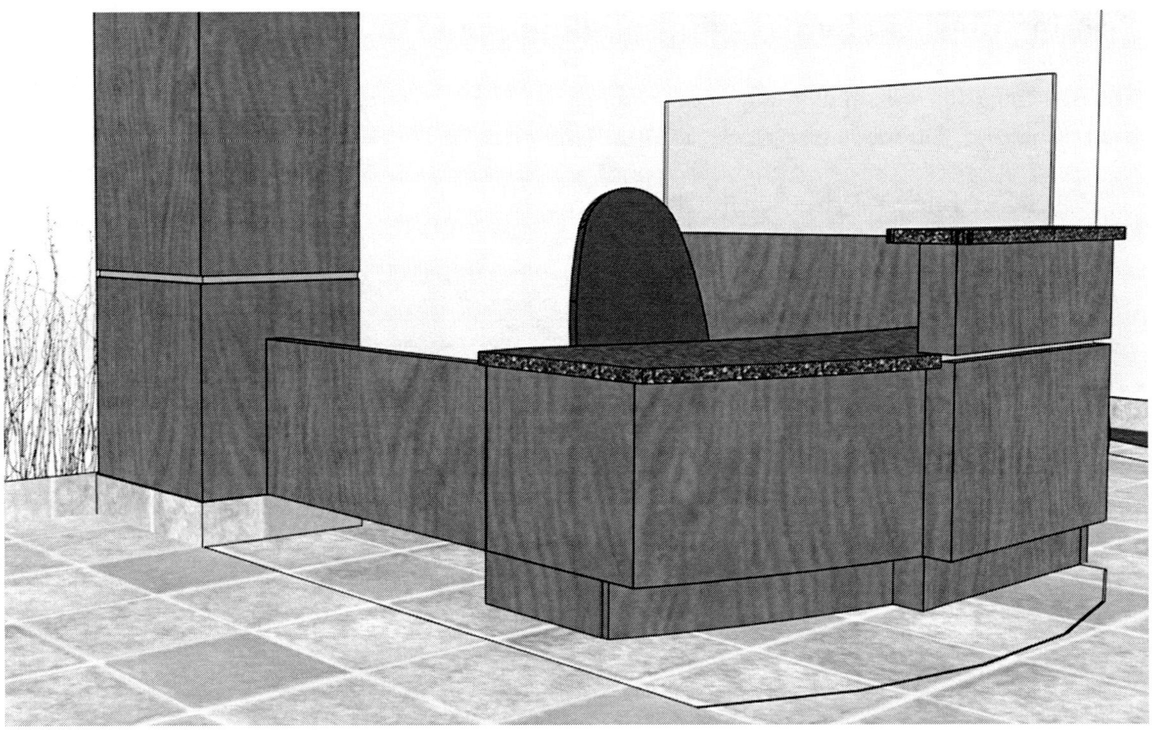

Project Example: Reception Desk. *Image courtesy of LHB; www.LHBcorp.com*

This first option allows the designer to start thinking about the big picture aspects of the project. Quickly working through multiple scenarios allows the designer to rule in and out various ideas. Oftentimes the end result is somewhat serendipitous; that is, the final solution was derived by taking elements from several random iterations to come up with an ideal design solution. This final solution might never have otherwise been found if the designer spent too much time worrying about sketching to scale and trying to explore these early design scenarios in CAD/BIM/SketchUp.

Another option is to print the floor plan to scale and engage in a more formal sketch-over process at your desk. This route can be taken if you, or the client, have a fairly strong notion of what the layout will look like given the program and the space.

Next you will learn how to create both types of prints.

Printing on small format printer (not to scale)

The first thing you should do is adjust the settings in the ***Print Setup*** dialog. This tells SketchUp what printer or plotter you plan to use, plus the paper size and orientation.

1. Select **File → Print Setup** from the menu.

You are now in the *Print Setup* dialog (Figure 14.1). Your floor plan is tall and narrow so you will want a *Portrait* orientation. The default size is *Letter*, 8½″ x 11″. Most small format printers can also print on *Legal* size paper, which is 8½″ x 14″. Some printers will print on *Ledger*, which is 11″ x 17″.

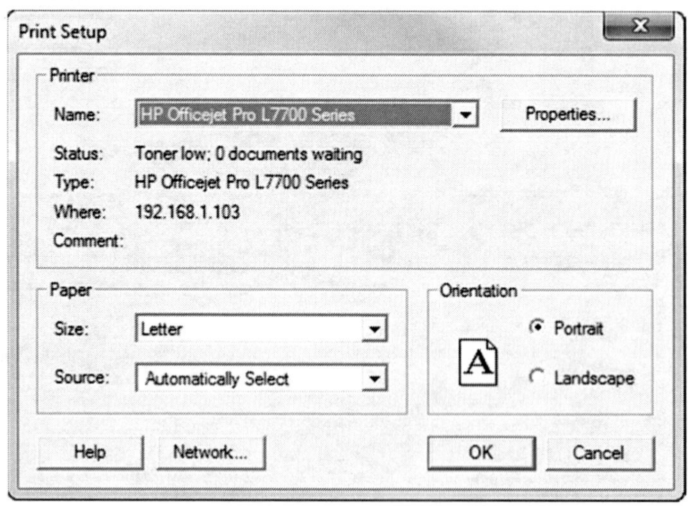

FIGURE 14.1 Print Setup dialog

2. Select the following in the *Print Setup* dialog:

    a. *Printer*: (select any small format printer you have access to)

    b. *Size*: Letter

    c. *Source*: Automatically Select

    d. *Orientation*: Portrait

3. Click **OK** to accept the changes.

Before printing you will temporarily turn off the visibility of the faces as you do not need to see them on the print.

4. Select **View → Face Style → Hidden Line**.

The faces should now be hidden.

With the *Print Setup* options selected, these settings will be the defaults when you open the *Print* dialog box.

5. Select **File → Print** from the menu.

6. Make sure the following options are selected (Figure 14.2):

    a. *Printer*: already set based on *Print Setup*

    b. *Fit to Page*: Checked

    c. *Use Model extents*: Checked

    d. *Print Quality*: Standard

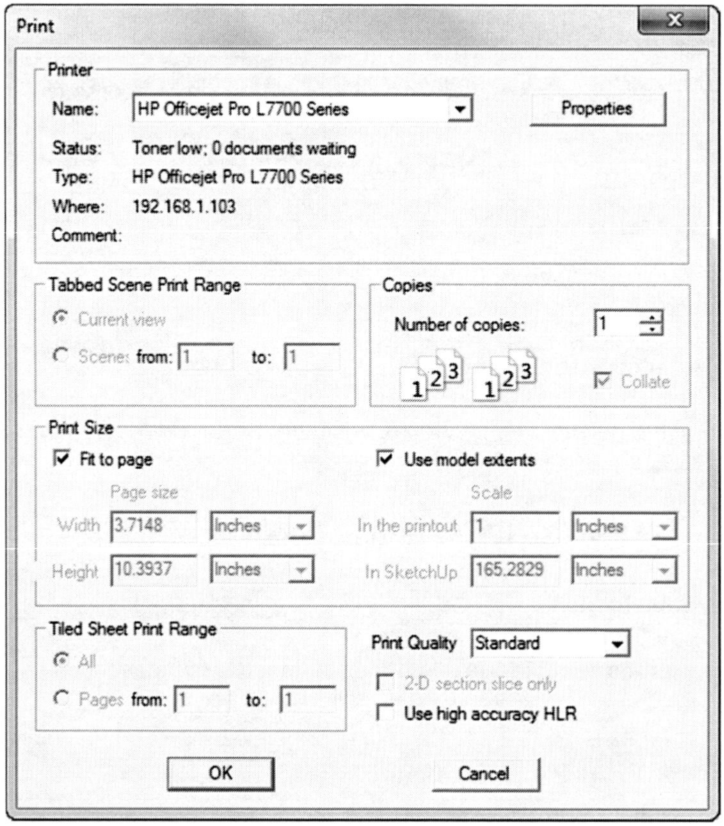

FIGURE 14.2 Print dialog

7. Click **OK** to print a copy of your floor plan.

At this point the *Print* dialog closes and your floor plan drawing is sent to the printer. It is a good idea to use the **Print Preview** option found in the *File* menu to visually verify what your print will look like before actually sending it to the printer. This saves time and paper! One common problem is with lines floating way out in space. When using the "extents" option, this will cause the main model to be small as SketchUp is trying to include extraneous lines in the print.

Both your print and the *Print Preview* should look similar to the image below (Figure 14.3).

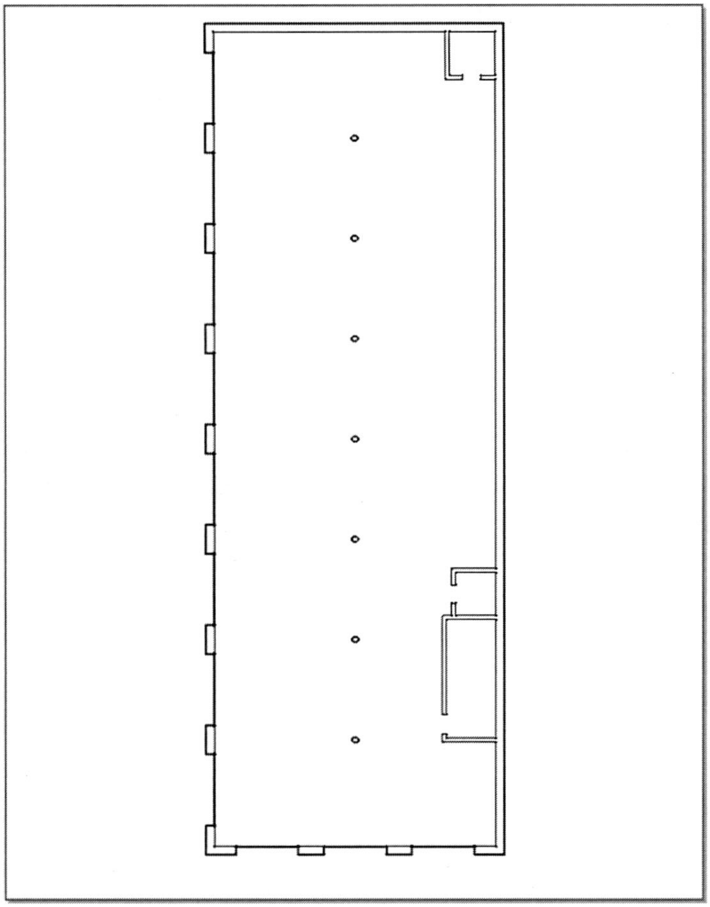

FIGURE 14.3 Print preview and "letter" sized paper

At this point you can use tracing paper to sketch over the floor plan printout or print a few copies and sketch directly on the printout.

You may want to write "not to scale" on the printout, or the letters "NTS", so you or others on the design team know the drawing is not to scale. It is possible that the printed drawing is really close to a standard scale and could create some major problems in terms of wasted time.

Printing on large format printer (to scale)

This section will show you how to print to a large format print, also called a plotter. You will also learn how to print to scale and create a PDF file, both of which could also be applied to the previous steps on creating small format prints.

To actually print to a large format printer, or plotter, you need to have access to one. However, to work through these steps you will learn how to print to a PDF file. This process is identical to actually printing; the only difference is you select a PDF printer driver rather than an installed printer/plotter while in the *Print* dialog. Once you click **OK** to send the print, you are prompted for the file name and location. Very simple.

Most computers do not come with a PDF printer driver. If you have Adobe Acrobat installed you will have this PDF printer driver appear in your list of printers. Another option is to download a free driver from the internet. There are several options; however, Adobe does not provide a free option for this feature. One free option is PDF995 (PDF995.com). The free version displays small, self-promoting, company advertisements every time you print to PDF. There are several other options; just do an internet search to explore.

You will need access to a large format printer or a PDF printer driver in order to follow along with the next few steps.

8. Ensure you have set the following options:

    a. Camera → **Parallel Projection**

    b. Camera → Standard Views → **Top**

    c. View → Face Style → **Hidden Line**

In order to print to a specific scale you must have **Parallel Projection** and a standard view selected. Perspective views cannot be printed to scale.

9. Select **File → Print Setup**.

10. Make the following adjustments in the ***Print Setup*** dialog:

    a. *Printer*: select a large format printer or a PDF printer driver

    b. *Size*: 22"x34" (also called ANSI D)

    c. *Orientation*: Portrait

11. Click **OK**.

Next you will do a *Print Preview* so you can determine what scale will fit on the paper size you have selected.

12. Select **File → Print Preview**.

13. Make the following adjustments to the *Print Preview* dialog (Figure 14.4):

    a. *Fit to page*: uncheck

    b. *In the printout*: ¼ (or .25)

    c. *In SketchUp*: 12

    d. *Print Quality*: Large Format

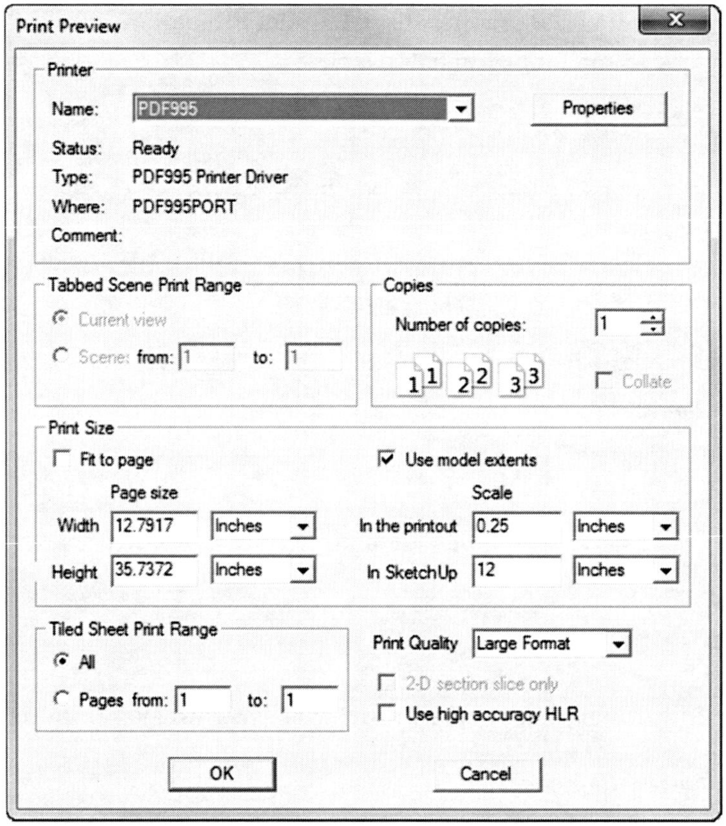

FIGURE 14.4 Print preview dialog

Notice, in Figure 14.4, that the page size for the printed drawing has updated when you specified a scale.

> ***TIP**: The page size does not update until you click into another field within the* Print *dialog.*

Note that the *Height* is 35.7″, which is larger than your 22″x34″ paper you intend to print on. Therefore the ¼″ = 1′-0″ scale will not work.

> ***FYI**: If you printed with these settings,* SketchUp *would tile the drawing onto multiple sheets of paper to print the entire drawing to the selected scale.*

Next you will adjust the settings to try another scale.

14. Change the **In the printout** option to **.125** in the *Print* dialog.

Notice the page size now fits on the desired paper size.

15. Click **OK** to see the *Print Preview.*

The preview image should look similar to Figure 14.5.

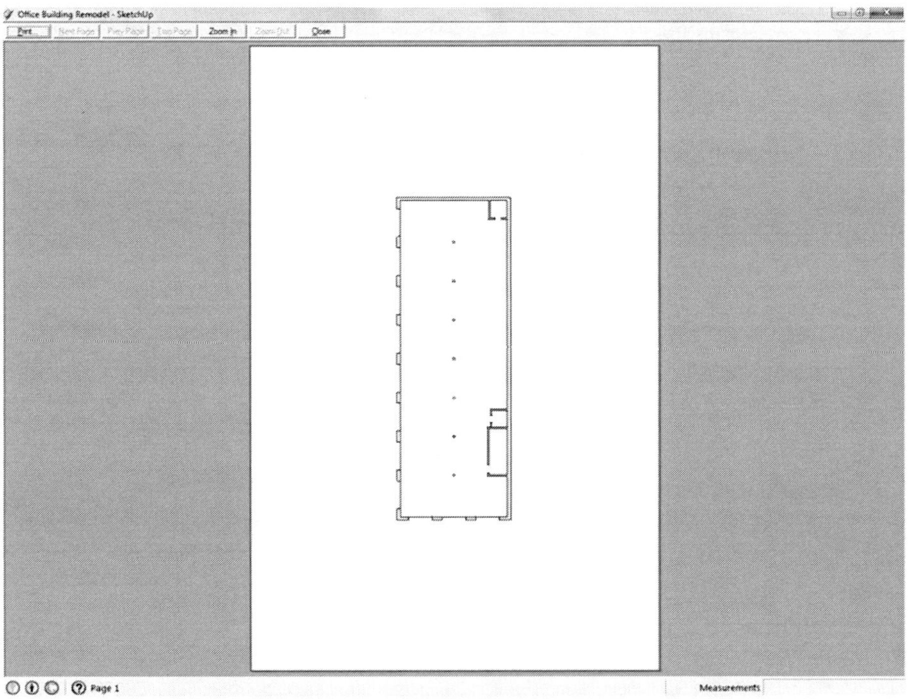

FIGURE 14.5 Print preview showing floor plan at 1/8″ = 1′-0″ on 22″x34″ paper

16. Click the **Print** button near the top of the application window to enter the *Print* dialog.

17. Click **OK** to print the drawing.

You now have a print out or a PDF that is to scale. You can use your architectural scale on it to read existing building dimensions or sketch proposed items.

Exporting Image Files

Before moving on, we will mention another way in which you may output your model. You can export your current view to a raster image file. SketchUp supports many different file formats. This file can easily be emailed to a client or printed.

These are the steps to export an image:

- File → Export → 2D Graphic
- *Export Type:* Set this to the type of file you wish to create (jpg, png, etc.).
- Click the **Options** button and increase the pixels, as needed, to create a higher resolution image (Figure 14.6).
- Specify the location and name for the new file.
- Click **Export**.

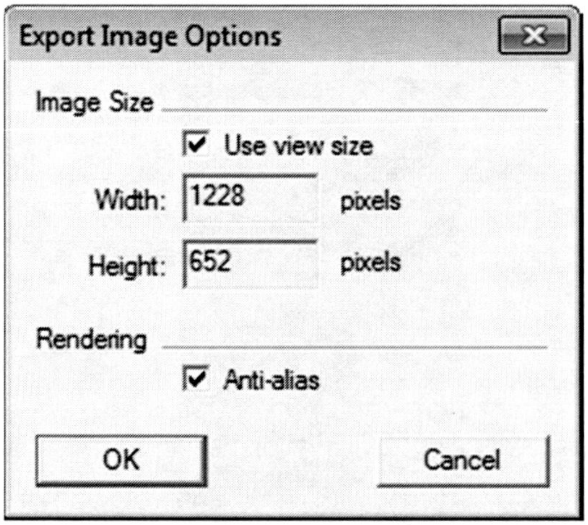

FIGURE 14.6 Export image options dialog

Section 15
Creating the 3D Model

With the framework of the floor plan established you can quickly turn it into a 3D model using the tools and techniques previously covered.

1. Open your **Office Remodel.skp** file.
2. On the *View* toolbar, select the **Iso** icon to switch to a 3D view.
3. Click the ***Push/Pull*** tool on the toolbar.

Next you will pull upward the enclosed wall areas, making them 12′-0″ tall.

4. Press and drag, upward, the corner shown in Figure 15.1.
    a. Release the mouse button once the wall is a few feet tall.
    b. The specific height is not important.
5. Type **12′** and then press **Enter**.
6. Repeat this for all enclosed wall areas (Figure 15.2).
7. Using ***Push/Pull***, drag the floor slab downward.
    a. Set the thickness to **5″**.

Now you are ready to work on the window openings. As you get more proficient with SketchUp, you will find much faster ways to do this. But for practice on the fundamentals, you will do everything manually and multiple times.

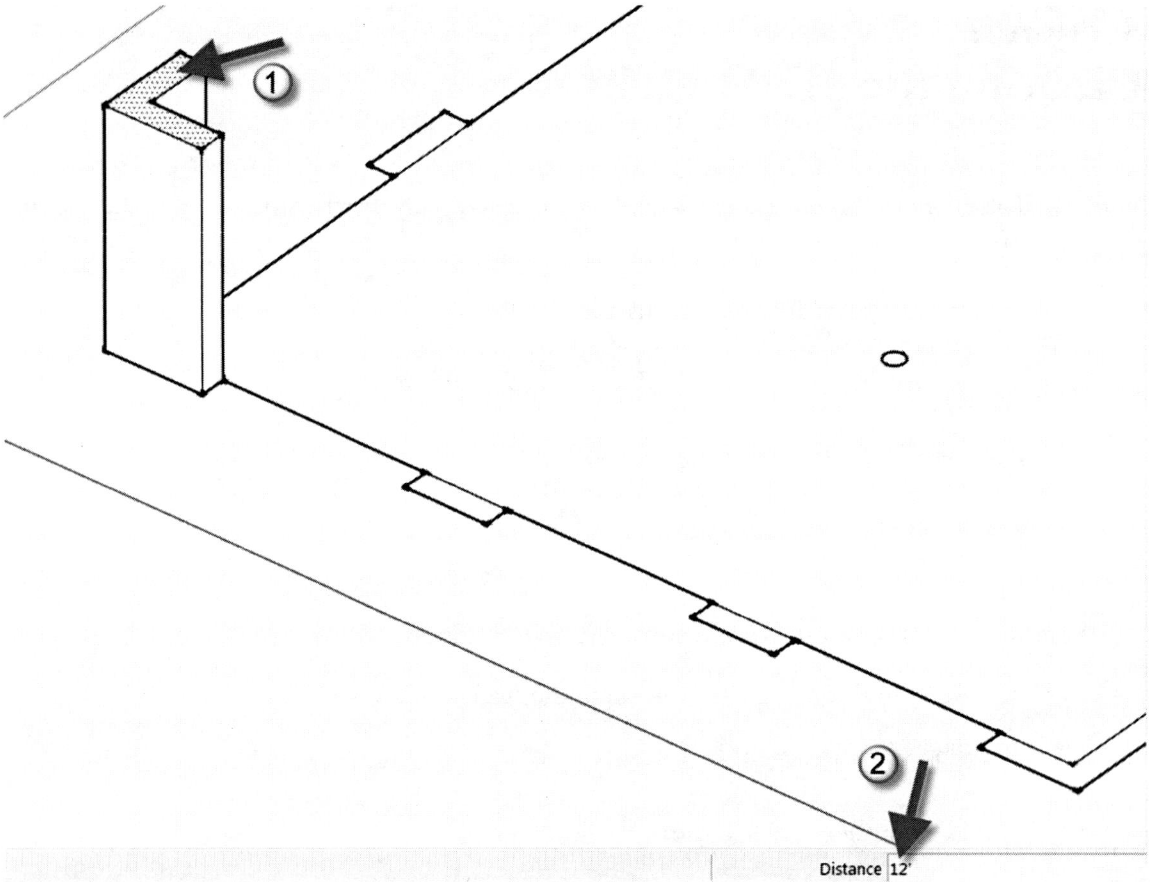

FIGURE 15.1 Raising the walls

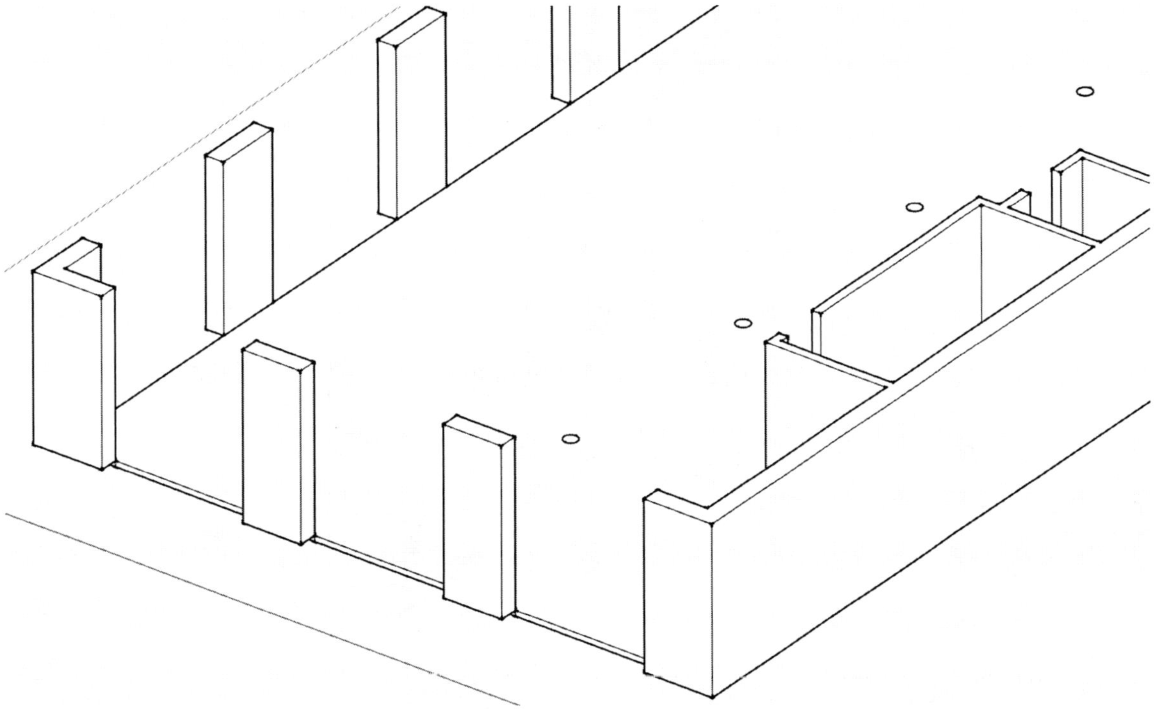

FIGURE 15.2 Raising the walls

8. Zoom in on one of the front windows.

9. Use the **Line** tool to draw a line from the floor straight up 3′-0″.

   a. See picks 1 and 2 in Figure 15.3.

10. Draw a **Line** 10′-6″ to the East.

    a. Step 3 in Figure 15.3.

***FYI:** 10′-6″ is the width of the opening; use the* Tape Measure *tool if needed.*

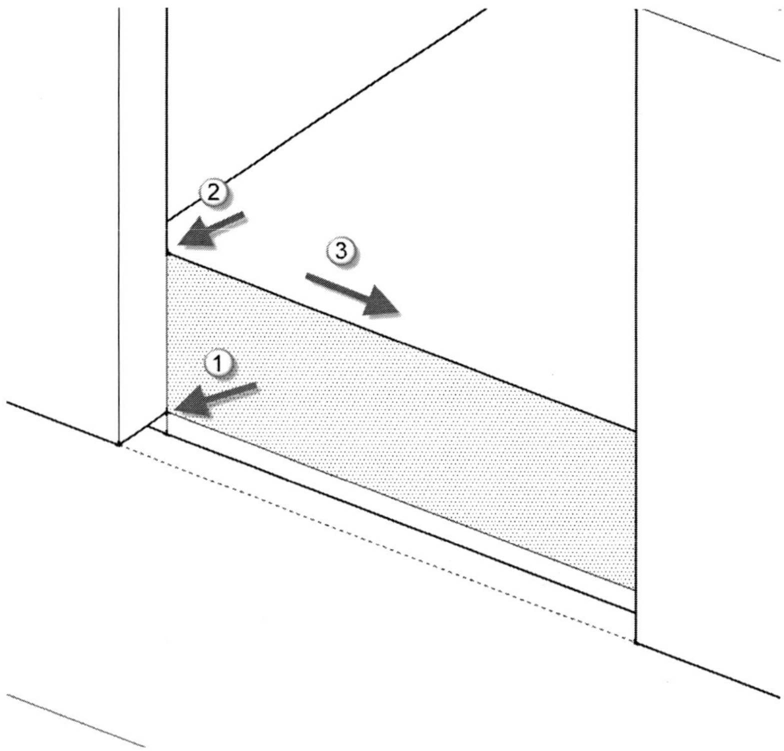

FIGURE 15.3 Adding window sill

You should now have a face which can be extruded out to create the portion of wall below the window. We will make this half the thickness of the main wall.

11. Use ***Push/Pull*** to create an 8″ thick wall below the window (Figure 15.4).

12. Repeat these steps for all exterior window openings.

As we continue to develop our preliminary plan, we will add a simple representation for the window and the portion of wall above.

The detail of the window can be developed later as the design becomes more refined.

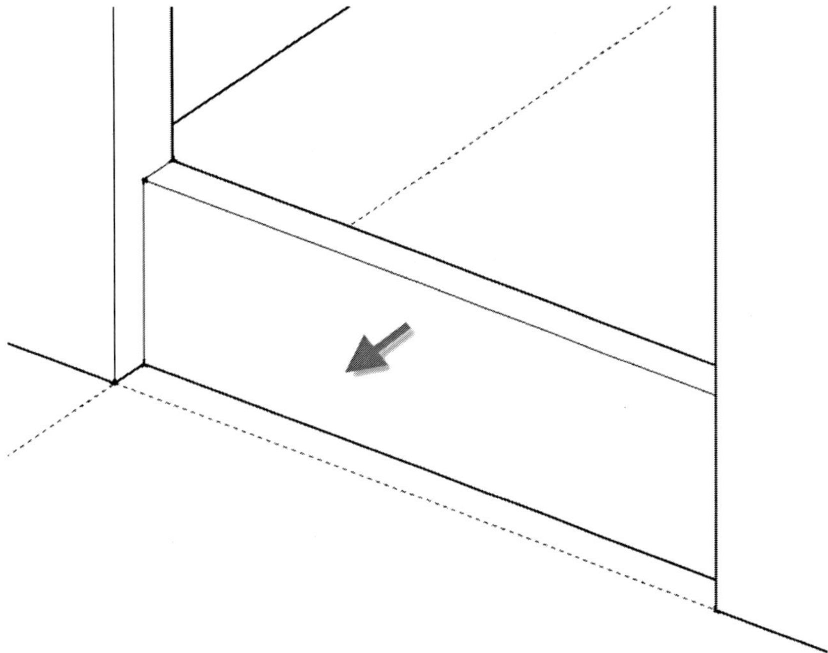

FIGURE 15.4 Creating wall thickness below the window opening

13. Draw two horizontal lines at each window opening (Figure 15.5):

    a. One at **5′-0″** above the bottom of the window (#1).

    b. The other aligned with the top of the wall (#2).

14. Use ***Push/Pull*** to create the **8″** wall above the window (Figure 15.6).

15. Repeat these steps for each window location.

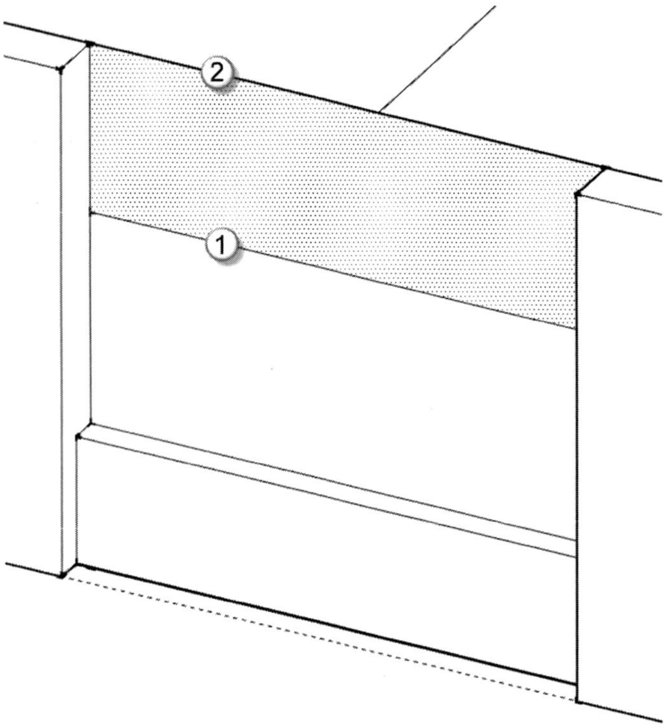

FIGURE 15.5 Creating wall above the window opening

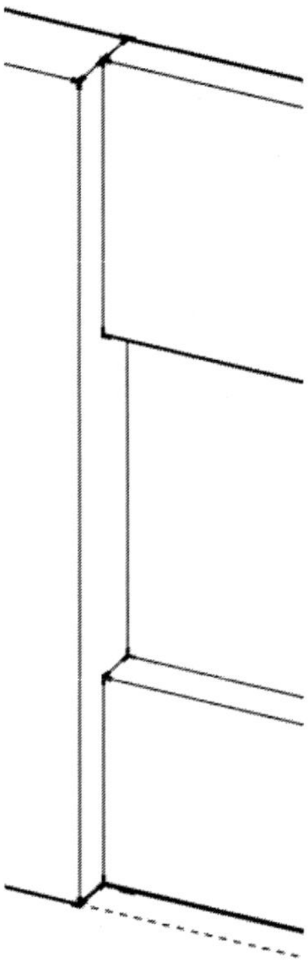

FIGURE 15.6 Wall thickness

Once you get to the last window, the open edge of your model will be completely enclosed so SketchUp will create a surface across the top (Figure 15.7). You do not want to cap off your model at this point so you will delete this face.

16. Use the **Select** tool to select the face closing off the top of the model.

17. Press **Delete**.

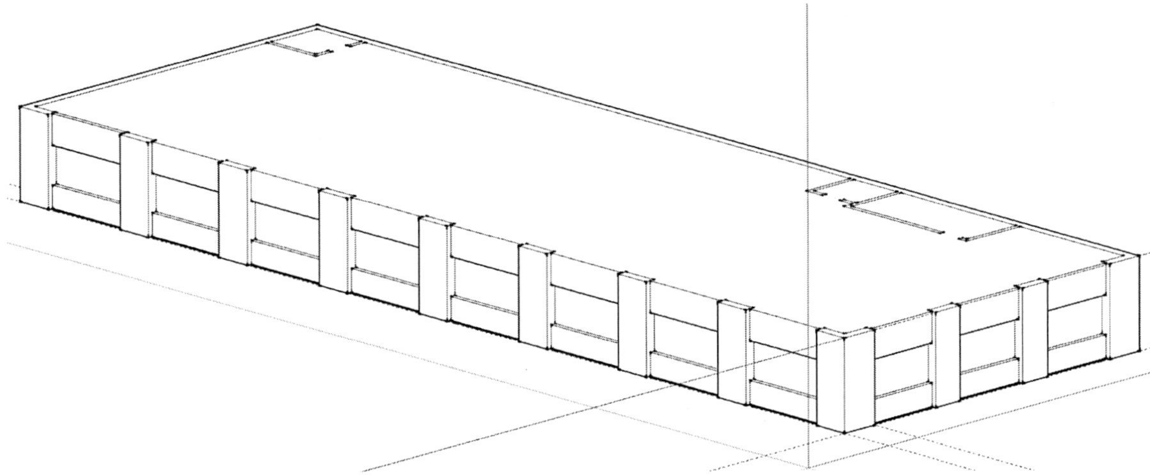

FIGURE 15.7 Windows added

The wall above the window needs a little work now that the "roof" is gone.

18. Use the ***Push/Pull*** tool to pull the wall back to the interior side of the wall.

    a. Do not pull the bottom part upward. Just select the back side of the wall and pull it back to align with the interior side of the main wall. While dragging the wall thickness back, move your cursor over the inside corner to snap to it.

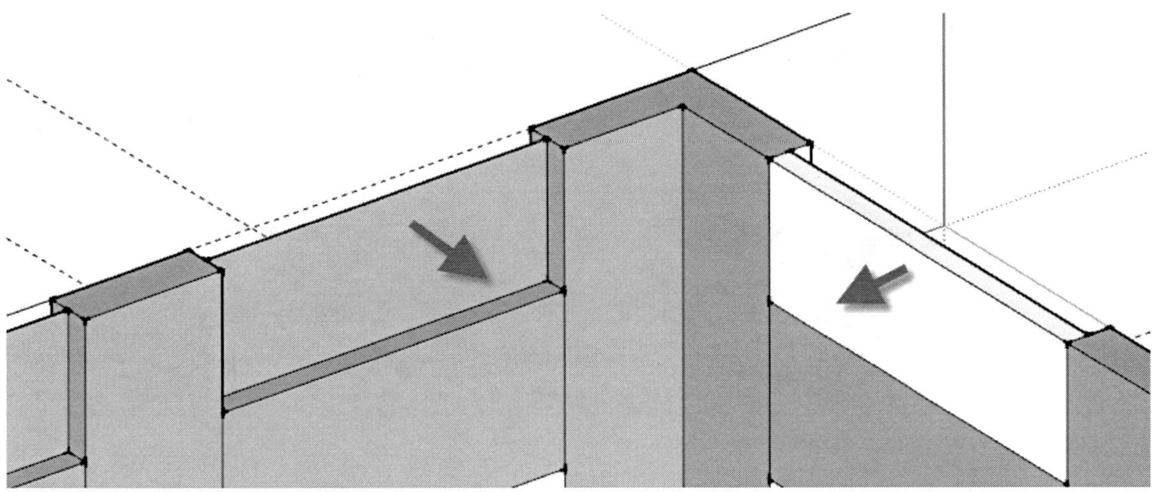

FIGURE 15.8 Windows added

Next you will add a few materials to round off this lesson.

19. Select **Windows → Materials**.

20. Add *Materials* to your model (Figure 15.9):

    a. Wood flooring

    b. Two colors on walls

    c. Sketchy material on top of walls

21. Turn **Shadows** on via the *View* menu.

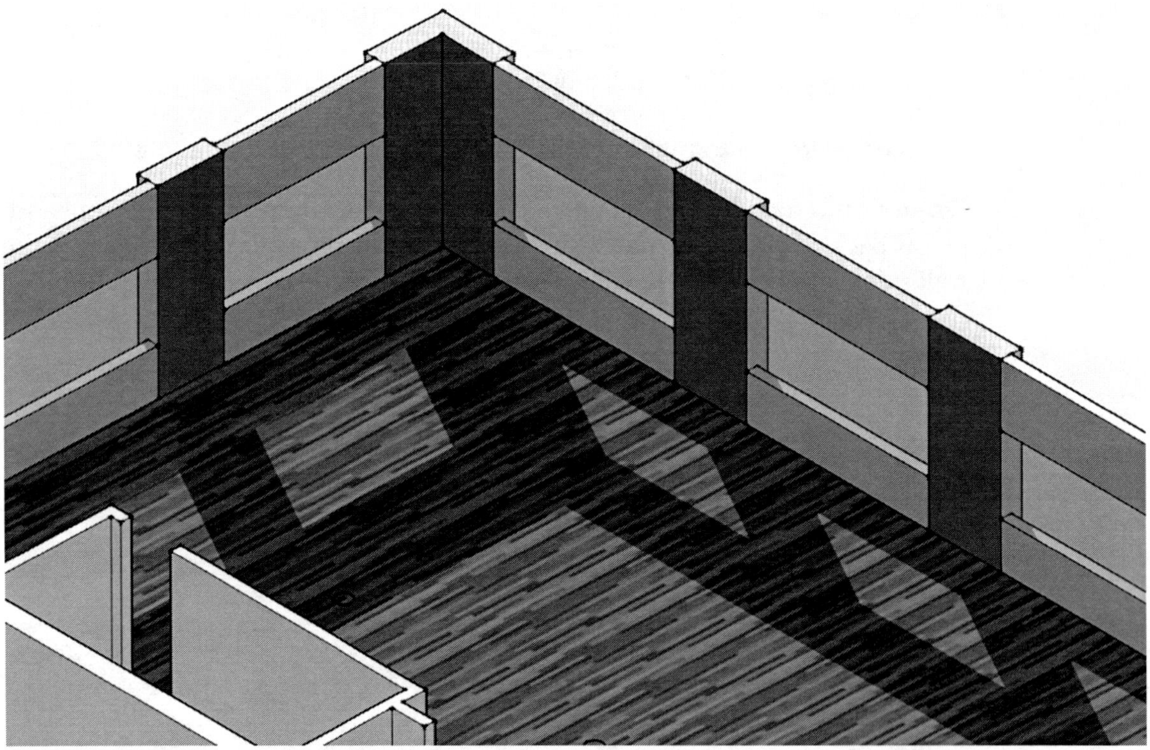

FIGURE 15.9 Windows added

22. Select **Camera → Perspective**.

23. Select **Camera → Position Camera**.

24. Drag the center wheel mouse button around and spin it to view the model from an interior perspective (Figure 15.10).

25. **Save** your project.

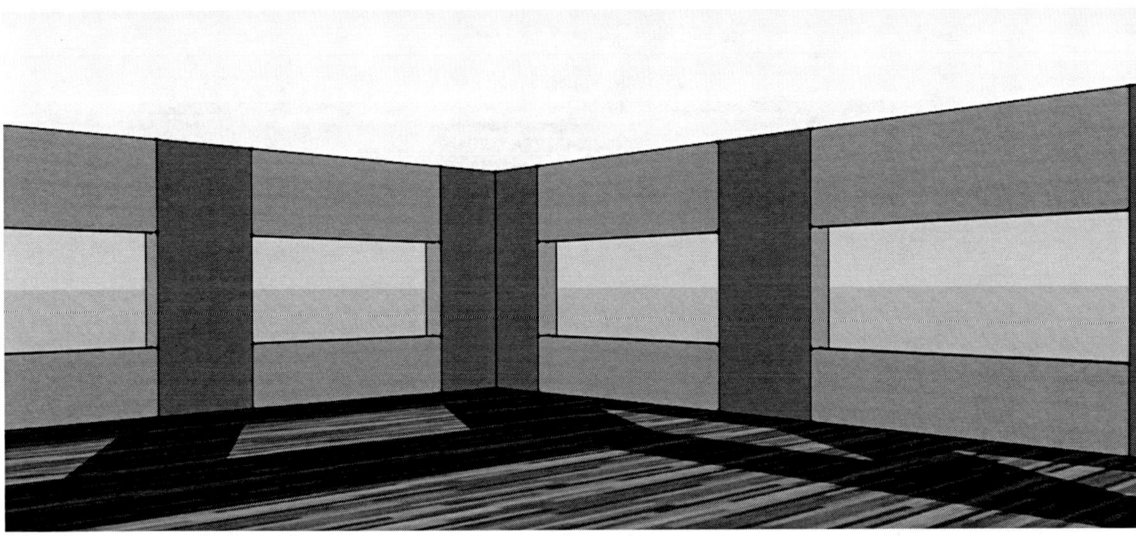

FIGURE 15.10 Interior view of space

You now should have a good handle on the basics of using SketchUp for interior design. If you want to continue working with this model, try making a few saved **Scene** tabs and generate an animation. You can also begin to develop new interior walls and place elements from *3D Warehouse*, as well as the furniture items you created previously in this book.

Good luck with your future SketchUp endevors!

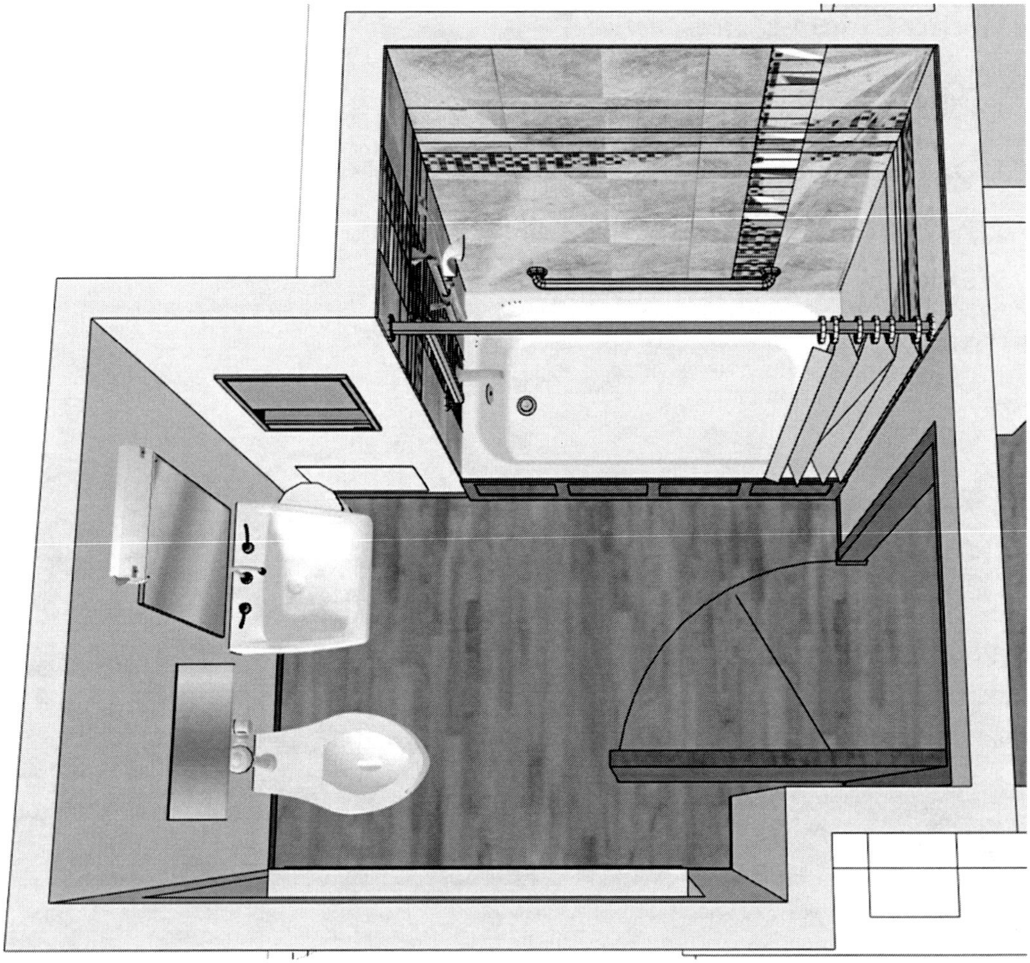

Project example: Walls Modeled. *Image courtesy of LHB; www.LHBcorp.com*

Section 16

Working with AutoCAD DWG files

It is fairly common to start a SketchUp model using an existing AutoCAD, DWG format, file. For years now, AutoCAD has had the largest market share for architectural design software. Therefore, there are a lot of existing buildings already drawn in AutoCAD. It is WAY faster to start with an AutoCAD file than it would be to sketch everything from scratch. It can take several days to accurately draw the existing conditions of a building, so having access to a DWG file is a big plus.

This chapter will walk you through the process of using a DWG file as the starting point for a SketchUp model. Most DWG files are 2D drawings; typically, one file for each floor of the building. SketchUp can import either a 2D or 3D AutoCAD file.

One more thing to point out before we get started... this feature, the ability to import a DWG file, is only available in the **Pro** version of SketchUp. **The free version of SketchUp cannot import AutoCAD DWG files.** This is probably the main reason most people buy the professional version. As was just mentioned, this feature often saves days' worth of work, so the cost is worth it. One nice thing about the *Pro* version for design firms is they can buy network licenses. If a company buys five network licenses, they can install SketchUp on one hundred computers, but only five people can be using the software at any given time. They can still buy standalone licenses, too; this is one copy for each individual computer.

> ***FYI:*** *This chapter requires* **SketchUp Pro**, *not the free version used in the rest of this book. Also, you will have to download the resource files from the publisher's website* (www.SDCpublications.com) *to follow along exactly. Otherwise, you can use another AutoCAD DWG floor plan file if you have one.*

1. Open a new SketchUp file.

2. Select **File → Import**.

> ***TIP:*** *If you do not have access to SketchUp Pro, you can still complete this section by downloading the file* ***Library.SKP*** *from* www.SDCpublications.com. *This file already has the DWG file loaded into it. Once the DWG file is in the SketchUp model, you no longer need the Pro version.*

3. Browse to the AutoCAD DWG file **Library – Level 01.dwg**; do not click open yet.

TIP: This file needs to be downloaded from www.SDCpublications.com. *Just browse to the page for this textbook and click on the* Downloads *tab.*

4. Click the **Options** button (Figure 16.1).

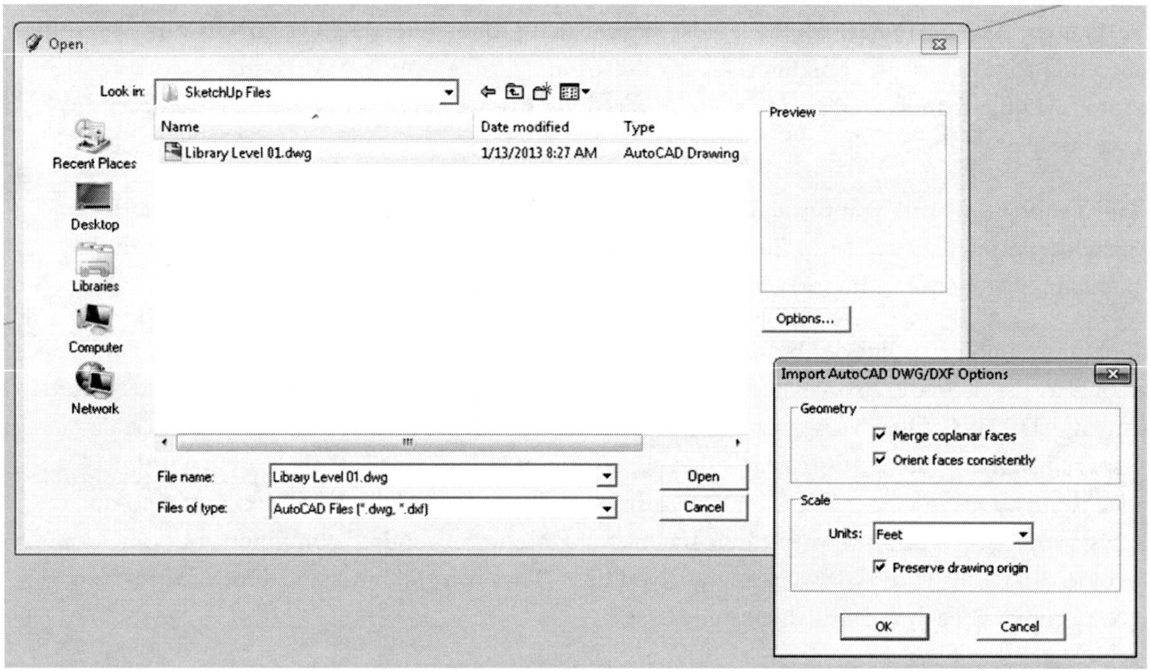

FIGURE 16.1 Importing AutoCAD DWG file

In most cases you will want both options checked, under geometry, to make sure you start with a clean and organized model. You will also check "Preserve drawing origin". This will align the AutoCAD drawing origin (0,0,0) with the SketchUp origin, which is the intersection of the *Axes* lines. This is nice in case you continue to receive updated/progress drawings, as they will always land in the same location. Otherwise you have to pick a place to insert the DWG.

5. In the *Options* dialog, make sure **all the boxes are checked** and *Units* are set to **Feet**.

6. Click **OK**.

7. Click **Open** to place the DWG file in SketchUp.

8. Take a minute to note the entities listed and then click **OK**.

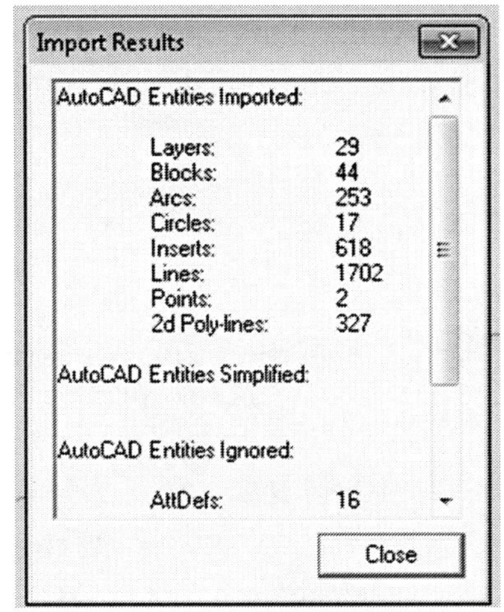

FIGURE 16.2 Import results

You should now see the first floor library plan as shown in the image below (Figure 16.2). Notice how the SketchUp person, near the origin, looks to be about the right size in relation to the imported drawing. This is a good clue that the model is the correct scale.

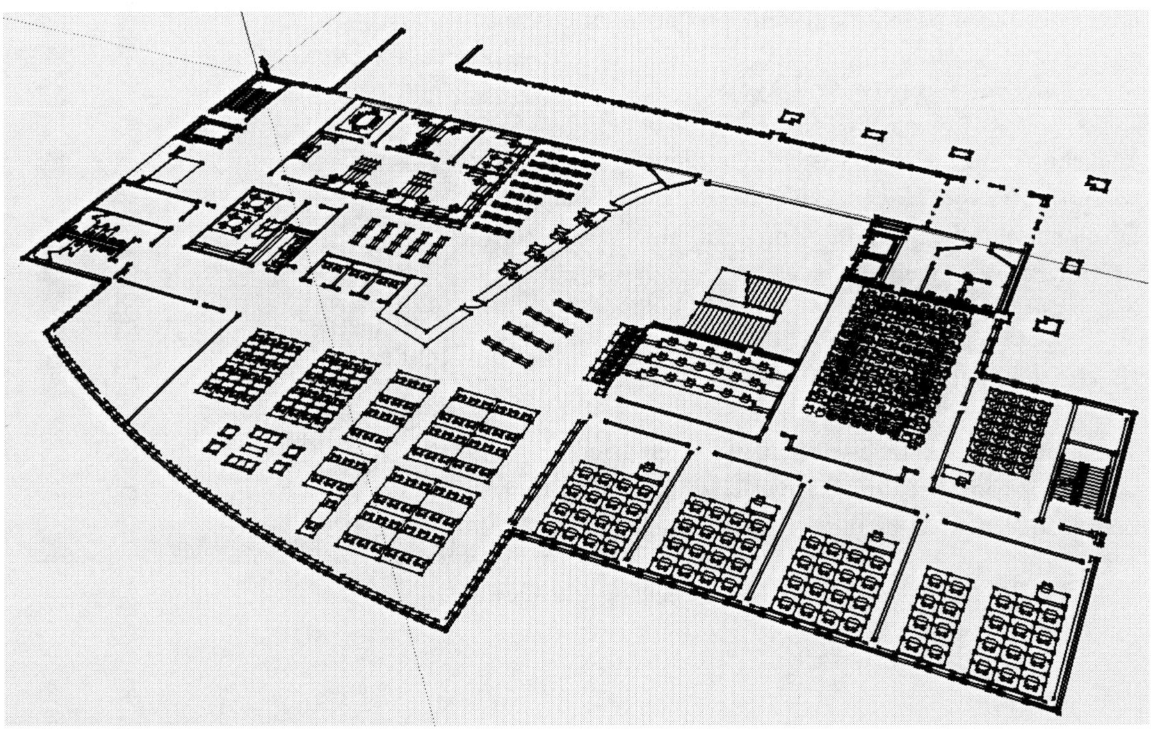

FIGURE 16.3 Imported AutoCAD DWG file

Next you will use the *Tape Measure* tool to verify the drawing came in at the correct scale.

9. **Zoom in** on a door opening into one of the classrooms in the Southeast corner of the building.

10. Use the **Tape Measure** tool to verify the doors are **3′-0″** wide (Figure 16.4).

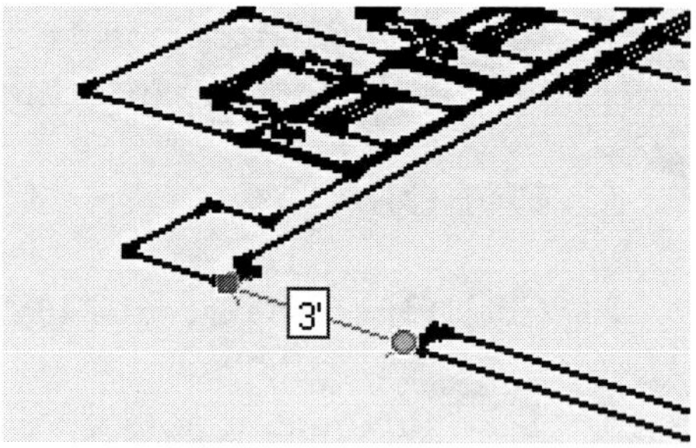

FIGURE 16.4 Tape Measure tool

> ***FYI:*** *The scale should be correct for this example, but when it is not, you will need to use the* Scale *tool to make it right.*

Next you will open the *Layers* window and notice several have been created. The AutoCAD user typically uses layers to control visibility and other properties of entities.

11. Select **Window → Layers**.

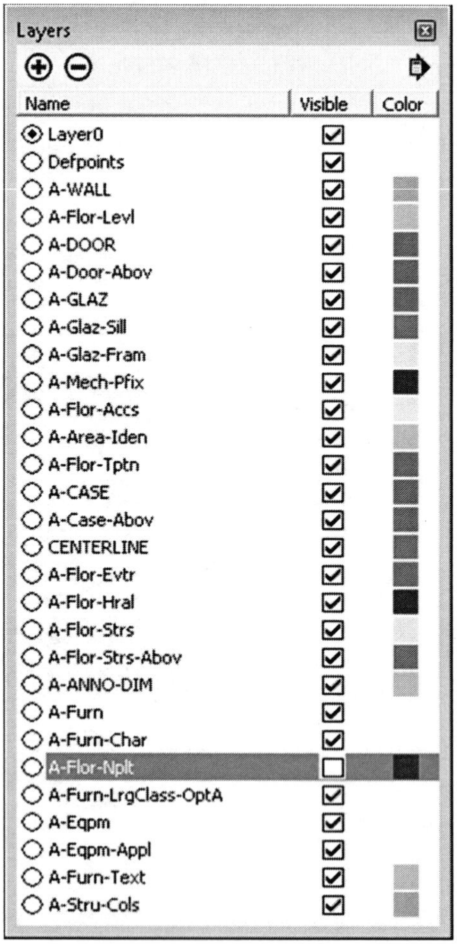

FIGURE 16.5 Layers window

You should see the Layers as listed in Figure 16.5. We will turn off *Layer* "A-Flor-Nplt" to hide the clearance lines built into the furniture. One might also want to turn off other *Layers* to reduce the visible lines to just walls, casework and windows.

12. Uncheck **A-Flor-Nplt**.

The *Layer* with the circle selected, in the left-hand column, is considered the current *Layer*. This is the *Layer* on which all new edges and faces are modeled.

13. **Close** the *Layer* window by clicking the "X" at the upper right.

Next, you need to decide if you want to **Explode** the DWG file or not. Right now, if you select the imported drawing, the entire thing highlights. Opening *Entity Info* shows that this is a *Component* (Figure 16.6). This is nice if we want to move it around, we don't have to worry about selecting hundreds of files and text. Or, if we want to replace it with an updated DWG file.

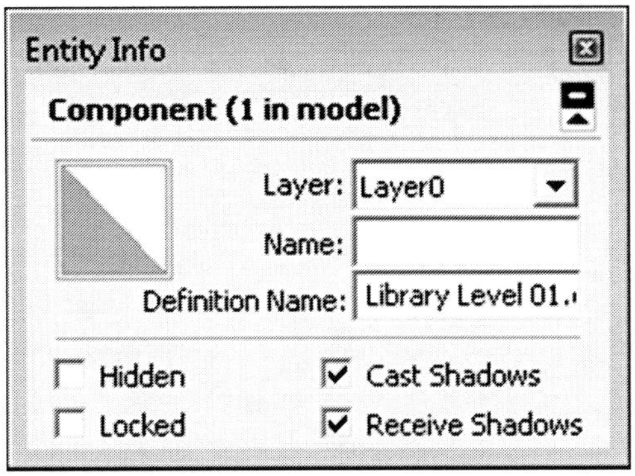

FIGURE 16.6 Entity Info for DWG Import

However, if we want to edit the lines or extrude them into the third dimension we will need to *Explode* the *Component*. In the next step you will explode the floor plan drawing.

14. Right-click on the floor plan drawing.

15. From the pop-up menu, select **Explode**.

Now, when you select a line, you will just be selecting that one line, not the entire floor plan.

After exploding the drawing, you will just have lines and no faces. To create faces you can sketch a line diagonally at a corner or on top of another line. Another option, when using the Pro version is to use a **Ruby Script**. This feature allows things to be automated in SketchUp. Here is one example of a tool which will create faces for you: **www.smustard.com/script/MakeFaces**.

Once you have faces you can follow the steps outlined in the previous chapter to create a 3D model!

16. **Save** your model as **Library.SKP**.

FIGURE 16.7 Right-click menu

NOTES:

Additional Resources

This is by no means an exhaustive list, but here are a few resources you may want to check out if you are interested in learning more and keeping up on the latest SketchUp info:

- **Within SketchUp**
    - **Help → Welcome to SketchUp** and then click on the "**Learn**" bar for links to *Video Tutorials* and *Tips & Tricks*
    - Don't forget about the **Help Center**
    - **Window → Instructor**

- **Online**
    - YouTube http://www.youtube.com/profile?user=SketchUpVideo&view=playlists
    - SketchUp.com
    - http://www.sketchupartists.org/

- **Blogs**
    - http://sketchupdate.blogspot.com/
    - http://sketchuptips.wordpress.com/

- **Components**
    - 3D Warehouse, via…
        - File → Google 3D Warehouse → Get Models
        - http://sketchup.google.com/3dwarehouse/
    - Plumbing Fixture Manufacturer example: http://sketchup.google.com/3dwarehouse/cldetails?mid=886afdb19cf5a0e12e8ae34ac2aaf4f2
    - Furniture manufacturer example: http://www.hermanmiller.com/design-resources/3d-models-cad-drawings/3d-models/seating.html

NOTES:

Index

O

P

R

S

T

U

V

W

X

Z